The Grizzly in the Southwest

A grizzly on the Fort Apache Indian Reservation in Arizona. Courtesy Arizona Game and Fish Department.

The Grizzly in the Southwest

DOCUMENTARY OF AN EXTINCTION

By David E. Brown

FOREWORD BY FRANK C. CRAIGHEAD, JR.

UNIVERSITY OF OKLAHOMA PRESS : NORMAN

BY DAVID E. BROWN

The Wolf in the Southwest (ed.) (Tucson, 1983)
The Biotic Communities of the Southwest: United States and Mexico Desert Plants (ed.) (Tucson, 1983)
Tales from Tiburon (co-ed.) (Phoenix, 1983)
Arizona Tree Squirrels (Phoenix, 1984)
The Grizzly in the Southwest: Documentary of an Extinction (Norman, 1985)

Library of Congress Cataloging-in-Publication Data

Brown, David E. (David Earl), 1938–
    The grizzly in the Southwest.

    Bibliography: p. 249
    Includes index.
    1. Grizzly bear—History.   2. Extinct animals—
Southwest, New—History.   3. Mammals—Southwest, New—
History.   I. Title.
QL737.C27B76   1985   599.74'446   84-28027
ISBN 0-8061-1930-6

The paper in this book meets the guidelines for permanence and durability of the Committee on Production Guidelines of the Council on Library Resources, Inc.

Contents

Part Four
Lore, Legends, and Adventures

Appendices

Illustrations

MAPS

Foreword

BY FRANK C. CRAIGHEAD, JR.

If we can learn from history, David Brown's documentary of the grizzly in the Southwest shows us the pattern of events that led to the great bear's extinction. It is abundantly evident that where the grizzly's requirements conflicted with man's economic interest there was no compromise—the bear had to go. As Brown points out, the grizzlies' numbers appear to have been overestimated, and the bears were gone before anyone realized or believed it. Their extermination from this vast area was abetted by government trappers and assisted by federal administrators under pressure from the Southwest's livestock industry.

This process of extinction through conflict, though now terminated in the Southwest, still continues elsewhere. It has been accelerating in the Northern Rockies and in the Yellowstone ecosystem over nearly two decades. Although efforts are now underway to reverse the population decline of this threatened species, a regional recovery is not yet in sight. Consideration of man's interests still prevails over that of the bear's. Habitat destruction and high annual mortality continue to retard recovery. The effect of the grizzly's low reproductive rate in population recovery does not appear to be fully appreciated, and there is a tendency to overestimate the grizzly population, just as occurred in the Southwest. Yet the historical, documented demise of the Southwest grizzly, along with the biological and ecological data now available, provides the information and, hopefully, the motivation to secure the grizzly's presence compatible with that of man's. A study of history should aid biologists and modern bear managers in making the fullest use of their accumulating knowledge. It is not yet a case of being too late.

Grizzlies and brown bears are abundant in Alaska where suitable habitats exist. However, where bear and human interests conflict, the same decimating process is operative. Take, for example, the Chilkoot State Park "problem" bear of 1984. Actually, the problem began a year earlier when a resident killed a brown bear sow in defense of life and property. The female's death left two motherless cubs, one of which returned to the area in the summer of 1984. Successful in foraging for food, the bear rambled through the Chilkoot campground more and more frequently. It also patrolled the adjacent Chilkoot River—timidly at first, then boldly snatching fish that anglers left lying on the banks. The bear made daily trips to scavenge the carcasses of salmon left by fishermen, alternating his foraging between campground and riverbanks—all populated areas. There were angry rumblings from fishermen forced to vacate favorite fishing spots. The young bear found an ice chest carelessly left beside a motor home and consumed one hundred pounds of halibut. The owner protested to park, state, and federal officials, even though it was he, not the bear, who was at fault. Campers were warned daily of improper food storage. Local officers did all they could to keep bear and man apart. A woman tried to feed the cute young bear a tuna sandwich. The bear knocked over a tent in search of food. He was definitely becoming habituated to the readily available human sources of food.

In an attempt to change the bear's habits, "cracker shells" were fired overhead to scare him. Bird shot in the rear end at thirty yards failed to scare him sufficiently to keep him from returning. Officials stated, "The policy that deals with habituated bears is to destroy the bears." Trapping and immobilizing were ruled out for a number of reasons, one of which was a shortage of funds—the economic factor. The use of a helicopter to relocate the bear was discussed, but policy would not allow it. The policy was based on the high percentage of relocated bears that had returned to their original area of capture, and had returned in spite of obstacles and long distances. The official opinion was that the bear had gotten out of hand. There was a problem of public safety. A distant boss gave the word, and the beautiful, inquisitive, adaptable—but problem—bear was destroyed at night in the parking lot of the campground.

The loss was real though subtle. It could possibly have been averted or perhaps postponed to another year. The death of the young bear would not have any significant effect on the bear population, as might have been the case if the population were low and the bear a mature female. It was, however, an example of the slow attrition that over a period of time led to the extinction of the grizzly in California, then in the Southwest. Perhaps we can learn a lesson from the history of the Southwest grizzly and use our knowledge, combined with understanding, to tolerate a magnificent creature whose greatest fault is that he competes with man.

Preface

I used to wonder over the term "natural history." I did not understand why the study of living organisms was history, or why history was called a social science. I had not yet learned that all study is science, and that all things natural are in the process of becoming history. The appropriateness of merging these two disciplines was to be revealed to me later in life.

The value of history came to me at a symposium on riparian habitat, held in Davis, California. Displayed at that meeting were old maps and photographs of the Sacramento and San Joaquin river system—as they were, and as they are. The greatness of the rivers was lost; most of the marshes and the best riparian forests were gone forever. Still, one could trace on aerial photographs the dim ghosts of the rivers that used to be. The remaining scraps and remnants, valuable as they were, were now somehow not enough. The present status of the rivers was depressing, and the future had no promise. The only excitement was in the past.

From the old maps and descriptions I could discover the California that I wanted to know. As I looked backward, the checkerboards of clean farms, angular canals, and residential sprawl gave way to marshy prairies, valley oaks, waterfowl, and grizzly bears. To me that was the lesson and the success of the symposium. When descriptive accounts are properly prepared and preserved, future generations can, with a little imagination, recapture the natural world we are losing.

Such is the case with the grizzly bear of the Southwest. There is none at present, nor will there probably be in the foreseeable future. What we have is the imperfect record of

those who were here and who noted his presence. The purpose of this book is to document as well as possible the
animal's regional life history, habits, and requirements and
try to communicate the adventure that went with him. This
is not a management study; such is no longer possible. What
is presented here is a historical study with a wildlife-management lesson. Thus the term "natural history" *is* appropriate; it is only through the retelling of our past that we
understand our present attitudes and actions. These will determine the great bear's future in the north, just as our past
attitudes have extirpated him from the south.

   This book is patterned in many respects after *California
Grizzly*, by T. J. Storer and L. P. Tevis, Jr., published in
1955; and *The Wolf in the Southwest*, edited by D. E. Brown
(1983). Like A. W. Schorger's *The Passenger Pigeon; Its Natural History and Extinction* (1955; 1973), these works are natural history studies made after their animal subjects had been
extirpated or become extinct. The research necessary for
such works is not unlike the work of a detective. The depo-
sitions of all the witnesses are examined and pieced together
with all the available evidence to re-create a past situation
—one might almost say to reconstruct a crime. In this instance the work was particularly difficult, because, unlike
the California grizzly *(Ursus arctos californicus)*, the Southwest grizzly (*U. a. nelsoni* et al.) went mostly uncelebrated.
There are no paintings of Southwest grizzlies—not even
sketches. Almost no mounted specimens exist, and there are
very few photos—almost none of live bears. There are, nonetheless, a number of skins and museum specimens, and a
substantial written record of bruin's presence is scattered
throughout varied literature. This is fortunate, for almost
all of those who personally knew Southwest grizzlies have
passed on.

   For a Southwesterner to meet a grizzly today, one must
travel either through time or space. I have done both. To
understand the grizzly's domain, I visited his former habitats in the White Mountains, on Escudilla, in the Mogollon
Mountains and the Gila Wilderness, and in the Black Range.

I climbed to the summit of his final strongholds in the Sierra del Nido and tasted the wilderness of the San Juans. I saw also the old headquarters of the GOS, Q, and Slash Ranches, out of where so many grizzlies were killed. Not content to see just where grizzlies had been, I went to Montana, the only conterminous state that still possesses a sizable population of "wild" grizzlies.

As impressed as I am with grizzlies, I am equally appreciative of those who work with them. I was most fortunate in being able to spend a week in the field with Keith Aune, Wayne Kasner, and Tom Stivers, working on a cooperative grizzly study on the East Front of the Rockies. These men graciously showed me the grizzly's preferred habitats and how they found, trapped, and tracked him. Most important, they shared their understanding of the animal's ways and freely gave me the natural history that they obtained through so much effort. These insights were essential for the preparation of this book.

Although this book will speak mostly of remarkable explorers, pioneers, and bear hunters long gone, it is today's biologists and their immediate predecessors—scientists like Adolph Murie, John J. and F. C. Craighead, C. J. Martinka, and Charles Jonkel—who are the real heroes in today's world of retreating bears and advancing civilization. And although it is too late for their work to save the grizzly in the Southwest, it is to their efforts that this book is dedicated. Should the United States lose its grizzlies, it will not be because no one cared or did not try.

In several previous publications (Brown and Lowe 1974, 1980; Brown 1982), the "Southwest" was defined and mapped for convenience as those portions of the southwest United States and northwest Mexico west of longitude 103°W, south of parallel 38°N, east of longitude 118°W, and north of parallel 26°N. Included are New Mexico, Arizona, Baja California Norte, Sonora, and most of Chihuahua, as well as most of trans-Pecos Texas, western Coahuila, southern Colorado, southern Utah, southern and southeastern California, and extreme northern Baja California Sur, Sinaloa, and Durango. For the scope of this work the Californias are deleted, for the history and status of the grizzlies in southern California and Baja California Norte are addressed in Storer and Tevis (1955) and Leopold (1959). Otherwise the boundaries of the areas to be discussed are as stated.

This is not the first account of Southwest grizzlies. Bob Housholder's *The Grizzly Bear in Arizona* (1966) was first published in 1961 as a three-part series in *Arizona Wildlife-Sportsman* (the publication of the Arizona Game Protective Association). Principally a summary of grizzly encounters, this book was an important contribution because Housholder had the foresight to interview many individuals who had actually known Arizona grizzlies. None of those whom he cited are alive today. The book's assemblage of the few existing photos of Arizona grizzlies is superb, and the descriptive accounts are informative.

For New Mexico material the accounts of Vernon Bailey (1931) provided an important nucleus. As a staff biologist and later senior biologist with the U.S. Biological Survey, Bailey was one of the few professional biologists to work in the Southwest when grizzlies were still extant. Moreover, as a major force behind the establishment of the Predatory Animal and Rodent Control (PARC) arm of the Survey, he knew and appreciated grizzlies. Bailey's accounts, therefore, not only are some of the most factual that we have but deal with bear biology. His summaries of the bear's status through the early 1920s also provided important historical data.

The excellent descriptions of grizzlies in Mexico of Charles Sheldon (1925) and A. Starker Leopold (1959) were consulted, as were the mammal texts for Arizona (Cockrum 1960), New Mexico (Findley et al. 1975), Chihuahua (Anderson 1972), Sonora (Burt 1938), Coahuila (Baker 1956), Durango (Baker and Greer 1962), Colorado (Warren 1942, Armstrong 1972), and Utah (Durrant 1952). These and the scientific bulletins accompanying collections or taxonomic descriptions (e.g., Coues and Yarrow 1875, Merriam 1918,

Poole and Schantz 1942, Miller and Kellog 1955) provided important distribution and descriptive data.

Studies on the life histories, requirements, problems, and status of extant grizzlies were also reviewed; they include the recent works of Craighead and Craighead (1971), Mundy and Flook (1973), Craighead (1979), Servheen (1981), and Murie (1981), and the reports of the Border Grizzly Project (1982). These studies and others, while about grizzlies outside the Southwest, gave valuable insight into the causes of the decline of those bears' more southern cousins. Especially valuable in this regard were the proceedings of the Bear Biology Association, published after international symposia in 1970, 1974, 1977, and 1980, and the comprehensive Grizzly Bear Recovery Plan (Brown 1982), published by the Office of Endangered Species of the U.S. Fish and Wildlife Service.

Then there were the bear hunters and bear stories. Carefully inspected, the useful and oftentimes excellent reports of Wright (1909), Stevens (1943), French (1965), Russell (1976), and many others, provided clues and evidence on the distribution, status, and biology of southwestern grizzlies. The collection of grizzly stories presented by Hayes and Hayes (1966) was also helpful, for it contains material from Arizona and the Southwest and some interesting commentary from Elliott Barker to Levon Lee, chief of game management in New Mexico in 1963. Also useful in this regard were Samson's *The Bear Book* (1979), O'Connor's *Hunting in the Southwest* (1945), and *John Spring's Arizona* (1966).

For early historic material I am greatly indebted to Goode P. Davis, Jr. Carefully researched and edited by Neil Carmony, Davis's summary (1982) of wildlife encounters and landscape descriptions in Arizona between 1825 and 1865 is must reading for any serious student of natural history. As to be expected, there are many references to grizzly bears during this period, several of which are included here. Goodman's *Arizona Odyssey* (1969), an invaluable annotated index of nineteenth-century Arizona periodicals, was another

excellent source of early material. Eventually I made contact with most of the region's historical societies and archives
and searched out their data on the grizzly.

More recent grizzly history was gathered from the annual
reports of the Arizona and New Mexico districts of the
PARC; the Arizona and New Mexico (Region 3) reports
and big-game estimates of the U.S. Forest Service; back
issues of *Arizona Wildlife-Sportsman;* and various newspapers
and periodicals. All these sources were combined with a
working knowledge of the Southwest to attain a vicarious
but more nearly complete relationship with Old Ephraim.

This book is the result of the help of many people over
many years. Of particular importance in its preparation were
Neil B. Carmony, Dale A. Jones, and Raymond M. Turner.
Their encouragement is as greatly appreciated as is their
material assistance.

Special thanks must also be given to the historical insti-
tutions and their cadres of professional curators and archi-
vists. Most helpful were Suzi Sato, Arizona Collections,
Arizona Historical Foundation, Arizona State University,
Tempe; Phyllis Ball and the personnel at the Special Col-
lections Department, University of Arizona Library, Tuc-
son; Paula Gussio, Northern Arizona University Special Col-
lections Library, Flagstaff; Joe Meehan, Northern Arizona
Pioneers Historical Society, Flagstaff; Mike Miller, Photo
Collections, Museum of New Mexico, Albuquerque; the
New Mexico Historical Society, Los Alamos; and the U.S.
Geological Survey Photographic Library, Denver.

The contributions and assistance of professional bear
biologists is also greatly appreciated and, as stated earlier,
was an essential ingredient in the compilation of this book.
In this regard the shared knowledge of Keith Aune, Tom
Stivers, and Wayne Kasner, of the Montana Department
of Fish and Game, and Thomas E. Waddell, of the Arizona
Game and Fish Department, was particularly valued. The
all-important technical review of the manuscript was provided by C. J. Jonkel, University of Montana, and Al Le-
Count, Arizona Game and Fish Department, two of the

West's foremost bear biologists. Neil B. Carmony reviewed the manuscript for historical content, and Peter Zager, Muskingum College, New Concord, Ohio, did the same for habitat descriptions. Especially valued was the review by Ing. José ("Pepe") Treviño for the spelling of Spanish terms and the accuracy of the account of the grizzly's status in Chihuahua.

Also helpful along the way were Jack Brooks, Bloody Basin, Arizona; Roger Bumstead, U.S. Forest Service, Albuquerque; G. W. Evans, Jr., Montosa Cattle Co., Magdalena, New Mexico; Kevin P. Ford and Jack Wight, Wildlife Studio Taxidermy, Phoenix; Bob Hernbrode, Jr., Colorado Department of Wildlife, Denver; Ted Knipe, Sonoita, Arizona; Kim Manning, Silver City, New Mexico; Homer C. Pickens, Albuquerque; Lendell Cockrum, University of Arizona, Tucson; and William Carrel, Dave Daughtry, James Brooks, John Snyder, Todd Pringle, Richard Glinski, Paul M. Webb, James Wegge, and Norman Woolsey, Arizona Game and Fish Department.

Special thanks also go to Phil M. Cosper, who is retired from the Arizona Game and Fish Department, and Nathan Ellison, of Cherry Creek, Arizona, for sharing their family history and some great bear stories; to Tom Hoffman and Duane Rubink, U.S. Fish and Wildlife Service, Animal Damage Control, for making available the well-kept files of the PARC reports for New Mexico and Arizona; to Bob Housholder, for the use of his outstanding collection of photographs and correspondence; and to Frances Nutt for her hospitality and willingness to share one of the few remaining mounted Southwest grizzlies.

For the all-important artwork for the maps and graphs, I am indebted to Matt Alderson, Phoenix. Marilyn Hoff Stewart, Mesa, Arizona, prepared the sketches.

With their help let us now return to that time not so long ago when grizzlies roamed the mountains and river bottoms of the Southwest.

Phoenix, Arizona   DAVID E. BROWN

The Grizzly in the Southwest

"It's Only a Mountain Now"

The government trapper who took the grizzly knew he had made Escudilla safe for cows. He did not know he had toppled the spire off an edifice a-building since the morning stars sang together.

The bureau chief who sent the trapper was a biologist versed in the architecture of evolution, but he did not know that spires might be as important as cows. He did not foresee that within two decades the cow country would become tourist country, and as such have greater need of bears than of beefsteaks.

The Congressmen who voted money to clear the ranges of bears were the sons of pioneers. They acclaimed the superior virtues of the frontiersman, but they strove with might and main to make an end of the frontier.

We forest officers, who acquiesced in the extinguishment of the bear, knew a local rancher who had plowed up a dagger engraved with the name of Coronado's captains. We spoke harshly of the Spaniards who in their zeal for gold and converts, had needlessly extinguished the native Indians. It did not occur to us that we, too, were the captains of an invasion too sure of its own righteousness.

Escudilla still hangs on the horizon, but when you see it you no longer think of bears. It's only a mountain now.
— *Aldo Leopold* (1949)

And so it was that the Southwest's mountains and canyons came to possess the grizzly only in the memories of a dwindling few. His later numbers appear to have been overestimated, and he was gone before anyone believed it. There were many who noted the great beast's passing, and some who regretted it, but almost no one resisted the final outcome. Soon there will be no one left who knew a Southwest grizzly. Yet it is an ironic fact that many today would cherish

3

a remnant population and ensure that it was protected and maintained.

There are those who say that the grizzly had to go, that his presence in the Southwest was incompatible with man's. There is some truth in this. Certainly there was no compatibility between the grizzly and the livestock industry — not at Southwest stocking levels. Like the wolf, the opportunistic grizzly was not about to forgo a new and readily available food source — not when this new-found prey had depleted the grizzly's natural food supplies.

It was too bad that all of the bear's habitat was grazed so heavily. This was especially so of the forests and the "high country" after these lands were withdrawn for forest reserves. If some of these areas had been withheld from grazing, as was done in some of the national parks, the grizzly might have persisted in the Southwest as he did in the regions of the Yellowstone and Glacier national parks.

The failure to provide for the grizzly was especially unfortunate after the mid-1920s, when a more enlightened attitude prevailed among U.S. Forest Service administrators and conservation-minded sportsmen. Instead, the federal government assisted in the taking of the few remaining grizzlies. It cannot be ignored that many of the last bears of record in Arizona, New Mexico, and Colorado were killed by the PARC's hound men and trappers. Perhaps even more important, their widespread use of predacides hastened the grizzly's disappearance.

As Ligon (1927) noted, the year 1924 was the low point in numbers of Southwest wildlife. Homesteaders, ranchers, and market hunters — and grazing — had taken their full toll. Both species of bears, grizzlies and black bears, were scarce; the U.S. Forest Service estimated that only 1,500 black bears were residing in national forests in Arizona, New Mexico, southern Colorado, and southern Utah. By way of contrast, more than 3,550 bears were estimated to inhabit the region's forests in 1941 (U.S. Forest Service Annual Summaries of Big Game Animals on National Forests). Other southwestern big-game species — pronghorn, elk, and deer — had also re-

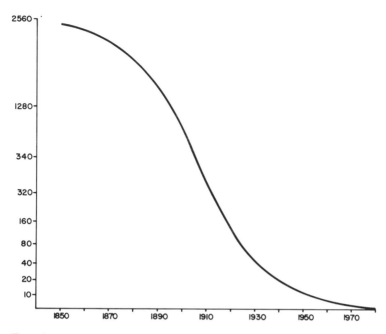

FIG. 1. *Hypothetical decline of grizzly bear populations in the South-west, as suggested by written accounts.*

covered some semblance of their former numbers, if not their ranges, by the late 1930s and early 1940s. This trend, which was general throughout the West (see, e.g., Picton and Picton 1975), was brought on by the abandonment of thousands of small homesteads, the reduction and stabilization of livestock numbers, and the promotion and enforcement of sound game-restoration programs. The grizzly, however, was not permitted to join in this recovery, even if his greatly reduced numbers had allowed him to do so (see, e.g., Craighead et al. 1982). The lack of any refugium made it impossible for the animal's low reproductive rate to recoup the constant attrition from the ranchers and their bear-hunting allies. Thus southwestern grizzlies slid into oblivion, a bear at a time (fig. 1).

Why was this allowed to happen in the conservation-minded era of the late 1920s and 1930s? The grizzly certainly adapted, abandoning open country and bold ways to become a secretive, nocturnal animal. It carefully used the heaviest cover and became the wariest of game. *Ursus arctos* has persisted in smaller and more "civilized" places. There are still small but viable populations in such intensively utilized countries as Sweden, Norway, Poland, Bulgaria, France, and even Italy (Martinka and McArthur 1980). Why could the American Southwest, whose culture is rooted in the frontier and which still possesses tens of thousands of acres of rugged public wildlands, not afford to keep a few grizzlies? The answer is cattle, and more specifically, the Southwest livestock industry.

Few regions of the world have been so dominated by the ranching way of life as has the Southwest. Not only was every acre subjected to grazing, but the attitude of the stockmen—cattlemen especially—pervaded all facets of southwestern culture. For more than forty years the livestock industry overshadowed all other economic enterprises. The ranchmen singlemindedly looked after their economic interests and jealously preserved their way of life. As a result, their political power and cultural influence was, and remains, correspondingly and disproportionately great. Add to this the heritage of the cowboy life-style, and some idea of their cultural influence can begin to be imagined. In that society killing grizzlies was a service. It is no wonder that even Boy Scouts aspired to the taking of a grizzly as the ultimate in meritorious achievement equal to capturing cattle rustlers and army deserters (Schultz 1920). To territorial and state legislators, to administrators of bureaucracies, to political organizations (even those of the sportsmen) the cattleman was indeed king. Nor has his influence greatly diminished until recently.

In 1973, I was resolutions chairman for the New Mexico–Arizona Section of the Wildlife Society. In this capacity I introduced a resolution to reintroduce the grizzly to the Southwest (Appendix A). After considerable and sometimes acrimonious debate the resolution passed by a narrow margin. It paved the way for a feasibility study by the U.S. Forest Service to determine whether the grizzly could be reestablished in New Mexico's Gila Wilderness. The findings of this study, while noting the habitats to be perhaps less suitable than formerly, were generally favorable to such a project and stated that the wilderness would support at least a small resident population (Erickson 1974, appendix B).

The New Mexico Game and Fish Department was understandably cautious, but not opposed to a reintroduction program if it could be made acceptable to adjoining ranchers (most of the grazing leases in the Gila Wilderness had already been purchased by the department for elk and other wildlife and retired from grazing). The job of obtaining the consent, if not support, of the cattle growers went to Dale Jones, U.S. Forest Service staff biologist for Region 3 and an ardent advocate of a grizzly introduction.

The chance to test the waters for such a proposal came at a cattlemen's convention in Albuquerque. Accompanied by Bill Humphries, assistant director of the New Mexico Game and Fish Department, Dale explained to a respected leader of the cattle growers how the reintroduction of America's premier big-game animal would reflect favorably on the public image of the grizzly's former adversaries. He went on to describe how any "renegade" bears that left the wilderness to feed on stock could be promptly controlled. More difficult to address was the potential problem of a grizzly attacking someone—but then all sorts of accidents happen on public lands every year; the risk of being mauled by a bear would be small by any standard.

The cattleman was respectful but silent as he pondered the proposal. When asked to state his reaction, the leader of the stockmen replied laconically, "Dale, I feel like my daughter just married a n——," and walked out. So much for support from the ranchers. As succinctly stated by Craighead et al. (1982), when it comes to transporting grizzly bears to reestablish a historical population, "The requisite technology is available; the legal, social, political, economic and philosophical requirements are not." It is instructive and indicative that the Office of Endangered Species of the U.S. Fish and Wildlife Service does not address the feasibility of reintroducing grizzlies to the Southwest or elsewhere in the Grizzly Bear Recovery Plan.

And so the future of the grizzly in the Southwest hangs on the belief—one might say faith—that a few of the great beasts are holed up in some remote part of Mexico or that a couple of individuals still hang on in Colorado's San Juan Mountains. These hopes are more the musings of late-night campfires than beliefs based on evidence. Unless a remnant population can be found in Chihuahua, the grizzly must be assumed to be biologically extirpated from this great region. Perhaps another generation will bring him back. I doubt whether mine will. Until someone does, the High Mogollon, the San Juans, the Black Range, the Blue, and the Sierra del Nido, like Escudilla, are only mountains.

PART ONE

Western Man Meets Old Ephraim

MARILYN HOFF STEWART

CHAPTER 1

Nomenclature and Taxonomy

The physiognomy of the grizzly bear is now well known to every serious student of American wildlife. The dished-in face, the prominent shoulder hump, and the long, slightly curved claws (three inches or longer) on the forepaws which prevent adult grizzlies from climbing trees—all these characteristics distinguish the grizzly from the black bear. The latter species tends to have a less pronounced brow, lacks the shoulder hump, and has short (less than two-inch), tightly curved, catlike claws on all four feet (fig. 2). These differences were not so apparent one hundred years ago. Because both grizzlies and black bears exhibit a great amount of pelage, size, and behavioral variation, it was widely believed that the western United States was inhabited by several species of bears of numerous varieties.

Today there is a better understanding of bear taxonomy, and field studies have provided a greatly expanded knowledge of the life history, population dynamics, habitat requirements, and behavior of both species. Recent studies of grizzly bears elsewhere in North America, and brown bears in Europe, have provided a basic understanding of grizzly biology, which, combined with the written record, makes the animal's former status, requirements, adaptations, and behavior in the Southwest more evident.

Bears that probably were grizzlies have at various times been descriptively called variegated bears (for the variation in pelt tones), white bears, gray bears, red bears, cinnamon bears, brown bears, silver bears, and silvertips. In Mexico, or among Mexicans, the grizzly was and is known as *oso gris, oso plateado, oso blanco, oso grande,* or simply *el oso* (Sheldon 1925, Leopold 1959). The more appealing names "Bruin"

11

FIG. 2. Above, *the foreclaws of a male grizzly from Chihuahua and,* below, *the foreclaws of a large male black bear from the Mazatal Mountains of Arizona (lower photograph courtesy of Bob Housholder). Grizzly foreclaws are longer and less hooked than black-bear foreclaws and vary from straw color to light brown. The black-bear foreclaw shown is almost 1½ inches long. Black-bear foreclaws are dark brown to black and are similar to the claws on the hind feet.*

and "Old Ephraim" were used in some literary accounts, including those of Theodore Roosevelt (1885). The original use of Old Ephraim was attributed by Clark (1952) to P. T. Barnum, of circus fame.

In earlier times men tended to confuse grizzly bears with the cinnamon phases of the black bear (see, e.g., Coues and Yarrow 1875, Way 1960) or to describe several species of bear based on variations in coat color or behavior:

The kings of our beasts are the grizzly and brown bear. Fortunately there are but few of these ferocious animals in the [Arizona] Territory. An occasional grizzly may be found in the highest mountain ranges in the northern part of the Territory, but the large brown bear, which in Arizona is about as large as a grizzly, may be found anywhere in the mountain ranges which reach an elevation of 7,000 feet and upward.

The brown bear of Arizona closely resembles the grizzly; his head is fully as broad as long, but his nose is more pointed, his hair is from four to five inches long, which hangs in tangled knots. During the first month or two after they come out in the spring, they are very ferocious, and if the hunter surprises him or gets in too close proximity he is almost sure to become the attacking party. We know of a number of instances in which prospectors and hunters have been attacked by the brown bear, some of which ran very narrow escapes. We ourselves have had an experience with the brown bear which we would not care to repeat.

There are a few cinnamon bear in the northern part of the Territory, but they are seldom found in any of the southern mountain ranges.

The little black bear inhabits most of the highest ranges of mountains. Last year they were plentiful in the Santa Catalinas. They are a beautiful little animal, with a coat of fine jet black hair, and are much smaller than the black bear of the north and Western States. ["Fauna of Arizona," *Mining and Scientific Press* 44 (1883):146]

This cavalier attitude toward speciation was not confined to miners and settlers. It was also found among early naturalists, some of whom thought that there were three or even four species of bear in the Southwest.

Less erroneous but leading to even more confusion was the lumping of both species as "bears" or "bar," by the mountaineers and stockmen. Even the Predatory Animal and Rodent Control (PARC) of the U.S. Biological Survey described all stock-killing bears, real or potential, as "big bears," a term used among stockmen to this day. This lack of differentiation also explains the lack of grizzly place-names in the Southwest among the numerous Bear Springs, Bear Wallows, Bear Canyons, Bear Creeks, El Oso, Los Osos, and so on.

The scientific taxonomy was even more muddled. Grizzlies are strongly sexually dimorphic (the males are much larger than the females), and there is a great deal of variation in the skulls of individuals. This last characteristic and the limited amount of material in museums led C. Hart Merriam (1918) to classify two genera of brown bears into fifteen groups including seventy-eight species and twelve subspecies. No less than eight species were described by Merriam for the Southwest from "type specimens" collected near the Santa Rita copper mines; near Fort Defiance, on the Arizona–New Mexico line; near Nogales, on the Arizona-Sonora border; in the White Mountains of Arizona; on Escudilla Mountain, in Arizona; in the Davis Mountains, in trans-Pecos Texas; near Colonia Garcia, in Chihuahua, Mexico; and on Mount Taylor, in New Mexico. In addition, the so-called Utah and Baird grizzlies were described as ranging, respectively, southward to the Pine Valley Mountains in Utah and the San Juan Mountains in Colorado (map 1).

These nominate classifications were not based on descriptions of a series of specimens or on any genetic or behavioral information. Most were based on the measurements of one or two skulls, usually those of large males, from which it is impossible to determine even racial characters, much less separate species. This untenable situation led recent mammalogists to follow Rausch (1963) in considering all grizzlies to be subspecies *horribilis* of the holarctic brown bear *(Ursus arctos)*, the conclusion that had been reached by the astute Elliott Coues almost one hundred years earlier (Coues and Yarrow 1875).

This does not mean that there was not a California grizzly or a Mexican grizzly, or that there is not a Rocky Mountain grizzly. Populations within geographic regions adapted to particular food sources and climatic conditions are often recognizable as *ecotypes* or *biotic types* (Brown 1983). Such populations may also display behavioral adaptations, and it is reasonable to assume that the more subalpine and montane grizzlies of the southern Rockies in Arizona and New Mexico differed somewhat from grizzlies in the Madrean evergreen woodlands of southern Arizona, southwestern New Mexico, Sonora, and Chihuahua. If there were indeed differences in the behavioral traits and physical appearances of these populations, the animals in sub-Mogollon Arizona and west-central New Mexico would have displayed intergrading characteristics of both Rocky Mountain and Mexican forms. Unfortunately, we will never know what characteristics, if any, differentiated the southwestern races; there is simply too little information available to conduct such a study.

CHAPTER 2

The First Encounters, 1540–1825

Bears are poorly represented in the Southwest's fossil record compared to members of the dog and cat families. Grizzlies must have been recent arrivals as there are no records of their remains in the region's Pleistocene caves, shelters, and gravel deposits. Although there are remains of a number of black bears, or *Ursus americanus* (Lindsay and Tessman 1974, Findley et al. 1975), grizzlies are uncommon in the region's pre-Columbian archaeological sites. A recent arrival is also suggested by evidence that grizzlies did not cross the Eurasian land bridge until an interglacial period around 50,000 years ago (Churcher and Morgan 1976 *in* Brown 1982).

EARLY ACCOUNTS

In contrast to their experience in some other parts of North America, the first Europeans found parts of the Southwest already settled at the time of their arrival (1525–50). Pueblo Indians and other descendants of Anasazi and Hohokam cultures were living in permanent villages and practicing both irrigated and dry farming (Martin and Plog 1973). Many of the region's river valleys supported relatively dense populations, leaving the mountains and plains a wilderness inhabited by roving Apaches, Navahos, and Comanches.

At the time of the Spanish Conquest, Coronado found large numbers of bears south of the Zuñi pueblos and bear paws in the possession of Indians at Zuñi (Winship 1896). Like most other Spanish chronicles, Coronado's accounts of wildlife are nonspecific and vague, and some or all of the animals to whom he referred could have been black bears.

For the most part, the Spanish and Mexican periods brought little change to the Southwest other than Spanish nomenclature and a reduction in the number of pueblos. The one exception was the introduction of livestock. In time this aspect of Hispanic culture was to permeate every corner of the Southwest and set the stage for the elimination of at least three of the region's primary large carnivores— the jaguar, wolf, and grizzly.

Administratively, in Spanish colonial times the region south of the Rio Grande and east of the Sierra Madre was included in the provinces of Chihuahua and Durango. "New Mexico" included all the lands north and west of the Staked Plains (Llano Estacado) as far north as the Taos pueblos, with the regional government headquarters at Santa Fe. The western limits of New Mexico were the indefinite boundaries of Apacheria. There was as yet no Arizona; the province of Sonora extended northward on the west side of the Sierra Madre from Cajeme (now Ciudad Obregón), near the California Gulf coast, to Tucson. The country between the Gila River and the Moqui pueblos had long been abandoned by the Anasazi and other sedentary Indians and was the domain of several tribes of Apaches.

That the Indians of Sonora differentiated between the black bear and the grizzly was affirmed by a Jesuit priest, Juan Nentvig, who wrote in 1764 an account of the wild beasts in the province: "Bears, which the Opatas call *mava*, are found in the higher mountains. And there is another variety which they call pissini" (Nentvig 1980:29). A more descriptive account was given in 1795 by another European churchman, Ignaz Pfefferkorn, in a discussion of the animals of Sonora:

Of the sonora bears some have black hair, others dark grey, and the smallest number are a reddish color. These last are the most cruel and harmful, according to the statements of the herdsmen. The herdsmen who often have the opportunity on the field and in the bush to observe the natural impulses of animals tell also that the cinnamon bears eagerly go after ants.

. . . Hence the Spaniards in Sonora call the reddish bear *oso hormiguero* [ant bear]. [Pfefferkorn 1949:107]

Pfefferkorn (pp. 106–107) also gave us the first southwestern account of a fight with a bear and filed the first depredation report:

The Sonora bear looks just as bold and frightful as the European bear, which it resembles in body shape, size, strength, and savagery. However, it does no harm to man because it finds enough to eat in the woods and meadows. If a man attacks it, however, its rage is frightful. I was once a sorrowful witness to this. A brave Indian took me on a journey, and on the way we saw pass us a terrible bear, on its way to hide itself in the nearby mountains. While I continued with my company, the bold Indian remained behind and, unbeknownst to me, followed the ferocious animal. He caught up with the bear as it was climbing the mountain and wounded it badly, as we afterwards saw from its bloody tracks. But thereupon the infuriated animal attacked him and tore him to pieces. These we found lying about when we turned back to look for him.

Bears are a special menace to stock raising, for they eat many a calf, and, if no smaller prey falls into their clutches, they will attack even horses, cows, and oxen. They delight especially in eating maize as long as it is still tender and soft. Woe to the field if a hungry bear breaks into it at night. He eats as much as he can and makes off with as much as he can grasp and carry in his mighty arms. In so doing he ruins even more of the field by breaking it down and treading upon it. The inhabitants of the country assert that a bear defends himself by throwing stones when one attempts to chase him away and that a stone hurled from his paws comes with much greater force than one thrown from the hand of the strongest man. This seems the more remarkable because the bear is supposed to throw the stones backwards. [Pfefferkorn 1949:106–107]

Erroneous information concerning bears was obviously as prevalent then as it is now.

Both the various Apache groups and the Navahos (a closely related Athapaskan-speaking people) avoided contact

Fig. 3. *A group of Navahos with a fresh bear hide, photographed outside Sam Day's Chinle Trading Post, Chinle, Arizona, about 1890. Note the musket, the lances, and the bows and arrows. Photograph by Ben Wittick; courtesy of Museum of New Mexico, Santa Fe.*

with bears. They believed that bears and certain other animals, such as coyotes, snakes, and owls, have sinister supernatural powers. It was thought that contact with a bear, or even its tracks or dung, could cause deadly "bear sickness" (Kluckhohn 1946).

The respected anthropologist Morris Opler quoted a Chiricahua Apache informant:

The bear, like the coyote, causes evil influence. It is killed only in self-defense, for no bear meat is eaten and we are afraid to skin a bear. If you come in contact with the track of a bear, or a tree where a bear has leaned, or bear manure, or if you sleep where a bear has sat down, or if you come in contact with a bear by smell, or touch, you can get sick. [Opler 1941: 224–25]

Most Indians had a healthy respect for bears, and some, because of its similarity to a human being when skinned, had almost a reverence for the bear and considered it taboo to molest one. Nonetheless, certain Pueblo and Navaho clans had bear-hunting cults and considered the claws, feet, and hide to have special significance (fig. 3). These hunts were mostly ceremonial, and with only occasional battles with bears over corn or stock, the Indians probably had little effect on bear numbers or distribution outside the immediate environs of the pueblos.

Of interactions between bears and the Hispanics we know little. The small, largely illiterate Mexican populations were mostly interested in religion and stock raising and paid scant attention to wildlife. If we can accept the prejudiced and somewhat arrogant reports of British and American visitors to Mexico's frontier provinces, life was mean and lacking in social graces. In their descriptions of Santa Fe, Chihuahua, Taos, and Tucson, Hardy (1829), Gregg (1844), and Ruxton (1847) make no reference to the grand hunts, the bull or bear fights, or any of the other cultural practices that graced Hispanic California. Although many New Mexicans and Sonorans were stockmen and some were hunters, they left few accounts of bears or even any descriptions of the occasional encounter with ferocious bears that may have been grizzlies. Only the folk tale of Juan Oso (Ruxton 1847, Dobie 1966) and other legendary bear stories survive in the written record of the Hispanic period. It remained for Americans— beaver trappers, explorers, and tradesmen—to give us written descriptions of bears and grizzlies in the Southwest.

CHAPTER 3

The American Exploration Period, 1825–1865

In 1821, Mexican Independence from Spain opened New Mexico to American trade. In 1822 and 1823 about 120 Americans took the trails across the plains to Santa Fe (Davis 1982) and points farther south. Taos and Santa Fe subsequently became important American trading centers. Most of the trade was in silver and beaver furs, for New Mexico had little else to offer in exchange for American goods.

Trade accelerated in 1824. One of the early entrepreneurs was James Ohio Pattie, a literate, if boastful, mountainman. Pattie was probably the first American to chronicle encounters with grizzlies in the Southwest. Pattie; his father, Sylvester; and a party of twelve Missouri fur trappers reportedly found plenty of bears when they entered New Mexico. In December, 1824, Pattie recorded: "The bottoms, through which we now passed, were thinly timbered, and the only growth was cotton-wood and willow. We saw great numbers of bears, deer and turkeys. A bear having chased one of our men into camp, we killed it" (Pattie 1833:52).[1] This event occurred on the Rio Grande, somewhere near present Socorro.

---

[1] Pattie's dates are almost certainly in error, and his numbers are exaggerated (he reported seeing 220 bears in one day along the Arkansas River). Such tales have led some to discredit Pattie's narrative as largely a boastful fabrication made up on his return in collusion with his editor, Timothy Flint. Pattie's accounts cannot be dismissed that easily, however. To his credit, he places his animals in not-unlikely locations, and he describes new species and locales too accurately to have made them up. Pattie's account should be thought of as indicative but not definitive. For a critical discussion of Pattie's narrative see Carmony and Brown's appendix in Davis (1982).

Pattie's party then headed west for the copper mines at Santa Rita. There they hired two Mexican guides and pushed on to their trapping goal, the headwaters of the Gila (called "Helay" by Pattie), in what is now the Gila National Forest. Once on the Gila, he wrote, "We saw during the day [December 15], several bears, but did not disturb them, as they showed no ill feeling towards us."[2]

Supposedly on the night of January 25, 1825, on the Gila near its confluence with Bonita Creek, Pattie and a companion came upon a cave in which a grizzly bear was hibernating:

I advanced cautiously onward about twenty yards, seeing nothing. On a sudden the bear reared himself erect within seven feet of me, and began to growl, and gnash his teeth. I levelled my gun and shot him between the eyes, and began to retreat. Whatever light it may throw upon my courage, I admit, that I was in such a hurry, as to stumble, and extinguish my light. The growling and struggling of the bear did not at all contribute to allay my apprehensions. On the contrary, I was in such haste to get out of the dark place, thinking the bear just at my heels, that I fell several times on the rocks, by which I cut my limbs, and lost my gun. When I reached the light, my companion declared, and I can believe it, that I was as pale as a corpse. It was sometime, before I could summon sufficient courage to re-enter the cavern for my gun. . . .

Four of us were detached to the den. We were soon enabled to drag the bear to the light, and by the aid of our beasts to take it to camp. It was both the largest and whitest bear I ever saw. The best proof, I can give, of the size and fatness is, that we extracted ten gallons of oil from it. The meat we dried, and put the oil in a trough, which we secured in a deep crevice of a cliff, beyond the reach of animals of prey. We were sensible that it would prove a treasure to us on our return. [Pattie 1833:57–59]

---

[2] Like most other early-day explorers, Pattie did not always carefully differentiate between species of bears. December 15 is late for either species to be out, and the date cannot be taken at face value.

Descending the Gila to the San Pedro River, Pattie's party followed the San Pedro upstream and then crossed the Galiuro Mountains to return to the copper mines, arriving there, he reported, on April 29, 1825. They worked the mines, and in July he said, "We passed our time most pleasantly in hunting deer and bear, of which there were great numbers in the vicinity" (Pattie 1833:74). Pattie also described an Apache Chief, "Mano Mocho," who had lost a hand bitten off by a bear.

In October, 1826, according to his account, en route again to the copper mines, Pattie had another encounter with grizzlies:

This day my course led me up the del Norte, the bottoms of which are exceedingly rich. At a very short distance from the Passo, I began to come in contact with grey bears, and other wild animals. At a very little distance on either side are high and ragged mountains, entirely sterile of all vegetation. I had no encounter with the bears, save in one instance. A bear exceedingly hungry, as I suppose, came upon my horses as I was resting them at mid-day, and made at one of them. I repaid him for his impudence by shooting him through the brain. I made a most delicious dinner of the choice parts of his flesh. My servant would not touch it, his repugnance being shared by great numbers in his condition. It is founded on the notion, that the bear is a sort of degenerated man, and especially, that the entrails are exactly like those of human beings. [Pattie 1833:112]

Once again at the copper mines (in the vicinity of present-day Santa Rita, near Silver City, New Mexico), Pattie rejoined his father and rested for more than a month. He passed much of his time in hunting and related another adventure with a grizzly:

As we approached the ridge, where he had killed the deer, we discovered the bear descending the ridge towards us. We each of us chose a position, and his was behind a tree, which he could mount, in case he wounded, without killing her. This most ferocious and terrible animal, the grizzly or grey bear, does not climb at all. I chose my place opposite him, behind a large rock, which happened to be near a precipice, that I had not observed. Our agreement was to wait until she came within 30 yards, and then he was to give her the first fire. He fired, but the powder being damp, his gun made long fire, whence it happened that he shot her too low, the ball passing through the belly, and not a mortal part. She made at him in terrible rage. He sprang up his tree, the bear close at his heels. She commenced biting and scratching the tree, making, as a Kentuckian would phrase it, the lint fly. But finding that she could not bite the tree down, and being in an agony of pain, she turned the course of her attack, and come growling and tearing up the bushes before her, towards me. My companion bade me lie still, and my own purpose was to wait until I could get a close fire. So I waited until the horrible animal was within six feet of me. I took true aim at her head. My gun flashed in the open. At two strides I leapt down the unperceived precipice. My jaw bone was split on a sharp rock, on which my chin struck at the bottom. Here I lay senseless. . . .

When I had come entirely to myself, my companion proposed that we should finish the campaign with the bear. I, for my part, was satisfied with what had already been done, and proposed to retreat. He was importunate, however, and I consented. We ascended the ridge to where he had seen the bear lie down in the bushes. We fixed our guns so that we thought ourselves sure of their fire. We then climbed two trees, near where the bear was, and made a noise, that brought her out of her lair, and caused her to spring fiercely towards our trees. We fired together, and killed her dead. We then took after the cubs. They were of the size of the largest rackoons. These imps of the devil turned upon him and made fight. I was in too much pain and weakness to assist him. They put him to all he could do to clear himself of them. He at length got away from them, leaving them masters of the field, and having acquired no more laurels than I, from my combat with my buffaloe calf. His legs were deeply bit and scratched, and what was worse, such was the character of the affair, he only got ridicule for his assault of the cubs. I was several weeks in recovering, during which time, I ate neither meat nor bread being able to swallow nothing but liquids. [Pattie 1833:112–14]

Again, the date in Pattie's account appears implausible. The fight is supposed to have taken place in November, when the cubs would have been much larger than raccoons (Wright 1909). Either the date or the size of the cubs must be in error.[3] The story itself, while a bit flamboyant, appears plausible enough.

Pattie also described incidents of bear depredations in cornfields. The following incident had a rather melodramatic outcome:

The country abounds with these fierce and terrible animals, to a degree, that in some districts they are truly formidable. They get into the corn fields. The owners hear the noise, which they make among the corn, and supposing it occasioned by cows and horses that have broken into the fields, they rise from their beds, and go to drive them out, when instead of finding retreating domestic animals, they are assailed by the grizzly bear. I have been acquainted with several fatal cases of that sort. One of them was a case, that intimately concerned me. Iago, my servant, went out with a man to get a load of wood. A bear came upon this man and killed him and his ass in the team. A slight flight of snow had fallen. Some Spaniards, who had witnessed the miserable fate of their companion, begged some of us to go and aid them in killing the bear. Four of us joined them. We trailed the bear to its den, which was a crevice in the bluff. We came to the mouth and fired a gun. The animal, confident in his fierceness, came out, and we instantly killed it. This occurred in New Mexico. [Pattie 1833:114–15]

After their sojourn at the copper mines Pattie and his father joined another party on a winter expedition to the Gila. After a less than successful trip they traveled as far as the Black (Salt) River, where Pattie and his party "killed

[3] Some have used Pattie's accounts to suggest that southwestern grizzlies may not have hibernated or may have had a more variable life history than that of more northern populations. There is nothing in the numerous later accounts to suggest this, however, and it must be assumed that Pattie's descriptions are often from memory and that the dates do not always match the events.

plenty of mountain sheep and deer, though no bears" (Pattie 1833:96). On their return they struck the Pecos River about twenty miles above its confluence with the Del Norte (Rio Grande). Somewhere up the Pecos, Pattie (1833:115) reported: "This day's travel was through a wild and precipitous country, inhabited by no human being. We killed plenty of bears and deer, and caught some beavers." Then "on our return [to the Pecos? the locale is vague] we killed several bears, the talons of which the Indians took for necklaces" (Pattie 1833:119). His final reference to southwestern bears is also indefinite regarding the locale, but it was probably somewhere on the middle Pecos: "We saw plenty of bears, deer and antelope. Some of the first we killed, because we needed their flesh, and others we killed for the same reason that we were often obliged to kill Indians, that is, to mend their rude manners" (Pattie 1833:121).

Pattie's accounts of bears in general, and grizzlies in particular, are most valuable as first accounts. Although the bears on the Pecos may have been black bears, the animal described on the Gila near Bonita Creek, the female and cubs near the copper mines, and at least one of the bears on the Rio Grande were almost certainly grizzlies. His descriptions of the animals in dense riparian forests along the main river channels are of more than casual interest. Because of the early disappearance of grizzlies from these riverine habitats, this documentation of their presence there is important.

The pugnacity of some of Pattie's bears is also of interest, and one wonders whether the more subdued response to human beings observed by later explorers and hunters was due to the demise of the more aggressive bears—or to less sensational reporting. Perhaps it was some of both.

An accurate chronicler of frontier Mexico and the Santa Fe trade was Josiah Gregg (1844). Gregg, who had a more than casual interest in wildlife, mentions grizzlies only once in his account of his extensive travels through the southern Great Plains, New Mexico, Chihuahua, and Zacatecas. In May, 1841, he stated that game, including the formidable grizzly, was considered abundant on Santa Fe Creek in the Sangre de Cristo Mountains (Gregg 1844:102). It should be noted that in his descriptions of wildlife in the southern plains of Oklahoma, Texas, and eastern New Mexico he mentions only the black bear as "common in the thickety streams" (Gregg 1844:377).

New Mexico, Chihuahua, and Sonora had been settled for some time before Pattie's and Gregg's visits, but the Mexican inhabitants appear to have been less inclined to hunt and explore the back country than were the Americans — or at least write about it. This was due in no small part to marauding Indians, whose attacks were forcing Mexico's northern frontier to recede in the first half of the nineteenth century. It was in this setting that an English adventurer, outdoorsman, and careful reporter of events visited Chihuahua and New Mexico. Like the American frontiersmen and traders, who were unaccompanied by women and were not tied to a piece of land, Lieutenant George Augustus Frederick Ruxton had no great fear of Indians. He kept his powder dry, maintained his nerve, and lived long enough to publish the journals of his travels in Mexico and the Rocky Mountains.

Ruxton (1847) correctly noted that there were two species of bear in Chihuahua: "the common black or American bear, and the grizzly bear of the Rocky Mountains." Ruxton (1847:155) believed the latter to be the more numerous and abundant in the mountains near Chihuahua. He considered the grizzly to be a mountain animal and, like Pattie, reported it to be a fierce adversary:

The grizzly bear is the fiercest of the ferae naturae of the mountains. His great strength and wonderful tenacity of life render an encounter with him anything but desirable, and therefore it is a rule with the Indians and white hunters never to attack him unless backed by a strong party. Although, like every other wild animal, he usually flees from man, yet at certain seasons, when maddened by love or hunger, he not unfrequently charges at first sight of a foe; when, unless killed dead, a hug at close quarters is anything but a pleasant embrace, his strong hooked claws stripping the flesh from the bones as easily as a cook peels an onion. Many are the tales of bloody encounters with these animals which the trappers delight to recount to the "greenhorn," to enforce their caution as to the fool-hardiness of ever attacking the grizzly bear. [Ruxton 1847:270]

It was Ruxton, incidentally, who first published the saga of Hugh Glass, the mountain trapper, who was mutilated by a grizzly and left to die by his comrade. Glass survived his terrible wounds and tracked down the partner who had left him for dead.

When the United States declared war on Mexico in April, 1846, New Mexico, including what was to become Arizona, was of little value except as a corridor between newly acquired Texas and coveted California. In 1846 a 1,700-man "Army of the West" under Colonel Stephen Watts Kearny was dispatched from Independence, Missouri, to gain control of the routes through the wilderness and capture the trading centers at the other end. This Kearny achieved when, on August 18, 1846, Santa Fe surrendered to the Americans without battle.

Kearny then divided his army into four units. One he garrisoned at Santa Fe to hold New Mexico. Another, composed of volunteers under Colonel Alexander Doniphan, was ordered to take Chihuahua and then head east and link up with General Zachary Taylor's forces coming up from Vera Cruz. A third unit, composed of Mormons seeking passage to California, was to open a wagon route across Arizona under the supervision of Captain Philip St. George Cooke. Kearny and 300 dragoons headed west for the action in California. This "California Column" included fourteen topographic engineers who were to chart for the first time the Southwest from the Rio Grande to the Pacific.

This seizure of Mexican territory and the events that followed were fortunate for our understanding of Southwest wildlife, although the more development-oriented society that eventually resulted hastened the demise of the grizzly.

Like their British forebears, many Americans had a strong interest in natural history and the literary ability to express it. A surprising number of American soldiers, explorers, travelers, and emigrants kept journals. To its great credit, the United States government was in the forefront of natural history inquiry. Almost every commissioned exploration, boundary survey, and transportation-route reconnaissance force was accompanied by a botanist or naturalist, who was also usually a physician (Brown et al. 1982).

Kearny's topographic engineers, led by Major W. H. Emory, found little game along the upper Gila River. Downstream game became more abundant, but the column's journalists passed through the state without recording any bears (Davis 1982). This is of some interest, for the column essentially followed Pattie's route of twenty years earlier and traveled during the early autumn, when bears should have been active.

The Mormon Battalion had better luck. After a rendezvous at the Santa Rita copper mines, the column headed south into what is now Hidalgo County, New Mexico. There Henry Bigler, one of the volunteers reported: "The country abounds with plenty of game, hardly ever out of sight of antelope and the black-tailed deer. One of the guides [former beaver trappers] shot a grizzly bear up in the mountain [the Animas Mountains?] to vary the camp fare" (Bigler 1932 in Davis 1982).

The Mormons then descended Guadalupe Pass to San Bernardino Ranch. In the San Pedro Valley they found thousands of feral cattle, mostly bulls (Davis 1982). It was now December, however, and no more bears were encountered.

Later, forty-niners bound for the California goldfields followed Captain Cooke's wagon route. After descending Guadalupe Pass, they too found wild cattle abundant, and one of the gold seekers, A. B. Clarke, reported an encounter with a grizzly on the San Pedro River on May 27, 1849:

Three of the men attacked a grizzly bear last night on the other side of the river. They felled him three times, but their ammunition gave out. He was running towards one of the men, whose gun was yet loaded with buck shot, when coming very near, he let it blaze into his face, when they all ran, the men in one direction and the bear in another; this was the last that they saw of him. In the morning, they went out again, and tracked him by his blood some distance. [Clarke 1852:82–83]

Another emigrant, Lorenzo Aldrich, noted a "large bear" prowling through the ruins of San Bernardino Hacienda in October, 1849 (Davis 1982). The ranch was situated near a cienega (swamp formed by springs) far from timber; this is one of the few accounts of southwestern grizzlies in open country.

Other travelers had "bear encounters"—too many to mention here (see Davis 1982). Most of their accounts are vague about the species of bears involved, and provide nothing unusual or instructive about the animals' natural history.

When the Treaty of Guadalupe Hidalgo was signed on February 2, 1848, ending the Mexican War, Mexico's northern holdings were transferred to the United States. Ambiguities in the treaty led to a series of boundary surveys. Each survey party invariably included someone who served in the role of field naturalist. The leader of the Boundary Commission in 1850 was John R. Bartlett, an enthusiastic, if not always precise, observer of wildlife. In May, 1851, Bartlett had this to say about the country around the Santa Rita copper mines, which he considered to be the southern end of the Rocky Mountains:

Bears are more numerous than in any region we have yet been in. The grizzly, black, and brown varieties are all found here; and there was scarcely a day when bear-meat was not served up at some of the messes. The grizzly and brown are the largest, some having been killed which weighed from seven to eight hundred pounds. These are dangerous animals. [Bartlett 1854, 1:256]

Taking Cooke's route, the boundary party headed south for the Animas Mountains. Approaching Guadalupe Pass from the east, they caught two large bears on a hillside in the open. Although chased on horseback, the bears outran their pursuers and escaped. This incident took place early in the summer of 1851 in a region with live oaks and cedars and good grass cover (Bartlett 1854:252).

Bartlett went as far south as the vicinity of Arizpe, in northern Sonora, and then returned to the copper mines. There his boundary arrangements were roundly condemned, and Bartlett set forth again. In late August, in an oak woodland on the west slopes of the Burro Mountains (on the western edge of present-day Gila National Forest) the party was outdistanced by another grizzly:

> While seated on a rock, . . . we were startled by the appearance of a huge grizzly bear, about fifteen rods distant, advancing in our direction. He discovered us at the same moment we did him, and seemed quite as much alarmed, for he suddenly sheered and made his escape at full speed along the base of the hill. We ran for our arms, which we had left with our horses a few yards below; but before we could get them he was too far off for a shot. He crossed directly in the rear of the train, when he made for the hills, followed by several of the party. Coming to a steep ascent, he ran up it with as much ease apparently as he did over level ground, and soon disappeared. The bear has a great advantage over his pursuers in this respect, as his large and pliable feet, and huge claws, enable him to climb the steepest acclivity with the same facility as a cat. The color of this animal was of a silvery gray, with a darker or a black stripe down his back. [Bartlett 1854, 1:363]

In September, Bartlett's party killed a "large black bear" in Arizona between the Whetstone Mountains and the San Pedro River, but it was not until almost a year later, on August 5, 1852, that he had an opportunity to see what may have been a grizzly "close up." Some emigrants wounded a "large brown bear" east of Guadalupe Pass. The bear holed up in a thicket, and one of the hunters was severely bitten on the leg before the beast was dispatched. Bartlett was impressed: "The skin of the animal lay before us, bearing authentic testimony to his immense size" (Bartlett 1854, 2: 335–36).

Bartlett was dismissed as leader of the boundary survey and replaced by Major W. H. Emory. In 1853, after the Gadsden Purchase, which established a new southwestern boundary line between the United States and Mexico, another survey had to be conducted. Full-time naturalists were assigned to the survey parties, and biological data were collected in a professional manner. One of these naturalists, J. H. Clark, collected a grizzly bear for the United States National Museum near the Santa Rita copper mines. This specimen was destined to be one of the several "type specimens" later described by Merriam (1918). Clark provided the first life history of grizzlies in the Southwest, published in 1859 in S. F. Baird's summary of the expedition's zoological data:

The . . . grizzly was found abundant in all the mountainous regions traversed west of Rio Grande. Late in the summer they leave the mountains for the open prairie, it is said by frontiersmen, for some plant which is relished much, and which ripens at this season. What that plant is I was never able to ascertain [biscuit-root?].[4] As far as my observation extended, they make an annual migration from the rugged and unfrequented mountains, which they habitually inhabit late in summer, and probably because the supply of acorns, pinones, and cedar berries, their principal food, is exhausted at this season. Its habitat in the mountains is marked by upturned rocks, which seemed to be displaced for the sake of insects and other animals harboring under them, and loose soil torn up in pursuit of the roots of the cedar and other trees. Notwithstanding its awkward and ungainly gait, where the country is at all rough and broken, it will easily outdistance a mule. I have known this bear, when surprised and suddenly startled, to make a snuffling blow, or a respiratory grunt, which is, I believe, the only sound

---

[4] Biscuit-root *(Lomatium cousei)* was a favorite autumn food of the grizzly, and one species, *(L. nevadense)* could be expected in this region (Kearny and Peebles 1950).

it is capable of producing. Once entering a grassy depression of prairie near the Cobre, I was surprised to see three of these bears sitting on their haunches at a short distance, to all appearances, calmly watching our approach; it was soon evident that they were only reconnoitering, for no sooner did they get the scent of us, than they put off at as rapid a rate as possible. As a rule, they avoid the vicinity of man; yet they have been known to come into camp after the offal after night, and even in day. [Clark in Baird 1859:58]

Clark also collected four black bears at the Santa Rita mines, which Baird (1859) called cinnamon bears because three of the four were more brown than black.

The other collector assigned to Emory's contingent, Dr. C. B. R. Kennerly, also collected a grizzly for the National Museum near Los Nogales, Sonora. He had this to say about the bears:

These animals were observed by us in greater or less numbers in the San Luis mountains, the Sierra Madre, and the Los Nogales; being particularly numerous at the first and last named localities.

The food of these animals, in this country, consists of acorns, walnuts, piñones (the fruit of the *Pinus edulis*), manzanillas, the fruit of an ericaceous shrub, and such animals as they are able to capture. [Kennerly in Baird 1859:28–29]

Arthur Schott probably wrote the following summary, also reproduced by Baird:

Grizzly bear; oso of the Mexicans; shaz of the Apaches. — Near the highest crest of the Sierra Madre, called "San Luis mountains," I had an opportunity to witness a rare butchery, by which, in less than one hour, a whole family of grizzlies was killed, without one offering the slightest resistance. It was about noon on the 11th of October, 1855, when our long train, coming from the Guadaloupe Pass, in the Sierra Madre, towards the San Luis springs, met on the plains these unexpected mountaineers. When surprised, they were lying on the ground not far from each other digging roots. The position in which they performed this work naturally caused long narrow strips of grassy lands to be turned up and searched as if it had been done by a bad plough. I could not learn what kind of roots they had been looking for [biscuit root?]. After taking off the thick skin of these root-diggers, we found them all in a very poor condition, and this may account for the want of that resistance which they failed to offer. The ungrizzly-like behavior of these poor brutes induced the majority of our party to doubt their being grizzlies at all. They evidently had descended from the surrounding mountains, where they have their stronghold in the rough trachytic recesses of this part of the Sierra Madre, the highest crest of which is densely crowned by a dark growth of pines. There their fruit stores had probably given out in the late season, and they were obliged to resort to roots to satisfy their hunger. [Baird 1859:29]

At the same time that the United States–Mexico boundary was being determined, transportation routes were being surveyed farther north. In 1851 a United States Army expedition left Santa Fe to determine a transportation route across northern Arizona and check on the navigability of the Colorado and Little Colorado rivers. The topographic engineer in charge was Captain Lorenzo Sitgreaves, and Dr. S. W. Woodhouse was attending physician and naturalist. Grizzlies were noted along the Little Colorado River and on San Francisco Mountain, but no specimens were obtained. Woodhouse reported: "This formidable animal is found in the mountainous portions of New Mexico and California. About the San Francisco Mountain, near the Little Colorado River, New Mexico, I have frequently seen fresh tracks without having met with the animal, although it was there quite abundant" (Woodhouse in Sitgreaves 1853:43–95). Woodhouse considered black bears "very common in the timbered portions of country in Texas and New Mexico" (Arizona was then still part of New Mexico).

Another government-sponsored southwestern expedition explored the thirty-fifth parallel during the winter of 1853–54 to determine a transcontinental railroad route. Placed under the command of Lieutenant A. W. Whipple, the expedition was well staffed with scientists, including two naturalists. One of these was Dr. Kennerly, who later joined Emory's boundary survey mentioned above. The other was Heinrich B. Möllhausen, an artist and naturalist who had been sent to America by Baron Alexander von Humboldt, the great German explorer-naturalist. While the party made camp at Zuñi, Kennerly and Möllhausen hunted for grizzlies. They were taken to a blind constructed at a spring for this purpose, but they were unsuccessful (Möllhausen 1858, 2:92), probably because it was late November and the bears were in hibernation.

It was late December when the party approached San Francisco Mountain. Near Mount Sitgreaves the naturalists noted the footprints of the "gray bear" and large numbers of what they thought were dens that had been abandoned only a few days before. Though ever alert to collecting opportunities, the expedition members nonetheless failed to meet a bear of either species (Kennerly 1856:6–8).

The next survey party to report bears was Lieutenant Edward F. Beale's expedition to test camels as transport animals and establish a wagon route from Fort Defiance to the Colorado River. Beale (1858) on September 11, 1857, reported seeing a "bear" on San Francisco Mountain and bear sign near the north end of the Juniper Mountains on September 29. However, the species could not be determined.

Möllhausen had another chance for a bear in 1858, when he accompanied Lieutenant Joseph Ives on his reconnaissance up the Colorado River to Black Canyon and then eastward to Fort Defiance. It was other members of the party, however, who first jumped a grizzly, at the headwaters of Cataract Creek, north of Mount Floyd. The encounter occurred on April 21, 1858:

A large grizzly bear—the animals whose tracks we had observed—was seen quietly ascending a hill near by, and half of the company rushed after the grim monster. He was unconscious of pursuit till the party was close upon him. Then he commenced to run, but the hill retarded his pace, and a volley of balls made the fur fly in all directions from different parts of his hide. Twice he turned as though meaning to show fight, but the crowd of pursuers was so large, and the firing so hot, that he continued his flight to the top of the hill, where he fell dead, riddled with bullets. His skin was taken off to be preserved, and the flesh divided among the party. It is rather too strong flavored to be palatable when roasted or broiled, but makes capital soup. [Ives 1861:112]

This was one of the westernmost grizzlies ever taken in Arizona. Later the party reported tracks of grizzlies along Partridge Creek (Ives 1861:113). In 1859, Möllhausen deposited the skull of a grizzly from the Fort Defiance area (the Chuska Mountains) in the United States National Museum, but the particulars of how the skull was obtained are not known; it may have been from the animal taken near Mount Floyd.

Government-sponsored naturalists were not the only ones who encountered southwestern grizzlies. Prospectors and hunters were also exploring the nation's new acquisitions for hidden wealth. Grizzlies were still found in riparian habitats, as, for example, when a party of prospectors killed two of the "brutes" in 1852 in a tributary of "Aravaipa Canyon," which was perhaps Booger Canyon (Thomson 1968).

That southwestern grizzlies hibernated was suggested in the March 10, 1859, issue of the *Weekly Arizonian* (Tubac), Arizona's first newspaper. In an item heralding the arrival of spring, the paper predicted, "It is about time also for grizzly bears and rattlesnakes" (the newspaper was actually about a month premature on both counts). Bears were newsworthy for the paper. An entry in the June 9, 1859, issue read:

A Man Bitten By A Bear.—A few days ago two Mexicans, one on foot and the other mounted, went into the Santa Rita Mountains, about six miles from Tubac to hunt stray horses. On coming to a cañon, where there was water, they came suddenly upon a large cinnamon bear, who, not liking an intrusion upon his retreat, showed fight. He sprang upon the man who was on foot, crushed him down, and bit his thigh; and one arm in a very severe manner. The poor fellow had a knife, but did not succeed in injuring the animal. The man on horseback having no arms, lassoed the bear, who, alarmed by such an unusual method of assault, dropped the man he was lacerating, and made off, breaking the lasso and nearly tumbling over the horse. The wounded man was brought to Tubac where he is being attended to by Dr. Hughes.

Also on June 9, 1859, the paper reported:

Several grizzly bear have been killed by persons working in the timber regions of the Santa Rita mountains, and the fires that are now raging in the canyons will have the effect of driving Mr. Grizzly into the more accessible regions. We should say that it is a good time for a bear hunt in those canons and localities in the mountains where the fires have not burned.

The *Arizonian* reported on June 23, 1859:

Ugly Visitors.—One night last week three bear, probably of the cinnamon species, came down and drank out of the Santa Cruz, within a few hundred yards of Tubac. The next morning they were seen on the trail to Santa Rita by a Mexican, who prudently rode around them and passed on.

That southern Arizona was well populated with "cinnamon" bears was also verified by a prospector with the unlikely name of Phocian R. Way (1960:283). In 1858, writing in his diary about the south slopes of the Santa Rita Mountains, he commented:

Bears are very numerous here of these species, the black bear, the brown or as it is called here the Cinnamon bear, and the fierce and dreaded grizzly. The brown bear is the most common and is almost as dangerous as the grizzly. It will attack a man without provocation, but it is smaller and not so hard to kill as the grizzly. The grizzlys are not so numerous but there are a good many of them. The black bear here as everywhere is cowardly and will run from the hunter, and will not fight unless he is badly wounded or cornered and cannot help it. It was this last species that Grosvenor and Fuller chased from our camp yesterday morning. [Way 1960:287]

Way described an encounter with what may have been a grizzly near their mining claim on July 6, 1858:

Yesterday 2 of our men, Randall and McCoy, had an encounter with a large cinnamon bear. They were cutting timber at the foot of a mountain close by, when they saw a bear on the side of the mountain feeding upon acorns. They crept up slightly within a hundred yards of him without being seen. When Mr. Randall raised his rifle, took deliberate aim and fired, the monster dropped on his knees, roared with pain, but recovered himself in an instant and discovered his enemies and darted like lightning down the mountain. They saw him coming and knew their danger. McCoy sprang into the fork of a low mesquite tree and he had hardly done this before the bear was at the foot of the tree with his mouth wide open, ready to drag him down. Mc snapped his revolver three times at him but it would not go off, and the bear would certainly have "wiped him out" if he had not caught a glimpse of Randall making fast time down the hill. Randall could find no tree to climb and was forced to depend on his legs for safety. The trees here are few in number and very small—not more than 10 or 15 feet high from the ground to the topmost branch. The bear, attracted this time by a new object, left Mc and pursued Randall. Mc at this moment succeeded in firing off his treacherous pistol and gave him another wound, but he would have caught Randall in a few more bounds if his vitality had continued; but fortunately for both parties he had "run his race" and dropped dead in his tracks.
All this transpired in less than a minute's time, and illustrates the great danger of bear hunting. At this moment Grosvenor came up and, anxious to have a hand in so glorious an affair, shot the prostrate brute in the head and "killed him again." They cut him open and found that the first ball had entered his flank and passed through his lights [lungs], liver and heart and lodged in his shoulder. It was a large ball from a Mississippi Yaeger. This is the wound which really proved

fatal, but if he had succeeded in catching both of the men he would have lived long enough to kill them. Their tenacity of life is truly wonderful. We have now killed a bear and a tiger in the short time we have been in the mountains of Santa Rita. Deer, we do not count them. [Way 1960:355–56]

Arizona was separated from New Mexico Territory in 1863, in the midst of the Civil War. The exploration period was coming to a close, and settlement was underway. Elliott Coues, an Army physician and biologist stationed at Fort Whipple, near Prescott, the Arizona Territory's first capital, summed up frontier conditions in his *Quadrupeds of Arizona,* published in 1867:

The wild and primitive region which constitutes the Territory of Arizona exhibits a remarkable diversity of surface of its mountain ranges, grassy plains, and desert wastes; and its Fauna and Flora are varied in a corresponding degree. The traveller meets, at each successive day's journey, new and strange objects, which must interest him, if only through the wonder and astonishment they excite. In every department of Natural History there is ample field for observation and study; and even at this late day, opportunities for discoveries in Zoology and Botany. First in importance, as they are also in general interest to the observant traveller, are undoubtedly to be ranked the quadrupeds of the country; and so savage and unreclaimed as its condition, that they are there to be seen in what is truly a state of nature. Their habits, and even their numbers have been as yet scarcely subjected to modifying influences by contact with civilization; and he must be stolid indeed, who, under such rarely favorable circumstances, does not look about him with interested attention, and learn something of the strange animals by which he is surrounded. [Coues 1867:1(6):281–82]

Although his major interest was ornithology, Dr. Coues assembled a formidable collection of mammals, including a grizzly from the San Francisco Peaks. Coues considered that the bears were already reduced in their numbers though not in their range:

Bears of at least two species are found, and are not uncommon, at least in all the wooded, and particularly the mountainous portions of the Territory. The vicinity of the San Francisco and Bill Williams Mountains was formerly noted for the
numbers of these animals found there, though they appear to
have somewhat decreased of late. The southern Rocky Mountains, and the ranges of California, seem to be particularly the
home of the huge Grizzly, . . . which becomes less numerous
farther north. A variety . . . extends into Mexico. The common
Black Bear . . . also includes Arizona in its very extensive
range. [Coues 1867:1(7):354]

CHAPTER 4

Settlement, 1865–1912

At the time of the Civil War both the American and the Mexican halves of the Southwest were largely uninhabited by whites. Bands of Apaches, Navahos, and Comanches attacked the few mining camps, farms, and ranches almost at will. These circumstances changed rapidly with the cessation of hostilities. Poor economic conditions in the East and the passage of the Homestead Act in 1862 were powerful incentives for settlement in the West.

For the protection of the settlers the Indians had to be subdued, tamed, and settled on reservations. To accomplish those goals, the army was sent west, and forts and camps were established. Many of these, such as Fort Davis, Fort Stanton, Fort Bayard, Fort Lowell (New Mexico), "old" Fort Wingate, Fort Tularosa, Camp Bowie, Fort Huachuca, Fort Apache, Camp Wallen, and Camp Verde, were in or adjacent to prime grizzly country (map 1). Bears were still relatively unsophisticated in regard to man, as illustrated by the following account of an incident that occurred at the northern end of the Huachuca Mountains in 1867, when the writer, John Spring, was stationed at Camp Wallen:

I had just entered upon this turn when I heard a noise to the right above me, and looking up perceived several rocks rolling down the mountain side, which was in places covered with small scrub oaks and creosote bushes. Presently there came into view what at first seemed a large tumbling fur ball rolling down the steep declivity. As it came nearer I made out that it was a bear running obliquely towards me. What astonished me not a little was the fast gait he was able to maintain while descending steep ground covered with loose stones,

41

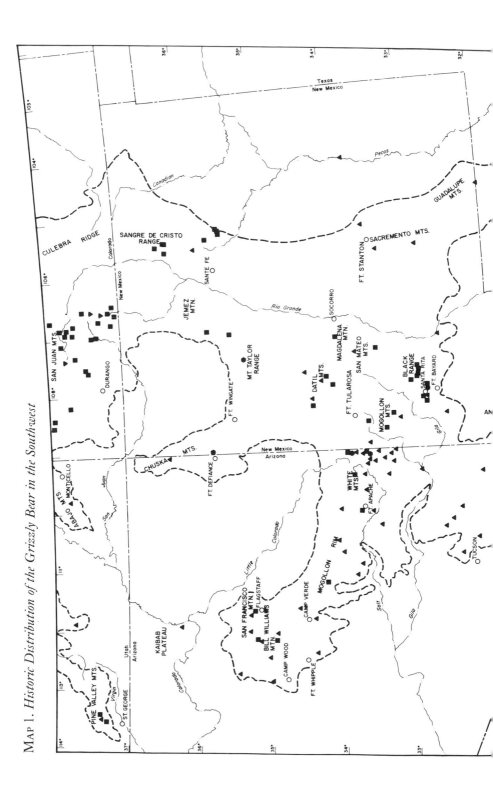

MAP 1. *Historic Distribution of the Grizzly Bear in the Southwest*

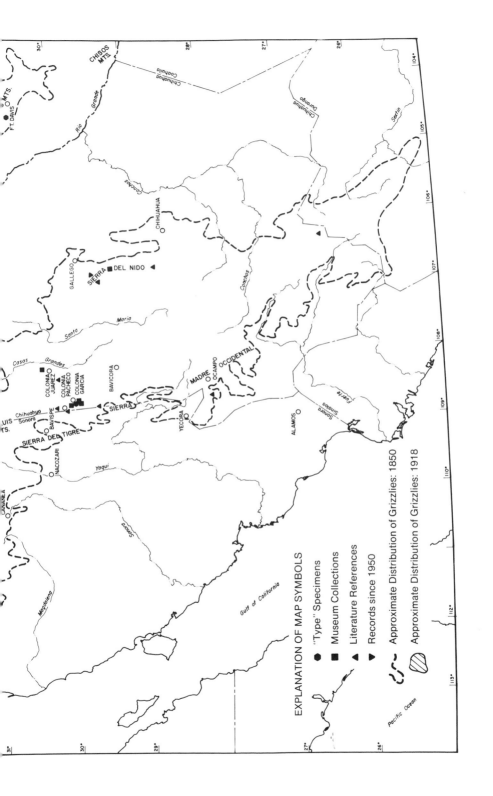

EXPLANATION OF MAP SYMBOLS

- ⬢ "Type" Specimens
- ■ Museum Collections
- ◀ Literature References
- ▶ Records since 1950
- ◠◡ Approximate Distribution of Grizzlies: 1850
- ◡◠ Approximate Distribution of Grizzlies: 1918

CHISOS MTS.

FT. DAVIS ● ○ MTS.

Rio Grande

Chihuahua
Coahuila

Chihuahua
Durango

Satin

CHIHUAHUA ○

Conchos

GALLEGO ○

SIERRA ■ DEL NIDO ◀

◀

Maria

Santa

Casas   Grandes

COLONIA ○
JUAREZ

COLONIA ◀
PACHECO

COLONIA ■
GARCIA

BAVICORA ○

MADRE   OCCIDENTAL

OCAMPO ○
○

◀

Chihuahua
Sonora

SIERRA ◀

LUIS ○
TS.

BAVISPE ◀ ■○ ◀

SIERRA DEL TIGRE

YECORA ○
○

ALAMOS ○

Sonora

Fuerte

NACOZARI ○

Yaqui

CANANEA
A ○

Sonora

Magdalena

Gulf of California

Pacific Ocean

30°
28°
27°
26°

104°
105°
106°
107°
108°
109°
110°
112°
113°

31°
30°
29°
27°
26°

a feat that no horse, not even the Mexican mustang, can accomplish. He reached the edge of the steep opposite bank of the ravine, and as I had stopped he stopped also, audibly sniffing the air, which probably carried to him the odor of the fresh meat upon my saddle. The ravine was fully thirty yards wide, and across this chasm we surveyed one another.

The bear was soon dispatched, and furnished several good roasts, for one of which I took half a hindquarter to camp in exchange for the beef I had brought. The bear was not large, probably not over three years old, and could hardly weigh more than 500 pounds "on the hoof"; but its meat was tender and juicy. The skin I have still, and regret to say that it contains more bullet holes than the desirable number, and certainly far more than are generally made in the killing of a cinnamon bear. [Spring 1966:111–13]

The grizzlies not only supplied fresh meat for the troops but sport for the posts' hunters. They had not yet become wary of man and were still sometimes caught out in open country:

On the 19th of June last [1871], Captain James C. Hunt, First Cavalry, and Captain W. S. Fuller, Twenty-first Infantry, with five mounted men, left Camp Apache, Arizona, for a short visit to the Zuni villages, or Pueblo Indians. The villages lie very nearly one hundred and thirty miles from Camp Apache, on the road to Fort Wingate, New Mexico, perhaps forty miles from that post. Early in the morning, just after the party had crossed the Rio Colorado Chiquito, on the bank of which they had camped the night before, they passed over an open plain that rose in slight undulations covered with a growth of sage brush and scattering scrub oak. On reaching the top of one of the swells an immense bear was discovered about a mile ahead, evidently coming down the trail to the river for water. The bear at the same moment catching sight of the party turned off to his right, and was heading for the foothills some eight or nine miles distant, as if desirous of gaining the timber. He struck a gait apparently of the clumsiest kind imaginable, but which when tested by the speed of the horses proved that at least for some distance a horse at full speed can hardly keep up with a bear—such ones as we find in the chain of the Rocky Mountains, or the continuations of that range.

By permission of Captain Hunt, Captain Fuller, with Corporal Hyde and Privates Armstrong and Haley, started out their horses to overtake the bear before he could reach the mountains or the rocks and timbers of the foot hills. With horses in good condition, and a free use of spurs, after a chase of four or five miles they succeeded in closing to a few rods distance, or about thirty yards. The party were armed with Spencer carbines and revolvers, with the exception of Captain F., who carried a heavy Army revolver only. Maintaining a distance of twenty or thirty yards, a lively fire from all was opened on Bruin, but without serious effect. It is not so easy as it may appear to hit an object even of considerable magnitude with carbines or revolvers from the saddle when both the rider and the object fired at are moving at a jump and run, and on rough ground at that.

Captain Fuller by good luck first succeeded in sending a ball through Bruin's hind leg. The effect was to cause the brute to run on three legs, with his right hind leg held off the ground, crimsoned with a free flow of blood. The bear at first rather increased his speed, but the wound soon began to tell on him, as he attempted after gaining a little distance to turn and bite at the wounded foot. A shot from Corporal Hyde's carbine again cut him across the ham. The whole party, keeping up their fire, had drawn up to within some twenty yards of him, when he whirled short round to the left and bounded toward the horse of Corporal Hyde. The corporal turned his horse and gave him the spur, but in a wonderfully short time, considering the clumsy movements of the bear, he overtook the horse and caught him by the flanks. The poor horse gave one desperate kick, for an instant throwing off the bear, but in a second more the horse was pulled down on his haunches, and with one motion of his paw the bear knocked Hyde out of the saddle. The horse galloped off wildly, while the corporal, without any weapons, was rolling on the ground struggling for his life in an actual and literal wrestle with a wounded bear.

It was a desperate position and unequal contest on the ground. Captain Fuller and Armstrong reined in their horses, while within three yards of their horses' feet was this enormous bear ferociously biting and tearing the limbs of the unlucky corporal. The weapons of the party had been discharged and were empty; and with the coolest of men it requires some little time to load a Spencer carbine or revolver while in the saddle. Corporal Hyde struggled manfully, striking with his fists and arms down the mouth and throat of the bear, while his own blood ran in streams from his wounds.

The bear rose twice on his hind legs, standing much above the corporal's head, and the two literally wrestled as two men would in a prize fight. The wounded leg of the bear was Hyde's salvation, or the claws in the brute's hind feet would soon have torn out his entrails. In ferocity and wildness nothing could surpass the horrible appearance of the brute, with bloody foam dripping from his jaws, while the poor man called to the party to help him for God's sake or he would die. No one had a load to fire. Armstrong, believing that there was a load in his carbine, jumped off his horse, and placing the muzzle of his piece against the side of the bear pulled the trigger, but it only snapped. The next instant the bear left Hyde and was tumbling Armstrong, biting and tearing him as he had done with Hyde, who was lying covered with blood a few feet distant. It looked in this position of affairs as if two of the party would receive mortal wounds before the others could assist them. But here Haley got one load in his pistol and fired it at the bear. The ball must have cut him, for he bounded away from Armstrong, and, with his leg held up, again ran for the mountains. The two men presented a dreadful sight, with pale faces, streams of blood running down them, and their clothing torn in shreds. Corporal Hyde only said, 'Here is my carbine; kill the d——d beast for me, captain, for God's sake!" pointing to his carbine that had been dropped a few yards off when the bear first attacked his horse.

As the rest of the party would soon be up, Captain Fuller and Haley reloaded the carbines, and, having done the best to make Hyde and Armstrong as comfortable as circumstances would admit, remounted and rode after the bear, who was making his way toward the hills, occasionally turning round to lick his hind quarters. The horses, pushed to a run, soon overtook the wounded brute. Riding up to a safe distance, Captain Fuller and Haley fired from their carbines, keeping their horses well in hand to avoid any rush of the bear. After a few shots from each and several attempts of the brute to get at the horses, he turned at bay under a scrub oak, evidently unable to go further and ready to fight. Still the bear's vitality was so great that a dozen more deliberate shots were required, each passing through some part of his body, before his head dropped and he expired.

The conformation of the ground, and the distance ridden in chase of the bear, had concealed these mishaps from the rest of the party, who were greatly surprised at the bloody result of the chase. The bear was of uncommon size, of a brown color, and displayed a boldness and ferocity not credited to that animal by naturalists. The wounds of the men were dressed as well as possible, and with much exertion they were able to reach Zuni villages the second day after the fight. [Correspondence, *Army and Navy Journal,* August 12, 1871]

While he was stationed in the Chiricahua Mountains in the 1880s, J. C. Hancock found bears "thick." Beef for the soldiers was butchered at Bear Springs, about three-quarters of a mile from Fort Bowie, in Apache Pass between the Chiricahua and Don Cabezas mountains:

One day one of the Indian scouts came into the butcher shop and asked Mr. M. L. Woods, who had the beef contract at the Post if he would want to "buyum bear." Sure said Mr. Woods, "How much?" "Two dolla," said the scout. All right said Mr. Woods, handing him the money, "you get the bear." "You come, me showum," said the Indian, and he led the way across the little ridge between the Post and the spring to where the slaughter pens were and there was a big silver-tip eating on the head of a freshly killed steer. "There your bear," said the Indian. Mr. Woods told me afterward that it was the one and only time he ever bought a bear "on the hoof." They came back to the post and got some of the boys and guns and went back and killed the bear and the next day there was bear meat issued instead of regulation beef. [Hancock 1930:17]

One effect of these encampments of armed men was an immediate reduction in the local grizzly populations. Of even greater significance were the mining communities. Not only did the wide-ranging prospectors kill any bears that they encountered but also the semiprofessional hunters who supplied the mining camps rarely passed up an opportunity to bag a bear:

> July 8th [1858].
> Yesterday Mr. Fuller and myself went out with our guns for a short hunt near the mining camp [at the south end of the Santa Rita Mountains]. When about a mile from our Ranche we saw a large cinnamon [bear] walking leisurely along, stopping occasionally to take a bite at the wild cactus. He was distant about 600 yards and had not seen us. We crept softly up toward him in the cover of a canyon until we were within a hundred yards of the spot when we had last seen him. When we clambered up the steep bank under a low scrubby tree, there was the monster in open view. He had evidently got wind of us, for he was snuffing the air and tossing up his head. They are very keen scented and when the wind is in their favour they can scent a man a long distance. We had no time to lose for the bear had already turned to run. We knew our only safety was to keep ourselves hid from his view, for if we wounded him he would be upon us in a moment if he should happen to see where the shot came from. It is true we might climb the [s]crubby tree (which was the only one near); but we could not see that we would get entirely out of his reach, and we would likely have hard fighting to do before we gained the victory.
> It was a critical moment and I felt we were standing on dangerous ground. Fuller, being the best shot, levelled his gun and fired. He struck the bear for he gave an awful grunt, reared on his hind legs, and looked around in every direction for his enemies. We were concealed by the rocks and lay still as mice. He did not see us. Becoming frightened at the stillness around him, [he] started to move off. I took courage at this and fired my sharp shooter at him, but this only made him run faster. He soon disappeared over the mountain. We tracked him by his blood about a mile and then gave up the chase. If we had come upon him suddenly it might have cost us our lives, so we followed him with great caution. [Way 1960:356–57]

By the 1870s and 1880s large cattle ranches and some sheep outfits were carving out enormous holdings in the public domain. Many of these were bankrolled by investors back east or in Europe, and not a few of the latter ranches were operated by remittance men, younger sons of wealthy British families whose operations in Canada, Australia, and the United States were subsidized with checks from home. By 1885 large spreads—such as Aztec Land and Cattle Company's Hashknife, southwest of Holbrook, Arizona; the Empire, in southeast Arizona; and the VT and GOS ranches, north of Silver City, New Mexico—all but covered the Southwest.

One such ranch was the SU, which was headquartered near Horse Springs, in west-central New Mexico and owned by a one-armed Englishman named Montague Stevens. Like his British neighbors forty miles south on the WS Ranch, Stevens was a gentleman rancher and was not forced to wrest a living from his range. Such ranchers considered their occasional livestock losses to grizzlies a nuisance and a business expense. To ranchmen like Stevens and William J. French, of the WS Ranch near Alma, bear hunting was more a sport than a necessity. French wrote:

One of our occasional pastimes in those days, and one that afforded us much excitement, was a bear hunt. These we enjoyed at the invitation of Mr. Tom Lyons of the L C Ranch. He had a motley collection of dogs which he called bear-hounds, and in company with his friend Dr. Barron of Tarrytown, N.Y., used to visit our section in pursuit of his favourite game. . . .

Our country was a favourite habitat for Bruin, both the Mogollon Range and the mountains to north and west of us containing a goodly number. There was some debate as to the best district to try, which was shortly decided in favour of the head waters of the Gila in the vicinity of the West Fork, and thither Trayler and his assistant Bob Stubblefield were sent with all the dogs except Gyp to make camp, while Lyons with Dr. Barron and Gyp and I were to follow them later.

Bright and early the following morning they discovered some huge footprints and put on the hounds. But they led into a country that was practically impossible for horses, so we all took posts of vantage at different points, hoping they might get Bruin afoot and drive him to us. These posts, owing to the nature of the country as well as to the custom of the quarry, were necessarily far apart and usually taken with a view to covering the most likely place to be followed by a bear in his descent from the high mountains. . . .

It took us more than half an hour to reach our destination, and when we got there we found a wide, open canyon, with scattered timber and large clumps of oak brush lying fairly close together. The park into which it opened was thickly timbered with pines and pinon and cedar scattered in between. The mountains rose up almost perpendicular on all sides of it, and it looked an attractive shelter for a solitary bear.

There being nothing to do but wait, we took up our stations close to a clump of brush, and sitting sideways on our saddles beguiled the time chatting in subdued tones. Gyp, as was usual with her, jumped off and was skirmishing around the brush in search of chipmunks or anything that might interest her and help to pass the time. We paid no attention to her, and as we could still hear the hounds a long way off had no idea of the close proximity of a bear or any other large game.

Our surprise consequently can be imagined when there came crashing from a clump of brush, not over forty yards up the canyon, a bear that looked to me almost as big as a full-grown steer. [French 1965a:195–200]

Like French, Montague Stevens hunted often between 1888 and the turn of the century. Stevens's SU and other operations covered some excellent grizzly range in the Datil, San Mateo, Magdalena, Tularosa, and other mountain ranges in what is now Catron County, New Mexico. Stevens became totally enamored with bear hunting. He developed a superb stable of hunting dogs and devoted much of his energy to the study of "Mr. Grizzly," his favorite game. Nonetheless, Stevens (1943) stated that it took him six starts on a grizzly to bring one successfully to bay. In his first ten years of hunting, he bagged only five grizzlies. Clearly, such totals would have done no permanent harm to the grizzly population. What threatened the grizzlies was what threatened the large ranches: the dreaded nesters' small cow outfits and the sheepmen.

With the coming of the railroads in the 1880s, the influx

of settlers to the Southwest became a surge. Congress, intent on settling the West, had endeavored to make it easy to obtain a ranch homestead. Although much of the country was unsuitable for farming, one could "prove up" a claim by raising a few vegetables next to a creek and, if the opportunity presented itself, start a ranch, using a long rope and a running iron, if necessary.

The Homestead Act of 1862 allowed the homesteading of 160 acres by anyone who would live on his claim and make improvements each year for five years. To make it even easier to homestead the West, the Timber Culture Act was passed in 1873. This law gave a homesteader an additional 160 acres if he maintained 40 acres in commercial trees. These so-called "timber claims" are relevant to this discussion because they encouraged the settlement of bear country by settlers with families (fig. 4).

Gardner (1893) and Housholder (1966) relate an incident—probably the same one—in which a grizzly was shot near Pinetop, Arizona, after it had killed farm animals, broken into a cabin, and frightened the family of a timber-claim homesteader.

Discouraged by the ruinously low cattle prices through the late 1880s and early 1890s and bedeviled by drought and grass-depleted ranges, the eastern and foreign investors in the large cow outfits wanted out. The big spreads were broken up and absorbed by smaller ranches. Most important, the large areas of public domain became available to any homestead with permanent "base waters" and "tenure" —that is, to established homesteaders. The newly created national-forest lands were thus apportioned out to the small ranchers, and the numbers of grazing leases proliferated through the turn of the century.

A colorful but not atypical account of the determination of these "newcomers," the conditions of the times, and their reactions to the grizzlies is provided in the memoirs of James A. Cosper (the son of Toles Cosper, referred to below):

Four brothers, three married (George, Ed and Toles) and

Fig. 4. A grizzly taken near Chloride, New Mexico, by Christian Olson in the 1880s. Note the shortage of grass cover here in the foothills of the Black Range. Photograph by Henry A. Schmidt; courtesy of Museum of New Mexico, Santa Fe (neg. no. 12241).

one single (John) left Abilene, Texas in covered wagons in the Spring of 1886 and landed in Magdalena, New Mexico that fall and settled there. They were there for about two years and Toles' first child was born there, Effie, and the first one for George. In about a year, George and Ed moved to Duncan, Arizona and settled there, taking up farms. Toles and John stayed in Magdalena for about another year and then they moved to Luna, New Mexico and settled there. All the while, they had this little herd of cattle they came along with, a few head of cattle. . . .

They were in Luna for a couple of years. Toles was made Justice of the Peace and ran cattle there. John worked for different outfits around, including an English outfit with thousands of cattle carrying the VT brand. Toles worked for an outfit that branded JTH and they went out of business. Toles and Bill Lee (no relation to the Mormon Lees) gathered the remnant (400–500 head) and sold them to a fellow over west of Tonto Basin. They had to deliver them over there and they went through there during that cattle and sheep war they had in there. They came off into a ranch. Before they came to the ranch, they held the cattle up three or four miles up on a big mesa or prairie. Toles went ahead to see if they could get through and as he pulled up at this ranch, there were two men hanging on a cottonwood tree. He rode on down to the ranch. There were 20 or 30 men around there, cattlemen. He told them his business and that he'd like to go on through. So they told him that was all right, to go right ahead. So he went ahead and delivered his cattle and went back to Luna.

There were a lot of wild cattle in the country. There was an outfit that had thousands of cattle and they branded a big Y on each shoulder and they called it the Y. Toles and a fellow by the name of Bill Jackson bought that remnant after they went out of business and they gathered on them for three or four years, gathered a lot of them, and they got a pretty good little start from that Y remnant. That was in about 1896 or 1897 when they bought the place. It was in 1897 when Toles bought the Y-Y ranch and he bought this remnant before he bought the ranch. He was there from then on. . . .

Toles [later called "Bear" Cosper] was a great hunter and had an old 42-70 that he killed a lot of bear with, and deer. And when these Winchesters came out, the 30-40, he got one of those. He killed one bear that got up on the horse behind him, got the cantle of the saddle and pulled all the leather off of it. It cut the horse's hip pretty badly. He got away from that one, got out there and got his rifle and killed the old bear. And another time, DeWitt, Johnny and Jim and Frank Balke were with him. They were just kids: Frank and DeWitt were probably 18 years old. DeWitt, Johnny and Jim were down under the hill and Frank and Toles on top of the ridge. De-Witt, Johnny and Jim scared a bear off of a cow that he had killed and he went right up to Frank and Toles. Toles jumped off his horse and started shooting at the bear. He wounded him and he was charging, fighting and trying to get to them. Frank Balke would run between Toles and the bear while Toles was reloading, and the bear almost got ahold of Frank a couple of times. Toles got his gun reloaded and finally killed the old bear. By the time he got him killed, DeWitt, Jim and Johnny were up there. Those were about the two narrowest escapes he ever had, although he killed several grizzly bears after that. He killed mountain lions and bear. They were quite a problem in those days—they killed lots of stock. But all the cowmen had lots of cattle—they could afford it. And the horses—every rancher had a bunch of mares and tried to raise his own horses, but the lions killed 75% of the colts. You could very seldom raise a colt. Toles built bear pens and caught a lot of them that way—lots of bears and lions both, in those pens. They built a log cabin about four feet high with a drop door in it [fig. 5]. Turkey and deer, goodness knows how many of them were killed. Of course, there were no game laws in those days. [Cosper 1969:1–4]

In 1909, Congress passed the enlarged Homestead Act, which provided for homesteading of up to 320 acres when crops were raised for three years. As Congress became more aware of the inapplicability of farming measures to the arid and mountainous Southwest, this act was supplemented by the Stock Raising Homestead Act, by which a ranching homesteader could gain title to 640 acres of grazing land. These acts were to have far-reaching effects on the grizzly, for they encouraged men and women to take up ranching in every part of the country (fig. 6). More homesteads were filed in Arizona and New Mexico's mountains between 1910

FIG. 5. *Remains of a crude but sturdy cabin trap built by Eugene ("Stutterin'") Charlie Johnson about 1880 in Wild Bunch Canyon in Arizona's Blue River drainage. Note the gun ports. Photographs taken in 1984 by Jim Brooks and John Snyder. Information supplied by Ed Stacy.*

FIG. 6. *Duett Ellison, later the wife of Governor George W. P. Hunt of Arizona, and a grizzly that she killed in 1907. This is one of the few photographs of a grizzly, and the only one known of a whole animal, from Arizona. Note the large head, claws, and long fur. Reproduced from the Roscoe Willson Photograph Collection; courtesy of the Arizona Historical Foundation.*

and 1920 than at any other time (Beck 1962, Faulk 1970, Bahre 1977).

By 1912, when Arizona and New Mexico attained statehood, the Southwest had been thoroughly settled. Almost every live stream, every arable piece of flat ground, every meadow possessed a ranch or a farm. Use of the range was universal, and there were more people in the mountains than there are now. Oats, pinto beans, and potatoes were important crops. Only on the Indian reservations and in Mexico was there still wild country to be "taken up," and even in those bastions of wilderness inroads were being made. Americans and Europeans now acquired Mexican ranches that were the size of small states (Machado 1981). Mormon colonists moved onto large tracts of the Sierra Madre, and their farms became a force in western Chihuahua and along the Río Bavispe, in eastern Sonora. The governments of both countries encouraged development of untapped natural resources. Sawmills, railroads, ranches, and roads invaded the backcountry.

The grizzly was everywhere under siege, and his numbers were being reduced. Yet a number of populations persisted. Although he had been removed from the riverbottoms and from some of the isolated mountains, the grizzly's primary range was still intact. Moreover, the establishment of the national forests in the period from 1907 to 1912 had the potential for his salvation. That was not to be only because of bad economics and good politics. More about that later.

MARILYN HOFF STEWART

PART TWO

The Southwest Grizzly at Home

CHAPTER 5

Pelage and Measurements

Southwesterners always had difficulty differentiating grizzlies from the lighter shades of black bears. Poor light, partial concealment, or the animal's rapid movement could make field identification difficult, particularly when the animal was a subadult. The larger size of the grizzly was also difficult to ascertain unless there was something to relate it to, and bears were often identified on the basis of sign.

Grizzlies throughout the Southwest varied in coat color from a pale buffy yellow to a chocolate umber, but were rarely if ever solid black (fig. 7). Unlike black bears, most grizzlies have variegated pelage, and on older animals the ends of the guard hairs are lighter colored—hence the name silvertip. Grizzly hairs are also distinctive (fig. 8). Typically they are longer, wavier, and silkier than the shorter, more uniform hairs of Southwest black bears, and their fur has a distinctive texture. An excellent description of the variation in the pelage of grizzlies in Chihuahua was provided by Sheldon (1925), who noted:

Observed from a distance when the sun shines on them, the buffy-colored bears appear white. This is the reason why Mexicans believe that two species of grizzly bears occur in the mountains, giving the name of *oso blanco* to the light colored ones, and *oso plateado* to the others. Also they often call either a dark grizzly, or a cinnamon colored black bear *oso alesan* [*alazán*]. [Sheldon 1925:159–60]

The colors of New Mexico and Arizona grizzlies, according to Bailey (1931), ranged from dull brown with yellow tips on the long hairs to grizzled brownish black. Other

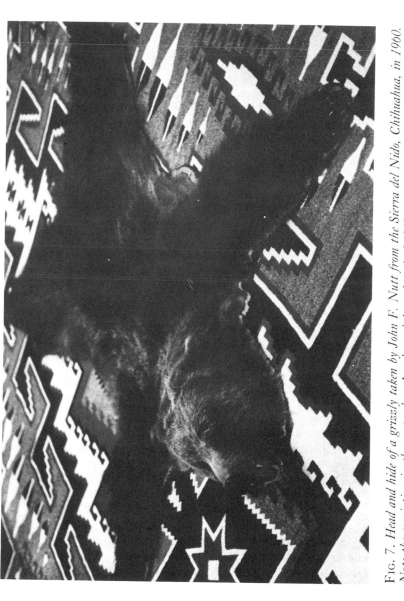

FIG. 7. *Head and hide of a grizzly taken by John F. Nutt from the Sierra del Nido, Chihuahua, in 1960. Note the variation in the coat color. Another adult male grizzly hide, in the possession of G. W. Evans, Jr., of Magdalena, New Mexico, taken in 1930 in the Black Range, is also variegated and dark, but has shorter hair. Although larger than the Nutt grizzly, the Evans grizzly appeared smaller than Montana and Canadian grizzly specimens examined.*

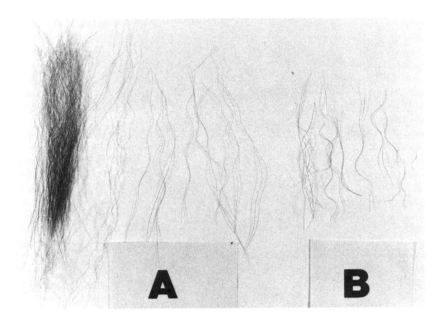

Fig. 8. *Grizzly neck hairs* (A and B) *compared with neck hairs of southwestern black bears* (C and D). *The longer, kinky hairs of the grizzly appear to be diagnostic. The hairs shown in* A *were taken from an Arizona grizzly; in* B, *from a Mexico grizzly; in* C, *from an Arizona black bear in winter in the cinnamon phase; in* D, *from an Arizona black bear in September in the black phase.*

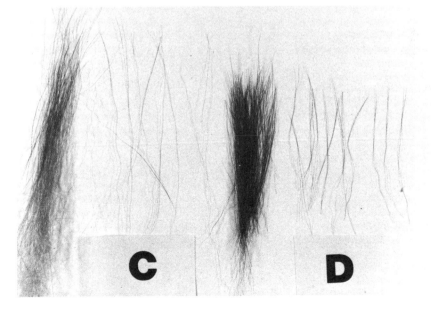

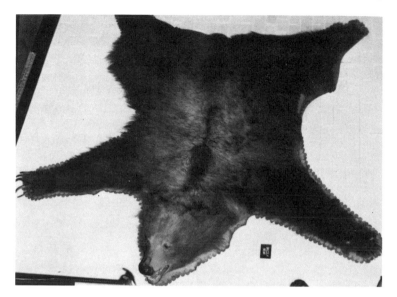

F IG. 9. *Skin of a female grizzly taken by a rancher in the Blue River area of Arizona in the early 1920s. Note the variation in pelt tone; the mane, or roach; and the long foreclaws. Photograph by Rich Glinski; courtesy of Ted Slinger, Buckhorn Mineral Baths, Mesa, Arizona.*

Southwest grizzlies were described as "roan colored" (Ellison 1968), "grayish white" (Merriam 1918), "dull pale brownish yellow" (Kennerly 1856), "dull brown with yellowish tips" (Bailey 1931), "uniformly chocolate brown" (Leopold 1959), and "dusky-dark brown" (Merriam 1918), and it appears that grizzlies showed great individual variations in coat color. A particularly dark old female from Arizona's White Mountains was described by Bailey (1931:366) as "darkest on rump, mane, ears, and legs; forehead, throat, and belly, light-yellowish brown; nose and face, light brown." Her cub, killed on the same date in midsummer, was similarly colored, and another cub taken in Taos County, New Mexico, on July 22, 1918, was also of various shades. Some grizzlies undoubtedly changed colors when they shed their coats, as do black bears (see, e.g., Waddell and Brown 1984). Also as with black bears, lighter-colored grizzlies were more often observed in the south and in the interior. There is no hard and fast rule, however, and a large male from New Mexico's Black Range is still variegated and dark thirty years after it was taken. An adult female from the nearby Blue Range in Arizona (fig. 9) is much lighter and closely resembles the female described by Bailey (1931) from the White Mountains.

Grizzlies are big animals. A large male might be as much as six and a half feet from nose to tail. Standing on his hind legs, he could exceed eight feet in height. Such a bear was an exceptionally large individual, however, and a five-foot animal was a typical good-sized adult.

There appears to have been a cline toward smaller bears from north to south, following Bergman's rule that the size of animals within a group is smallest in the south and largest in the north. Although their measurements are not always indicative, because of the great amount of variation among individuals and between sex and age classes, Merriam (1918), Sheldon (1925), and Leopold (1959) stated that Chihuahua contained the smallest grizzlies. Merriam's (1918) "type specimens" of his "Nelson's" and "Texas" grizzlies were "size small" and "rather small," as in the case of Kennerly's (1856) "Sonora" grizzly. Merriam (1918) considered the "Coppermine," or New Mexico, grizzly "medium size"; the "Arizona" grizzly, "rather large"; the "Mt. Taylor grizzly," "very large"; and grizzlies in Colorado and Utah, "large."

Although the weights of many grizzlies have been reported in the literature, almost all are estimates, and probably on the heavy side. Accurate weights of southwestern grizzlies were, for obvious reasons, difficult to come by, but Leopold's (1959) range of 300 to 700 pounds for adults is not unreasonable, given recent studies of Rocky Mountain grizzlies in Montana. Measurements of these presumably larger bears show that adult females range from 300 to 350 pounds, and males 350 to 500 pounds (Aune and Stivers 1980). Six-hundred-pound bears are rare, and most adult males are in the 400-to-600-pound range (Switzer, personal

TABLE 1. *Characters distinguishing skulls of adult Arizona grizzly and black bears* (Adults are defined as animals having all their permanent teeth and teeth having more then three annuli of dental cementum (3+ years of age)

Character	Grizzly Bear	Black Bear
Second Molar (M_2)	Broadest at anterior end	Broadest approximately halfway between anterior and posterior margins
First Molar (M_1)	One or more cusplets medially in valley between metaconid and entoconid	No cusplets
Fourth Premolar (P_4)	With median accessory cusps	Without accessory cusps
Length of rostrum	Long; rostral length > 7.0 inches; palatal length > 6.4 inches	Short; rostral length < 6.5 inches; palatal length < 6.2 inches
Breadth of rostrum	Broad; width across incisors > 1.7 inches	Short; width across incisors < 1.7 inches
Ascending coronoid process of lower jaw	High; > 4.0 inches	Low; < 4.0 inches
Length of ramus	Long; from posterior alveolus, M_3, to anterior alveolus, I_1, > 5.9 inches	Short; from posterior alveolus, M_3, to anterior alveolus, I_1, < 5.5 inches
Frontal shield	Wider; width across postorbital process > 4.4 inches; least interorbital breadth > 3.0 inches	Narrower; width across postorbital process < 4.3 inches; least interorbital breadth < 3.0 inches

Source: D. F. Hoffmeister, *The Mammals of Arizona* (Tucson: University of Arizona Press, 1985).

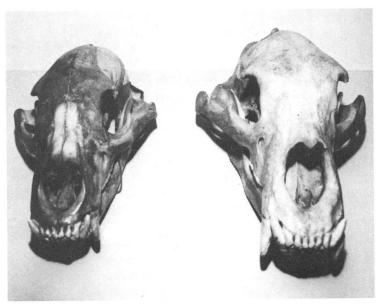

FIG. 10. *Skulls of a large male black bear* (left) *and a young male grizzly from British Columbia* (right). *The skull structure in the two species is remarkably similar, and even one experienced with both bears may need to take measurements and consider the animal's relative age before assigning species to a skull. Grizzlies and black bears have the same dental formula, except that the second molar (M²) of the grizzly is broadest at the anterior end, while the black bear's second molar is broadest approximately halfway between the anterior and posterior margins. The rostrum length in adult grizzlies exceeds 7 inches, while in black bears it is less than 6½ inches (Hoffmeister 1985). Photograph by Tom Britt.*

communication). So much for all the "800-to-1,000-pound" grizzlies estimated from the squared feet of hide.[1]

Even a small adult grizzly greatly exceeded the black bear in size (table 1; fig. 10). Southwestern male black bears uncommonly exceed 300 pounds, and females are usually

---

[1] Biologists can now estimate grizzly and black-bear weights by measuring the chest girth with a tape and comparing the measurements with a scaled ratio of animals of known chest circumference and weight (see, e.g., LeCount 1977b, Aune and Switzer 1981).

Fig. 11. *Grizzly scats. Formed droppings greater than two inches in diameter or more than two and a half quarts in volume are usually considered to have been made by a grizzly. Fecal deposits smaller than these are made by small grizzlies or large black bears (Hamer et al. 1981).*

under 160 pounds (LeCount 1977b, Waddell and Brown 1984). Bear hunters could therefore sometimes differentiate grizzly sign from that of black bears even when prints of the longer claws of the grizzly's front feet were not discernible. If the length of the hind footprint exceeded seven inches, or if the width of any print was five inches or greater, the track was considered to be a grizzly's.

Although scats of the two species of bear cannot be consistently differentiated (Hamer et al. 1981), scats more than two inches in diameter, or exceeding two and a half quarts in volume, are considered evidence of a grizzly in the Rocky Mountains (Aune and Switzer 1981; fig. 11). Less conclusive evidence of grizzlies there, and formerly in the Southwest, was a great amount of digging activity; deeply clawed "marks" more than six feet above the ground on trees, logs, and wooden signs; and the killing of large cattle (Stevens 1943; Baker 1963 in Haynes and Haynes 1966).

CHAPTER 6

Life History

The following life-history accounts were gleaned from the references noted in earlier chapters and the specific sources cited below. There were no designed studies of Southwest grizzlies when the bears were extant.

HIBERNATION

Several accounts have suggested that Southwest grizzlies may have hibernated irregularly (e.g., Bailey 1931:359). This is emphatically refuted by Sheldon (1925), a careful and experienced investigator, who found grizzlies in Mexico to have much the same denning habits as those animals farther north:

> From November to April they hibernated far within the ranges; they did not leave the interior recesses of the mountains until near the first of May. [Sheldon 1925:160]
> Although I frequently traveled through the mountains in winter, I never saw sign of bears during the months of hibernation. But Mexicans, who had spent most of their lives in or near the mountains, and also Johnny Bell, told me that during warmer days in winter, bears often wandered about for short distances from their dens. [Sheldon 1925:169]

Montague Stevens (1943) stated that New Mexico grizzlies began hibernating about November 20 and did not leave their dens until the middle of March. This is consistent with the findings of Aune and Switzer (1981), who found that grizzlies on the east front of the Rocky Mountains denned between November 2 and November 23 and

FIG. 12. A subalpine riparian thicket of willows, hawthorns, and thin-leafed alders on the North Fork of the White River, Apache Indian Reservation, Arizona, elevation about 8,500 feet. Such habitats were haunts of the grizzlies both in the early spring and in the fall, when raspberries and currants augmented the succulent streamside vegetation.

emerged between March 10 and April 29, moving away from the den site between May 28 and May 13. Servheen (1981) found that grizzlies denned in Montana's Mission Mountains between November 2 and 22, and Gillespie and Jonkel (1980) reported den entry on the South Flathead River between November 2 and 26. With the exception of a sow and three yearling cubs taken by government hunter T. T. Loveless on December 18, and a big male noted by bear hunter Ben Lilly on March 11, all Southwest grizzlies of record were taken between mid-April and November. Given the occasional forays of denned bears and the possibility of killing bears in their dens, it appears that the denning dates of Southwest grizzlies were much the same as those of northern grizzlies. This is also true for black bears (LeCount 1977a).

Young grizzlies everywhere are born about February 1. Dens are often in cold, north-slope locations or in secure locations high in the mountains. Besides providing security, these sites allow the bears to come out of hibernation to find spring conditions on south slopes and downslope well advanced. Den emergence is a critical time for the bears; they must find foods high in protein to compensate for weight lost during hibernation. These needs are supplied by carrion, and such green herbaceous vegetation as spring beauty *(Claytonia lanceolata = C. rosea)*, cow parsnip *(Heracleum lanatum)*, sedges (*Carex* spp.), horsetails (*Equisetum* spp.), dandelions (*Taraxacum* spp.), and new growth of cool-season grasses (e.g., *Melica porteri*). The search for food sources draws the grizzlies downhill, usually following a drainage; and riparian habitats are much used to obtain green vegetation and other early food supplies (fig. 12).

BREEDING SEASON

There is nothing in the literature to indicate that the breeding habits of Southwest grizzlies differed from those of grizzlies farther north. In their search for food and mates male grizzlies come in contact with other bears, and should a

FIG. 13. *Fruits of the prickly-pear cactus* (Opuntia phaeacantha), *a favorite autumn food of Southwest grizzlies and black bears.*

female be in estrus, a brief courtship may ensue, the mating takes place in early summer or midsummer (see, e.g., Herrero and Hamer 1977). Females breed no more than every other year and do not come into estrus while they are nursing cubs. If one or more cubs survive their first year, breeding cannot be expected for still another year or more. Adult grizzlies prefer to remain alone or in matriarchal family groups (Wright 1909, Switzer personal communication). Siblings may remain together for up to four years even without their mother.

As the summer progressed, southwestern grizzlies, like their northern brethren today, roamed throughout their range feeding on carrion, yampa roots *(Perideridia gairdneri),* onions *(Allium* spp.), green vegetation, and ants. Canyons and riparian bottoms were still especially favored as feeding sites (Sheldon 1925), but generally the bears were moving upslope. By midsummer the bears were in aspen stands and making heavy use of high-elevation meadows, rockslides, and outcrops. There they grazed on vegetation green from the summer rains, dug for tubers and small mammals, tore open logs in search of insects, and fed on early thimbleberries *(Rubus neomexicanus)*, raspberries *(R. strigosus)*, currants (*Ribes* spp.), and other fruits.

With the approach of fall the grizzlies concentrated in areas where mast was available. The range of daily movements expanded or contracted, depending on local food supplies. Accounts have the bears feeding on piñon nuts *(Pinus edulis, P. cembroides)*, acorns (*Quercus* spp.), manzanita berries (*Arctostaphylos* spp.), juniper berries (*Juniperus* spp.), carrion, and prickly-pear cactus fruits (*Opuntia* spp.; Bailey 1931, Way 1960, French 1965; fig. 13).

In autumn, when they had sufficiently fattened, the bears sought out den sites in mountain recesses. Although they sometimes used natural cavities, most dens were dug on slopes by the occupants, who may have used the same sites in previous years (Craighead and Craighead 1972). By mid-November most of the bears had denned.

RECRUITMENT AND MORTALITY

The grizzly has one of the lowest reproductive rates of the terrestrial mammals. Grizzlies normally do not reach sexual maturity until they are four and a half years of age; females may be mature even later (see, e.g., Brown 1982). Mean litter size is about two cubs per female, with a period of two to seven years between litters (Craighead et al. 1974). Given a typically even sex ratio and a population made up mostly of nonbreeding animals, a population of twenty animals is necessary to sustain a loss of only one or two grizzlies a year. Considering the effects of the vagaries of weather on food supplies and the importance of food to breeding condition and successful cub rearing, the removal of even a few females could be devastating to a local grizzly population.

Wild grizzlies have been known to live more than twenty-five years (Craighead et al. 1974). Bears over twenty years old invariably show dental problems, however; and ages much beyond twenty must have been unusual. Bears, incidentally, are aged by counting the annuli of the cementum of sectioned teeth by a technique similar to counting tree rings. Each annulus represents a year's growth. Although this is considered a modern aging method, the annuli phenomenon was first noted by the almost legendary Grizzly Adams, who kept a stable of captive California grizzlies (Hittel 1911).

HOME RANGE

Grizzlies do not defend established territories; rather, they have overlapping cruising ranges, which vary with individuals, circumstances, and seasons (Brown 1982). The range of males is generally two to four times that of females and varies greatly with individuals and types of habitat. Average home ranges for males in the northern Rocky Mountains generally exceed 180 square miles, while females have ranges of less than 100 square miles (sources cited in Brown 1982). Densities range from eight to sixty square miles per grizzly.

SOCIAL HABITS

The grizzly is not a social animal. An adult generally treats other bears as interlopers and will kill or drive away any bear encountered, grizzly or black, that is smaller, is not a potential mate, or is not protected by its mother. This behavior appears to be an adaptation to scarce food supplies and is modified in areas where food is plentiful; communal feeding behavior has been documented in swamps, at garbage dumps, and at ranch boneyards (see, e.g., Craighead 1979).

The grizzly is highly intelligent, secretive, and, when associated with modern man, nocturnal. Aune and Stivers (1982) found that grizzlies on the east slope of the Rocky Mountains did not become fully active until between 9:00 P.M. and midnight and retired between 6:00 and 9:00 A.M. Thus the period when they were feeding and traveling was less than nine hours a day. Bears in more remote areas that had less contact with man were more crepuscular; i.e., active in the early evening and early morning.

Like black bears, grizzlies make well-defined pathways to and from characteristic bedding sites in heavy cover where they avoid the midday heat. These bedding sites are interconnected to favorite foraging areas and escape retreats by a system of well-worn paths that facilitate rapid movement with a minimum of noise. Trails and typical bedding sites were described by Dyche (1893 in Edwords 1893):

The [bear] trail led into a deep fir forest and it was almost dusk under the trees. The pines interlaced at the top and the ground was covered with a thick bed of needles, shredded fir-cones that had been opened by squirrels looking for the seeds, and leaves, which formed a carpet in some places three feet thick. In this mass of debris were found many bear beds, where the animals had scooped out great hollows and made comfortable sleeping places. [Dyche in Edwords 1893:69]

Often in dense vegetation, such as aspen thickets or willow-lined riverbottoms, these trailways take on the appearance of tunnels and are virtually invisible to a man on horseback (Stevens 1943). Once discovered, however, the paths can, and were used to trap the bears in "trail sets."

CHAPTER 7

Abundance and Distribution

Although Southwest explorers reported a number of encounters with grizzlies (Pattie 1833), (Davis 1982), it appears that these bears were never as numerous in the Southwest as they were in early-day California. It is also thought that the reason early travelers reported more encounters with grizzlies than with black bears in the Southwest was that both explorers and grizzlies frequented the more easily traveled riverbottoms. In the mountains it was different. J. H. Clark collected four black bears and one grizzly in 1855 near the Santa Rita copper mines, at the south end of the Mogollon Mountains, suggesting that black bears were more numerous than grizzlies in montane habitats, a situation consistent with northern Rocky Mountain areas where both species still occur.

After the Civil War most reporters definitely considered black bears more abundant than grizzlies. Reports of bears in the riparian thickets along the larger watercourses ceased, doubtless because these areas were the focal point of early settlement and riverine bears were quickly eliminated. A typical report of the time is that of Farrar (1968) for the period 1871 to 1875 in the Raton Mountains on the New Mexico–Colorado border, about fifty miles east of Trinidad, Colorado: "We saw black bears every few days and occasionally a grizzly came along."

Consider also the statements by Hinton (1878) in a handbook summarizing what was then commonly known about Arizona's resources: "Grizzly bears are common at Camp Apache, and have been killed near Bill Williams mountain. The Coyotero, Mogollon and White mountains are the homes on cinnamon and black bears, which are also found in the hilly and wooded country of Arizona generally."

An exception may have occurred in Chihuahua, in the wooded mountains east of the Sierra Madre, where Ruxton (1847) and Sheldon (1925) unequivocally reported the grizzly to be the more abundant bear species. It is tempting to think that these grizzlies and those reported in 1855 by Kennerly to be numerous along the United States–Mexico boundary, from the San Luis Mountains west to Los Nogales, may have been sustained by livestock carrion (Baird 1859). The border area was reported to harbour large populations of feral cattle (Davis 1982), and the enormous ranches of Chihuahua were casually managed (Sheldon 1925). Such artificially sustained populations have been suggested for the California grizzly by Storer and Tevis (1955), and there is no reason why they could not have occurred in the Southwest also.

Stevens (1943), who hunted grizzlies in the 1880s and 1890s in the mountains of east-central New Mexico and knew bears well, stated that grizzlies were usually above the black bears: "At about 8500 ft. elevation, the timber changes to spruce, balsam [Douglas fir] and quaking aspen thickets, and here the grizzly makes his home."

By the turn of the century Bailey (1931) also considered the grizzly an animal of the high mountains: "In this region [northern New Mexico] the grizzly bears seem to be almost entirely mountain-forest animals, keeping in the dense growth of timber, especially in the deep canyons and almost impenetrable jungles of windfall and second growth, which follow the burning of forest areas."

Even in the oak-studded grasslands of southeastern Arizona and Chihuahua, which conjure up many comparisons with the evergreen woodlands and grizzlies of California, the grizzly was to be found "higher up." As Sheldon (1925) stated: "The grizzly bear was most abundant in the northern Sierra Madre. At that time [ca. 1898–1902] some of these bears might occasionally wander outside of the mountain in the pinyon-juniper belt, but their haunts were within the main sierra."

This does not mean that grizzlies were confined to high mountain peaks. Then, as now, the animals ranged widely and used a great variety of habitats. A bear in a montane meadow one day could be in a canyon bottom the next, and in alpine tundra the day after. Grizzlies followed food sources, and because they were less forest animals than their black-bear relatives, they were more likely to be in open grassland, meadows, or rockslides. When they were startled, however, they would invariably head upslope to dense aspens and other mountain-forest retreats (e.g., see Stevens 1943).

LOCALITY RECORDS

The known museum records and literature references of grizzlies are shown on map 1. Summaries of these occurrences by state are as follows:

Arizona.—In the United States National Museum there are grizzly specimens from the Fort Defiance area (a male sent in by H. B. Möllhausen in 1858); the San Francisco Mountains (sent in by E. A. Goldman in 1903); Bill Williams Mountain in Bear Canyon (a male collected by R. Patterson and J. Norman in 1922); the White Mountains (a male collected by Ben Lilly in 1913); Escudilla Mountain (a male collected on September 7, 1908, and a male taken on September 3, 1911); the Blue Range (B. V. Lilly, no sex 1905); and near Green Valley, an area eight miles north of Payson (1913) (Merriam 1918, Poole and Schantz 1942, Miller and Kellog 1955). The Museum of Vertebrate Zoology, in the University of California, Berkeley, has a grizzly that was taken in September, 1925, at 10,000 feet on the southwest slopes of Mount Baldy near the head of Hurricane Creek, on the Fort Apache Indian Reservation (Cockrum 1960). There are no Arizona grizzlies in the University of Arizona mammal collection.

There are also many reliable records and accounts in the literature for southern Arizona, and grizzlies have been reported from the Peloncillo Mountains (Allen 1895), the Chiricahua–Dos Cabezas Mountains (Hancock 1930), the Huachuca Mountains (Bahre 1977), the Santa Rita Mountains (e.g., see Davis 1982), and the Catalina-Rincon Mountains (Baily 1889 in Lange 1960, O'Connor in Housholder 1966). Housholder (1966) provides additional creditable records for the White Mountains, Escudilla Mountain, the Blue Range, the Chuska Mountains, the Fort Apache Indian Reservation, the Galiuro and Winchester mountains, and sub-Mogollon Arizona westward from the Apache Reservation through the Sierra Ancha to the Juniper (Camp Wood) Mountains.

There are no definite records for the chaparral-covered Pinal Mountains, the Mazatal Mountains, or the Bradshaw Mountains, although grizzlies may well have occurred there. Conner (1956) and Housholder (1966) report possible grizzlies for the Bradshaws, but none of the animals were killed and examined. Lawton Champie, a long-time resident rancher in the Prescott area, was widely reported to have killed the last grizzly in the Bradshaws. In a personal interview with Champie on February 1, 1975, however, he revealed that he had "had to kill a female and young black bear" that were killing his cattle in the 1920s. He stated that he had never known of a grizzly from the Bradshaw Mountains.

Records of grizzlies are almost nonexistent for the Arizona Strip and the plateaus north and south of the Grand Canyon, perhaps because these regions lack riparian areas. The only account of a grizzly on the North Kaibab is a marginal one related by Rasmussen (1941): "According to reports believed to be authentic, a grizzly bear was killed by an Indian boy in South Canyon on the east side of the plateau about eighty-five years ago [ca. 1855]. This is the only record of this species reported by either Indians or whites."

The heart of the grizzly country in Arizona was unquestionably the east-central part of the state—the White Mountains, Escudilla Mountain, the watershed of the Blue River, and the Fort Apache and San Carlos Indian reservations. This was where grizzlies were reported to be the most numerous and persisted the longest. There are almost no records at elevations below about 3,500 feet, and very few below 4,500 to 5,000 feet. The grizzly populations disappeared from those areas well before the turn of the twentieth century.

New Mexico.—Several specimens and many records of grizzlies in the literature are available for west-central New Mexico, including the Mogollon, Tularosa, San Francisco, Saliz, Gallo, and Pinos Altos mountains, the Datil and Gallinas mountains, the Magdalena Mountains, the San Mateo Mountains, and the Black Range (Bailey 1931, Findley et al. 1975). The National Museum possesses skulls of two males collected on October 10, 1911, and June 20, 1918, from the Mogollon Mountains complex; two females collected in 1893 from the Pinos Altos Mountains; a male sent in by V. Bailey and V. Culbertson in 1895; an animal of unknown sex sent by V. Bailey and H. H. Hotchkiss on June 14, 1906; a female and cubs taken on December 16, 1918; a female taken on May 6, 1920; and a male taken in April, 1930, all from the Black Range (Mimbres Mountains). Other animals in the museum include one taken at Kid Springs in the Datil Range on October 13, 1905, and a male from Magdalena Baldy, dated 1935. The National Museum also has a female and two cubs taken by J. T. McMullin in the Sangre de Cristo Range. There are records in the literature for northern New Mexico in the Chuska, Gallinas, Jemez, San Pedro, San Juan, and Zuni mountains, as well as the Sangre de Cristos (Bailey 1931). Less well documented but reported to be grizzly range, were the Guadalupe, Sacramento, and El Capitan mountains.

The occurrence of grizzlies in the Peloncillo, San Luis, Animas, and Guadalupe mountains in the southern part of the state near the Arizona-Sonora-Chihuahua border is well documented (Bailey 1931); but the status of grizzlies in the Manzano, Sandia, and San Andres mountains is less certain. Pattie (1833) reported a number of grizzly encounters along the major waterways, but succeeding records are from montane habitats, and there is no evidence of a "Plains grizzly" east of the Pecos.

Texas.—The only actual record of a grizzly from the trans-Pecos region is that of a large male killed in a gulch near near the head of Limpia Creek in the Davis Mountains, Jeff Davis County, by C. O. Finley and John Z. Means, on November 2, 1890 (Bailey 1905). This was the "type specimen" of Merriam's (1918) nominate *texensis* race. The bear was described as brown with gray tips on the hairs. Bailey (1905), who worked in Texas at the turn of the century, stated that this animal was the only grizzly that he had heard of taken in the state. Bailey (1931) later observed tracks that he attributed to a grizzly near the New Mexico-Texas state line at the head of Dog Canyon in the Guadalupe Mountains, but he stated that no grizzlies had been killed there for some time.

O'Connor (1945) stated that grizzlies were once abundant in the Davis Mountains and adjacent foothills before being extirpated from West Texas, but does not elaborate on this statement and provides no other locales. Early natural-history observers such as Gregg (1844) failed to record grizzlies anywhere in Texas.

Despite a relatively good history for the Big Bend country (e.g., see the bibliography in Wauer 1973), there are no records of grizzlies in the Chisos or other West Texas mountains. It therefore appears that grizzlies in Texas were restricted to the Davis and Guadalupe mountains—the only ranges having Rocky Mountain montane conifer forest.

Coahuila and the Sierra Madre Oriental.—There are no specimens of grizzlies from Coahuila, or anywhere in the Sierra Madre Oriental. The evidence presented by Baker (1956) for including this animal in the state's fauna is unconvincing. The absence of any reference to grizzlies in the accounts of early bear hunters, such as Ben Lilly, and early naturalists, such as W. P. Taylor, both of whom spent time in the Sierra del Carmen and Serranía del Burro when those ranges were in a relatively pristine state, indicates that the species had not yet crossed the Rio Grande from Texas. Other forested mountains, such as the Sierra San Marcos and the Sierra Madera, are limestone and lack riparian areas and the grassy rolling foothills associated with Mexican grizzlies. It therefore appears prudent to omit this area as part of the former range of the grizzly.

Chihuahua and the Sierra Madre Occidental. — Authenticated records indicate that in Chihuahua the grizzly was confined to the Sierra Madre and the high interior ranges on the east. The specimens in the National Museum were collected in an area near Gallego (Ben Lilly, ca. 1910) in the San Luis Mountains, where, in 1892, E. A. Mearns (1907) reported "numerous Sonoran grizzly bears" and collected two males; in the region of Colonia García (a male and three females collected by Mormon hunters for E. W. Nelson and A. E. Goldman during the summer of 1899): and in an area near Colonia Juárez (a male taken by W. W. Wood in May, 1903, near Casas Grandes. Sheldon (1925), who was much interested in the distribution of big game in Chihuahua, noted a "progressive scarcity of bears toward the south, none being found south of the latitude of Ciudad Chihuahua, except in a very small section including some outlying ranges south of Carichic." Later Leopold (1959) documented the past occurrence of grizzlies in the Cerro de la Hiedra, near Los Metates; the Sierra del Nido; the Sierra Santa Clara; the Cerro La Campana; and the stretch along the western border with Sonora west of Colonia Pacheco. Other literature references place grizzlies near Colonia Chuhuichupa (Sonnichsen 1974), west of Ocampo (Parker 1979), and near Colonia Juárez (Young and Beyers 1980).

The inclusion of parts or all of Durango as grizzly range by López and López (1911), Allen (1942), and Leopold (1959) is not based on collections, kills, or actual observation. The evidence supplied by Baker and Greer (1962) for including the Sierra Madre Occidental in northern Durango as former grizzly range is also tenuous, and they admit that, although the residents of the mountains recognize an *oso grande*, they "had never heard that any had ever been present in Durango." Lumboltz (1902) does not differentiate between species, but his discussions of bears suggest few or no grizzlies south of extreme northen Durango. Why the grizzly was not found in likely appearing habitats in Durango, Zacatecas, Nayarit, and the transvolcanic district is open to speculation; perhaps as recent palaearctic invaders they had not yet had time to spread southward when their invasion was halted by the events following upon the Conquest.

Sonora.—Except for Kennerly's specimen of 1855, collections of grizzlies from Sonora are lacking. It seems logical, however, to assume that the grizzly was present in the Sierra San José, Sierra de los Ajos, the Sierra de Cananea, the Sierra del Tigre, the Sierra del Manzano, and the Sierra de los Piñitos. O'Connor (1945) repeats a report that grizzlies were present about 1870 in the riparian bottoms of the Altar River, a drainage of the Pajarito and Cibuta mountains. Grizzlies appear not to have been present in the relatively dense forests on the west pediments of the Sierra Madre Occidental; at least there is no mention of them in these ranges by the Lumholtz (1902) expedition, by Burt (1938), or by other investigators.

Nevada.—There are no reliable records of grizzlies occurring anywhere in Nevada (Hall 1946). Hubbard and Harris's (1960) tale of a single grizzly that ranged the enormous arid area of the El Dorado Mountains, the North Rim of the Grand Canyon, and the region south of Searchlight, Nevada, is not plausible. The White Mountains of Nevada and southeastern California were apparently too arid or isolated for grizzlies, and the animal is not known to have occurred east of the Sierra Nevada.

Southern Utah.—The only museum specimens of grizzly bears in Utah south of 38 degrees north latitude are from the Pine Valley Mountains. The more recent of these two males was obtained by a U.S. Forest Service ranger in September, 1907 (Merriam 1918, Durrant 1952, Hubbard and Harris 1960). Joseph H. Porter (1926 in Young and Beyers

1980) describes cowboys killing a grizzly that had been wounded with a set gun in the Escalante Mountains in the spring of 1916.

Hubbard and Harris (1960) tell of a grizzly killed by prospectors in 1885 in the Abajo Mountains, now in the Manti–La Sal National Forest. That this is the only report of the grizzlies in southeast Utah is not surprising, since these ranges (the Abajo Mountains, Elk Ridge, the Henry Mountains, and Navajo Mountain) were relatively unknown to science until the 1920s. The former occurrence of grizzlies in these ranges is therefore largely undocumented.

Colorado south of Parallel 38°N.—A number of specimens and many records of grizzlies are available from the San Juan Mountains, and the Rio Grande and San Juan national forests have always been considered "grizzly country." Cary (1911), Warren (1942), Tully (1970), and Armstrong (1972) cite animals collected from Dry Creek Basin, North Mesa across Naturita Valley from Lone Cone, and Lone Cone Mountain (the last taken at 11,000 feet on May 26, 1907), all in San Miguel County; the West Dolores River, in Dolores County; the area north of Vallecito, in La Plata County; Rio Grande Pyramid, at the head of Pine (Los Pinos) River, in Hinsdale County: Middle Creek south of Creede, Lake Creek twenty miles south of Wagon Wheel Gap, Goose Creek, Red Mountain Creek, Window Lake, Coldwater Creek, and upper Piedra River, all in Mineral County; Pagosa Springs (three), Navajo Mountain (four) near Chromo, Iron Creek, and Chama Peak, in Archuleta County (four); and Burro Mountain near Elwood, in Rio Grande County.

In addition, since 1950 three known grizzlies have been taken in the San Juan Mountains of southern Colorado. A sheepherder killed a young grizzly near Plataro, in Conejos County, in August, 1951. In September, 1951, a federal government trapper took a two-to-three-year-old male in the Rio Grande Wilderness Area just northwest of Rio Grande Reservoir, west of Creede. Most recently, in 1979, an animal was killed on the headwaters of the Navajo River in the San Juan National Forest near Blue Lake, in Conejos County.

No museum records exist of grizzlies from the Sangre de Cristo and Culebra ranges east of the Rio Grande, but their occurrence in these mountains southward in New Mexico is well documented.

Armstrong (1972) noted that with few exceptions grizzlies in Colorado were from mountainous areas and along wooded watercourses. The few early records from the plains region were confined to the streams and rivers, and evidence for a separate race of "plains grizzlies" is again lacking.

From both the preceding accounts and later sources it becomes obvious that Southwest grizzlies were basically montane animals. The exceptions were almost all encountered in dense riparian vegetation. This distribution is similar to that of extant grizzlies northward in the Rocky Mountains, and there is little evidence that southern grizzlies were foothill or plains inhabitants like the California grizzly (Storer and Tevis 1955). Quite the contrary, most Southwest grizzly records are from mountains capped by conifers.

CHAPTER 8

Southwest Habitats

Like grizzlies of other regions, the grizzlies of the Southwest
required a wide range of habitats. An individual bear could
either use a relatively small, diverse area, such as a mountain
mass with its canyons and foothills, or roam over a larger,
homogeneous range with local areas of seasonal importance.
Large mountains with their steep reliefs and elevational variations generally possess a greater array of habitats than those
of similar-sized areas of less topographic relief. Either way
it took a large amount of land and a number of habitats
to support a grizzly population.

   Habitats are described on the basis of their vegetative
components, that is plant structure and composition. Vegetation is the observable plant response to integrated climatic
and evolutionary controls, which in turn, determines the
kinds of animals that are present. Vegetative communities
in a particular regional environment, together with their
animal components, are collectively termed "biomes" or
"biotic communities" (Lowe and Brown 1982). The following biotic communities have been identified as used by grizzlies in the Southwest.

ALPINE TUNDRA AND GRASSLAND

In the Southwest alpine communities are limited to the highest elevations of the San Juan and Sangre de Cristo mountains, to Sierra Blanca in the Sacramento Mountains, and to
the summits of the San Francisco Peaks. Although these
habitats are widely used by grizzlies in the northern Rocky
Mountains, specific records of grizzlies in alpine tundra in
the Southwest are lacking. Nonetheless, grizzlies were pres-

86

Fig. 14. *Subalpine forest and grassland: Bear Flat Meadow at 9,300 feet in Arizona's White Mountains, as it appeared in July, 1933. Note the herbaceous character of the grassland opening within the overall forest of Engelmann spruce (Picea engelmanni). This was some of the best and last grizzly country in Arizona. Photograph by Laurence M. Huey; courtesy of Special Collections, University of Arizona Library, Tucson.*

ent in all mountain ranges possessing alpine tundra, and it may reasonably be assumed that grizzlies frequented alpine areas in midsummer as they do farther north (Aune and Stivers 1982, Craighead et al. 1982). Bailey (1931:367) noted that grizzlies in the mountains of northern New Mexico ranged from "*timberline* to the lower timber," but that that distribution circa 1904 to 1906 may have been entirely artificial and forced because of their long-term, vigorous persecution by hunters.

SUBALPINE CONIFER FOREST

There are many references to grizzlies in boreal forests, and subalpine conifers were important habitats for the bears (fig. 14). Bailey (1931) referred to grizzlies in spruce (*Picea* spp.) and other subalpine vegetation and called this "the breeding zone of the bears." Stevens (1943) stated that "at about 8500 ft. elevation, the timber changes to spruce, balsam [Douglas fir], and quaking aspen thickets, and here the grizzly makes his home."

As the grizzles came out of hibernation, the riparian bottoms of the high country were used as cover, and the bears fed on early green marsh plants, such as sedges (*Carex* spp.) and rushes (*Scirpus* spp., *Juncus* spp., *Eleocharis* spp., etc.) (fig. 15). Beavers (*Castor canadensis*), too, were taken. In spring and early summer the subalpine meadows provided green herbaceous vegetation, as well as roots, ants, gophers, and other burrowing small mammals. The conifer forest with its deadfalls, blowdowns, and old burns was excellent escape cover and provided some of the best berry-producing areas; of special importance were quaking aspen thickets (*Populus tremuloides*), for their herbaceous understories provided a reliable food source close to cover.

MONTANE CONIFER FOREST, SCRUBLAND, AND MEADOW

At lower elevations, below the subalpine forest, the grizzlies

FIG. 15. *Herbaceous vegetation along a streamside in the Gila Wilderness Area, New Mexico. Such habitats were of critical importance to grizzlies emerging from hibernation.*

Fig. 16. *High elevation meadow and cienega habitats within montane conifer forest: North Fork of the White River, White River Apache Indian Reservation. Wet meadows and aspen thickets were important foraging habitats for grizzlies in the spring and early summer. The surrounding trees are ponderosa pine (Pinus ponderosa). Commonly considered "bear country," the extensive ponderosa pine forests of the Southwest were and are, in reality, poor bear habitat because of the lack of screening cover. Photograph by Laurence M. Huey, June, 1932; courtesy of Special Collections, University of Arizona Library.*

used the dense, mixed conifer forests of Douglas fir (*Pseudo-tsuga menziesi*), white fir (*Abies concolor*), aspen, and ponderosa pine (*Pinus ponderosa*) as cover and bedding sites. In more open areas where grasses and forbs flourished, the forest was of at least seasonal importance for feeding. Monotypic stands of ponderosa pine, however, are generally poor habitat for bears, and the key habitats were montane meadows, aspen patches, steep slopes, and canyon bottoms (fig. 16).

Here the bears found the sedges, horsetails, and other herbaceous plants that were of importance to them in early spring. Goldman (1951:122) described the virgin pine forest and mountain meadows of the Sierra Madre: "The pine forest is open, with very little undergrowth, but grasses and herbaceous plants are abundant. Beautiful parks or open meadows, some with an area of several square miles, occur here and there, and in them wild flowers in great variety abound during the rainy season." Later, as the season progressed, the bears worked the meadow edges and canyons for grass, currants (*Ribes*), raspberries, and thimbleberries (*Rubus* spp.). Gambel oak (*Quercus gambeli*, both as trees and in shrub-form in thickets) supplied acorns, shade, and if the occasion required, escape cover.

MADREAN EVERGREEN WOODLAND

Woodlands dominated by evergreen oaks found south of the Mogollon Rim in Arizona and New Mexico provided seasonally important habitats for grizzlies. Bartlett (1854), Baird (1859), Way (1865), and Sheldon (1925) found grizzlies in these warm-temperate environments. Some of the last grizzlies killed in the Sierra del Nido, Chihuahua, were taken in these oak woodlands (fig. 17). The periodic abundance of mast from several species of evergreen oaks (*Quercus* spp.), piñons (*Pinus cembroides*), and alligator-barked juniper (*Juniperus deppeana*), combined with the proximity of grassland and chaparral, made the encinals attractive to the grizzlies in late summer and early fall. Perhaps because of the open nature of much of this habitat, there are few reports of grizzlies in

FIG. 17. *An open Madrean evergreen woodland of oaks and pines in the Sierra del Nido, Chihuahua. Such habitats were important foraging sites for mast-feeding grizzlies, particularly in early fall. As grizzlies became more experienced, they avoided these open habitats and kept to denser cover.*

Madrean evergreen woodland north of Mexico after about 1890.

CHAPARRAL

Especially in later accounts, there is frequent mention of grizzlies in high-elevation chaparral communities (above 5,500 feet) adjacent to montane habitats (see, e.g., Bailey 1931, Housholder 1966, Ellison 1968). There are many references to grizzlies using manzanita thickets (fig. 18) as escape cover (see, e.g., French 1965a, 1965b), and of bears feeding on the mast of manzanita berries and other chaparral plants. It is speculated that with the deterioration in the quality of riparian and grassland habitats after 1880 the griz-

FIG. 18. *A manzanita thicket near the summit of the Mazatal Mountains, in central Arizona. Like aspen thickets, these communities provided both dense cover and foraging sites for Southwest grizzlies, who commonly used them in the fall months. These communities are found from central Arizona and New Mexico southward.*

Fig. 19. *A spring-fed cienega adjacent to Oak Creek, Yavapai County, Arizona, about 3,800 feet. Now rare, such marshy streamsides were once important foraging sites for grizzlies. Herbaceous plants present at this ungrazed location in July, 1982, included rushes, sedges, horsetails, several species of grass, and numerous forbs.*

zlies tended to use this biome even more than they had in previous times. By then the abundance of livestock provided a ready source of protein that allowed the bears to remain in heavy cover and thereby gain some protection from man and his dogs.

PLAINS AND SEMIDESERT GRASSLAND

Most references show grizzlies in grassland most often in late summer (Pattie 1831, Baird 1859, French 1965, Housholder

1966), and these accounts are more prevalent before 1880 than later. Even in the early accounts the grizzlies were near woodlands and riparian communities, and it is suspected that they made these forays to obtain the new growth of summer-growing grasses, roots, and later in the year, cactus fruit. Baird (1859) makes mention of a root particularly sought by grizzlies—perhaps biscuit-root, which is, as mentioned earlier, a favorite late-summer food of grizzlies in the Rocky Mountains. A biscuit-root also grows in grasslands near the United States–Mexico border (Kearney and Peebles 1960).

RIPARIAN COMMUNITIES

There are many accounts of grizzlies in riparian deciduous forest and other temperate riparian communities (e.g., Pattie 1831, Way 1865). Indeed, these and other wetland communities were key habitats for Southwest grizzlies, as they are to their more northern brethren today. In early spring, streamside vegetation, marshy cienegas, and cottonwood (*Populus fremonti*) stands possessed an understory of greens that were not yet available on the uplands (fig. 19). The willow- and cottonwood-timbered bottoms were also a source of cover and, as the summer progressed, furnished cool retreats—an important consideratrion for these holarctic animals. Here, too, the grizzlies could find the occasional tidbit of opportunity—a deer fawn, a lodge containing young beavers, or a floundered cow. Unfortunately for the bears, these were also the habitats first affected by the white man's exploitation of the Southwest—which was to play an important role in the grizzly's extirpation.

MARILYN HOFF STEWART

PART THREE

The Inevitable Conflict

The death knell for the grizzly in the Southwest was tolled not by a church bell but by a train whistle. The completion of the transcontinental railroads across the Southwest in the early 1880s opened the region to an orgy of stock raising, the effects of which are felt today. The "iron horse" connected the previously remote Southwest with markets east and west, and huge herds of livestock were quickly shipped in to take advantage of the "new" grazing lands. The ranges were soon denuded, and much of the grizzly's habitat was deteriorated. Beginning in the spring of 1884, torrential floods triggered by barren watersheds initiated a cycle of erosion that destroyed much of the region's wetland cienegas and riparian vegetation.

Changing economic conditions, new homesteading laws, and cheap rail travel resulted in an ever-increasing influx of settlers, who eventually penetrated to the remotest corners of the region. These pioneers were determined to protect their herds from real or imagined depredations, and the great predators, the grizzly included, melted away before the onslaught. What follows is a brief account of that destruction.

By the mid-1880s the ranges were greatly overstocked as a result of the cattle boom that began in 1881 (Wagoner 1952). In 1885 the cattle market collapsed. Ruinously low prices and the drought of 1885–87 aggravated already strained range conditions, and in 1886, for the first time, more cattle were shipped out of the Southwest than in. Investors withdrew their money, and the big cattle outfits were broken up; the day of the gentlemen rancher was over.

Two other events in 1885–86 worked against the large

ranches and prevented any improvement in range conditions. First, Congress passed a bill prohibiting the fencing off of any of the public domain, thereby opening the holdings of the large cattle ranches to sheepherders, other cattlemen, and homesteaders. Also, Geronimo and his Apaches had been subdued at last, and ranchers on the watersheds of the upper Gila no longer had to worry about Indian incursions on their ranges (Wagoner 1952).

Between 1888 and 1890 the southwestern ranching industry recovered somewhat. Although floods seemed to occur more often, there was an abundance of rain, and prosperity was once more upon the land. Again the "limitless" rangelands were stocked beyond capacity. Year-long grazing was practical, and a ranch in the high country could also have winter range downslope. Virtually every acre was destined to be tried for grazing at some time or other.

In 1891 the market price of beef fell, and cattle were again retained on the range and held back from the markets. Many cattle died in the spring of 1892 when another dry period set in. By the summer of 1893 cattlemen were experiencing the worst drought in memory. More than 200,000 cattle were shipped out of southern Arizona alone, and still there were great losses; more than half of Arizona's cattle herd died of thirst and starvation (see, e.g., Brown 1900, Brown and Ellis 1977). Cattle were held on the higher, wetter mountains as long as possible. The years 1894 through 1904 saw a repetition of the disaster-recovery pattern produced by southwestern climate and Wall Street prices.

There were other threats to the rangelands. Sheep were now on the range in increasing numbers. The price of wool was more stable than that of beef, and some ranchers turned to sheep raising as a matter of necessity. Because sheep were grazed at the highest elevations and in conjunction with horses and cattle, their effects on the grizzly's habitat were severe. Sheep were an excellent food source for Bruin, but with terminal consequences. Goats were also introduced by increasing numbers of homesteaders, and even the steepest slopes were subject to overgrazing and erosion.

The influx of homesteaders to the Southwest was small in comparison to that on the Plains, but the trickle grew ever larger—a trend that was to continue until the early 1920s (Bahre 1977). The perennial shortage of water in the Southwest, coupled with the lack of arable land, led the nesters to the mountain homes of the grizzly. They built rough cabins at springs, grew potatoes on the few patches of alluvium, planted montane meadows in barley, and turned their stock loose to roam the forests. They vigorously protected these investments in time, labor, and cash against predators, and any game that showed itself was at once added to the larder. Times were hard on wildlife in general and on the grizzly in particular. In 1901 even the Apache Indian reservations were opened to grazing (McGuire 1980). With a grazing lease went an implied right to protect the stock against predators. No ungrazed sanctuary remained.

The big floods came in 1904 and continued into 1905. The alluvial banks along the streams were washed away, the stream channels, already incised, became deeply entrenched, the cienegas were headcut and drained. The Blue, the San Francisco, the upper Gila, the Verde, the Mimbres, the Pecos—all these high-country drainages and their tributaries were forever altered and degraded. With them went some of the richest and most productive habitats for the grizzly.

By 1905 habitat encroachment and man's persecution had largely eliminated the grizzly from Arizona south of the Gila; from the Chuska and Lukachukai mountains; from the Guadalupe, the Sacramento, and other major mountain ranges in New Mexico; and from nearly all of the bear's riverbottom haunts. Populations elsewhere were also greatly reduced.

In summary, the period 1885–1905 saw the Southwest rangelands denuded of their grass cover. Streamside vegetation was much altered or destroyed. The large cattle ranches were broken up, and they were struggling for survival. The numbers of sheep on the public domain increased, and each year there were more settlers and ranching homesteaders. It was during this period that the Southwest lost most of its grizzlies (Bailey 1931; fig. 1). The stage was set for extirpation.

It was certainly true that the grizzly was by then incompatible with the livestock industry. The big cattle outfits had formerly sustained the loss of occasional animals to predators, but to the newer ranchers the loss of one cow or sheep was a great concern. Yet this incompatability was more subtle than is commonly believed. There is no question that grizzlies fed on cattle, sheep, and hogs, and the meat was not always carrion. What is less well known is that the cow and sheep were actually the primary predators and that herbaceous vegetation was the first victim. The relationship between Southwest grizzlies and livestock was therefore complex and circular.

Grizzlies are omnivores. Under natural conditions, without the presence of livestock, more than 90 percent of their diet can be herbaceous vegetation (Mealey 1980). Much of the remaining animal material is composed of rodents that are grass- or grassland-dependent. Because grizzlies are inefficient grazers, good growth of green, tall, protein-rich succulent vegetation is required to support them. The pre-green-up period in spring, when the animals emerge from hibernation, is a critical time. Lack of protein-rich herbs and carrion is a major factor limiting bear distribution and numbers (Craighead et al. 1982). It also causes bears to roam widely in search of substitute food sources.

CHAPTER 9

Depredations and Control Methods

Grizzlies—and black bears, for that matter—have been justifiably accused of despoiling cornfields; raiding beehives; killing sheep, hogs, and cattle; and breaking into cabins, stores, caches, and trap sets. It was their actual and alleged attacks on cattle and sheep that earned them the enmity of Southwest ranchers. Opinions about the severity of their depredations varied. Some competent ranchers and observers considered the grizzly's reputation as a stock killer undeserved, particularly on the larger ranches before overgrazing became widespread. Consider French's (1965) opinion about grizzlies and cattle on the WS Ranch in the middle 1880s:

> In those days encounters with bears were not infrequent. They really are most interesting animals, and despite what a great many people maintain I never could find that they were destructive to cattle. My personal experience is that they never molest them until they grow old and the procuring of other food becomes difficult, and cattle are not much afraid of them. The same cannot be said about hogs, however, which seem to be the tastiest dish for Bruin, for I have known them to break into a pen and push the hogs out in front of them.

Sheldon (1925) was even more inclined to doubt that grizzlies were a threat to cattle ranching, but his observations were made on William Randolph Hearst's Babicora Ranch, where cattle numbers were limited by the amount of available water and grazing lands were in good supply:

> I never found an authenticated case or reliable report of one of these bears killing cattle. In fact, the Mexicans themselves

who continually ranged through the bear country looking for
stock, maintained that grizzlies never molested live cattle, and
that the latter did not fear them. Johnny Bell [manager of the
Babicora Ranch] also held the same decided opinions.

This benign relationship apparently ended with the over-
stocking of the ranges in Arizona and New Mexico after 1885
and in Mexico after 1945. Even before then, the grizzly's
penchant for carrion made him a likely suspect whenever
his tracks were found around a carcass of a cow that might
have died from any of a number of causes. Nonetheless, its
need for ready protein when it came out of hibernation made
the grizzly a potential stock killer. This was especially true
where grass was scarce and cattle were plentiful.

The attitudes of later ranchers were summed up by Vic
Culberson, owner of the GOS Ranch, to Vernon Bailey
(1931): "The destruction of these grizzlies was absolutely
necessary before the stock business of the region could be
maintained on a profitable basis. . . . The grizzlies were at
one time almost as bad as the big wolves in their depredation on the range cattle."

By 1900 all grizzlies in the southwest United States were
considered stock killers. Barker (1963) echoed the opinion
of most ranchers after 1900: "I feel very strongly that the
assumption that grizzly bears originally fed on carrion and
rarely attacked or killed cattle themselves is entirely wrong.
My personal experience and the experiences of others in
New Mexico will not bear out any such theory."

Numerous others shared this view. In fact, most ranchers
couldn't imagine a time when the big bears would not take
livestock. Mired animals, calves, cows with calf, newly weaned
calves, and unfolded sheep were all susceptible to attacks
by grizzlies, as they are today. Unlike lions and wolves,
grizzlies selected large cows if these were the easiest to obtain. Cattle were often taken in spring and fall, but depredations were noted at all times of the year that the bears
were active. On the other hand, oftentimes grizzlies were in

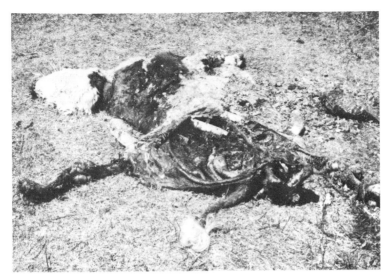

FIG. 20. *A cow carcass fed on by a grizzly, Wayne Golloehon Ranch, adjacent to Ear Mountain Game Range, Montana. The intestines and rear portions of the animal have been eaten first, and the hide peeled back and turned inside out.*

close proximity to ranching operations for years without incidents.

The descriptions of grizzlies slapping cattle across the head and breaking their necks, while colorful, are imaginative. Grizzlies generally grab and pull their victims toward them, biting them on the backs and neck. The massive jaws often break back and neck vertebrae; hence the descriptions of broken necks (see, e.g., Stevens 1943, Leopold 1959). Carcasses fed on by bears are readily identifiable, for the hide is peeled back in a characteristic manner, and little hide or hair is consumed (fig. 20). Oftentimes cattle killed by grizzlies are found close to water as if they had been ambushed while drinking (Stevens 1943). Unlike black bears, grizzlies may drag a kill to a chosen site and partly bury it (Roy and Dorrance 1976).

Sheep losses in the Southwest, in contrast to cattle losses,

FIG. 21. *Professional hunters skinning a bear in the Guadalupe Mountains, New Mexico, about 1895. Courtesy Museum of New Mexico, Santa Fe (neg. no. 14955).*

were greatest from midsummer to the end of the grazing season. A sheep-killing grizzly might take one to three sheep over a period of several days, though as many as two dozen sheep might be killed at a time (Johnson and Griffel 1982). Like attacks on cattle, most sheep depredations took place at night or in the very early hours of the morning.

The grizzly is an opportunistic feeder and readily takes to cattle, sheep, or garbage if any of these items are easily obtainable (Murie 1948, Johnson and Griffel 1982). Once an individual bear learns to take livestock, he becomes a stock-killer. Thus habituated, such grizzlies were easily trapped, for they almost always returned to feed on their kills. The greater the number of stock killed, the greater the vulnerability of the grizzly to the trap (Johnson and Griffel 1982).

BOUNTIES AND TRAPPERS

Even after the decline of the beaver trade in the 1830s, professional hunters and trappers were scattered throughout the Southwest. These latter-day mountain men eked out a living trapping fur-bearing animals, supplying game to mining camps and military posts, and living off the land (fig. 21). Few in number, they were nonetheless so pervasive that some believed that game was abundant in the mountains of west-central New Mexico and eastern Arizona into the twentieth century simply because Geronimo and his Apaches kept such hunters out of the country (e.g. French 1965a, 1965b; Flader 1974).

With the advent of ranching these men readily turned to bounty hunting as a means of making a living. As stockmen often did not have the time or expertise to rid their range of predators, the issuance of bounties became increasingly popular. A hunter could shop around for an area where predators were abundant or where the local ranchers were offering lucrative bounties. Although fraud was widespread, the predators usually were reduced only temporarily, bounty hunting became so much a part of life in the Southwest (Brown 1983) that in 1893 the Arizona Territorial Legis-

FIG. 22. *George Hockderffer and what appear to be a sow grizzly and two yearlings. San Francisco Mountain, about 1885. Note the rifle: one trigger opened the breech, the other fired the cartridge. Photograph courtesy Northern Arizona Pioneers Historical Society collections, Special Collections Library, Northern Arizona University.*

lature passed the Territorial Bounty Act, which enabled
counties to appropriate monies for bounties on "predatory
wolves, big bears, mountain lions, bobcats, and coyotes."
Such monies were irregularly appropriated, however, and
oftentimes individual cattlemen or livestock associations
found it necessary to offer additional bounties for specific
areas, particular species, or even individual animals. Grizzlies
were often the targets of these "sweetners," and amounts
of up to three hundred dollars were paid for individual
bears (Young and Beyers 1980). That was good money at the
turn of the century and attracted professional bear hunters
from a wide area.

TO KILL A GRIZZLY

Before the ranching period, most grizzlies were taken by
hunters traveling through the country in search of other
game or were shot as opportunities presented themselves.
For such chance encounters it was necessary to be equipped
only with a large-bore rifle firing a heavy ball propelled by
a suitable amount of powder (fig. 22). Of the several breech-
loading rifles available after the Civil War, the most popular
weapons were the U.S. Army Springfield .45-70 (.45 caliber
and 70 grains of black powder), the .45- and .50-caliber
Sharps single-shot Plains rifles, and later (after 1880) the
larger-caliber Henry and Winchester repeating rifles. As
hunters began specializing in bears, unusual guns possessed
of strong hitting power became the favorites of individuals.
The single-shot trap-door Springfield .45-70 (fig. 23) was
commonly used because it was reliable, inexpensive, and
widely available. Other popular weapons were the .44-40
Winchester and the .33- and .35-caliber Winchesters. There
never was a specialized gun for bears, or "grizzly gun."

To hunt for bears, the hunter could trail them, hoping
that when and if he caught up with one, the animal would
be out in the open and would afford him a stalk and a shot.
Otherwise, if the bear had not winded him, the hunter might
come on his adversary in heavy cover and get off a quick

Fig. 23. *Springfield .45-70. This single-shot top-loading rifle was widely used on the American frontier after the Civil War and accounted for many grizzlies. Gun loaned by James R. Wegge.*

FIG. 24. *A bear brought to bay with hounds, two airedales, and a pointer. After the bear was shot, the dogs were rewarded by being allowed to "wool" the carcass. Photograph by T. Harmon Parkhurst; courtesy Museum of New Mexico, Santa Fe (neg. no. 8175).*

shot before the bear disappeared or charged him. The latter alternative could be dangerous, as well as generally unproductive, and a more common practice was to make a stand over bait. Using this method, the hunter either staked out a carcass that showed signs of having been recently fed on or established his own bait station in hopes of attracting a bear. After a wait of several hours or several nights, and if the wind was right, one might get the reward of a shot. Both stalking and hunting over bait became less productive as grizzlies became scarce and more sophisticated. Grizzlies that rarely exposed themselves and foraged almost entirely at night were hard to get and required more specialized techniques.

Professional hunters had long known that a pack of good

FIG. 25. *A grizzly harassed by hounds in a spruce forest in the Sangre de Cristo Mountains, New Mexico, in 1918. Note the trap on the left foreleg. Photograph courtesy of Frank Hibben and Bob Housholder.*

bear dogs was essential for a successful bear hunt. Well-trained hounds, followed by one or more men on horseback, could trail a bear whenever a fresh track was found. There was no set breed of bear dog. Most were bluetick hounds, but bloodhounds and other trailing breeds were sometimes used or mixed in with the pack (see, e.g., Stevens 1943). It was not unusual to include some "fighting dogs" to worry the bear when they cornered him (fig. 24).

Once the dogs hit a fresh trail, their barking and baying led the hunters toward the bear. The grizzly's response was usually to head uphill to try to shake his pursuers in heavy cover or rough country (Stevens 1943, Ellison 1968). Because a grown grizzly cannot climb trees, a tired bear would often make his stand at the base of a tree or under a ledge of rock (fig. 25). According to Stevens (1943), cornered grizzlies tended to attack individual dogs, while the smaller black bears rushed at the collective pack.

The grizzly has tremendous endurance, and the chase could cover up to thirty miles. It was also not unusual for the grizzly to make several stands before the hunters could catch up. This was hard on the dogs, and if night fell before the hunters arrived, or if the dogs or horses gave out, the bear escaped. Stevens (1943) estimated that only one such bear chase in ten ended in success. Still, it was an effective hunting technique. The last grizzlies of record in Arizona, New Mexico, and Texas were all taken in this manner.

Bear hunting with dogs was a specialized sport, and maintaining a pack of hounds was expensive. It also required a high degree of endurance and many long days in the field. The training of the dogs was almost a career in itself. The average rancher therefore usually hoped to solve his bear problems by hiring a professional or by paying a bounty. The smaller rancher or homesteader normally could not afford such a service, and unless he had a bear-hunting neighbor to help him, or a professional hunter was working in the area, he usually attempted to catch the bear himself by setting a trap.

Professional hunters had long since developed and perfected the "cabin trap." Made of heavy logs and securely roofed, it did indeed resemble a small cabin (fig. 26). A drop door, also of sturdy construction, was sprung when the carrion bait at the rear of the cabin was pulled or jerked. Once trapped, the bear was secured until the trapper arrived or the animal could dig or break his way out. Although cabin traps were effective, particularly with inexperienced or hun-

Fɪɢ. 26. A cabin trap, about 1910. Note the drop door. Photograph courtesy of Arizona Historical Foundation.

gry bears, they were time-consuming to build and limited the hunter's area of operations.

Of great service therefore was the steel leghold No. 6 grizzly trap developed by Sewell Newhouse, a gunsmith and trap manufacturer from Oneida, New York (fig. 27). Weighing forty-two pounds and nicknamed the "Great Bear Tamer," the No. 6 was generally available in southwestern hardware stores in the early 1880s. This double-spring trap was extremely strong and durable and had a good reputation for holding grizzlies. It was never supplanted, and it remained the only commercially available grizzly trap, although a variety of hand-forged traps were also used (see e.g., Housholder 1971).

Grizzlies were not especially difficult to trap. Sets were made at a freshly killed carcass on a well-traveled bear trail or at a baited "cubby," a cache with an opening or entrance designed to allow a bear access at a particular location (fig. 28). The bait consisted of chunks of "ripe" animal parts wired to the inside of the cubby or to a tree off the trail. Unlike sets for wolves or coyotes, scents were of little use.

The more experienced trappers buried their traps in manure or boiled them in a tea of manzanita or some other pungent shrub's bark or leaves. Such caution was not usually necessary for any but a "spoiled" bear, for the grizzly was in no way as cunning as the wolf. Still, most professional trappers used leather gloves and a cowhide setting cloth when preparing their sets to mask any human scent adhering to the trap or ground (fig. 29). Under no circumstances was the trap ever oiled or greased.

Because of their large size, these traps were difficult and dangerous to set. For this reason they came with special setting clamps which, when applied to the springs, allowed the trap to be set with a few turns of the screws and the pan to be adjusted without danger. As a matter of frontier etiquette, warning signs were placed nearby, and a clamp was always left in reach should someone be so unfortunate as to step in the set.

The trick to a successful set was to make it look as

FIG. 27. *The No. 6 Newhouse trap, or "Great Bear Tamer." Note the setting clamp on the lower spring of the trap. Photograph courtesy of Arizona Historical Society.*

natural as possible. A shallow pit was scooped out near the carcass or at the entrance to the cubby, and the trap was laid inside. The clamps were then applied to the springs, and the trap was set. The hunter took care that the area below the pan or pad was clear of any obstruction. A twig was propped under the pan to prevent a smaller animal from tripping the set. Then a setting cloth was laid over the pan, and the jaws were opened. The trap was laid just below the surrounding ground and perfectly level. It was attached to a six-foot chain by a swivel or clevis, which was in turn attached to a large tree (not less than fourteen inches in diameter), a metal stake driven into the ground, or a drag. The drag could be anything from a large metal hook to a stump—anything that would hang up in brush, trees, or rocks. For obvious reasons a stationary set was preferred for grizzlies.

The entire set was now buried in the same dirt that had been excavated to lay the trap. Pine needles, grass, and other forest debris were laid over the set and chain, and the area was made as unobtrusive as possible. Sticks were placed around the trap to encourage the bear to step on the smooth ground over the pan of the trap.

There were of course, many refinements to this basic technique, and each trapper had his personal flourishes. What caught a grizzly one time might fail the next. The cost and weight of the trap demanded that each set be made with the greatest care and as though the intended bear were the most cautious animal alive.

Less popular was the even more dangerous practice of using a set gun. This was a shotgun or rifle placed at right angles to a well-worn bear trail or near a freshly killed carcass. The gun was strapped, or otherwise secured, to a tree or to stakes set out for this purpose, and a bait was placed on the muzzle. Attached to the bait was a string that led through a screw eye that was attached somewhere below the breech and tied to the cocked trigger (Young 1944). When the bear pulled or tugged at the bait, the gun discharged in his face. This was the method used on Escudilla Mountain by C. H. Shinn to take "Big Foot," the grizzly celebrated by Leopold (1949).

Another method, not usually associated with taking grizzlies, was poisoning. Strychnine, the lethal product of the nux vomica bean, was widely used to kill wolves and other predators. In a sulfate or alkaloid form the poison is a white, crystalline powder extremely bitter to the taste. For this reason it was usually wrapped in suet cubes, or sprinkled

FIG. 28. A cubby built to catch a grizzly. The bait (a white-tailed deer carcass) is inside at the apex of the V formed by the base logs. Traps are set on the trail and at the entrance.

FIG. 29. Setting a grizzly trap—in this case an Aldrich foot snare. The trap or snare was laid in a shallow pit, and small sticks were interlaced over the set. These sticks were then covered with grass and duff from the forest floor to make the site as natural-appearing as possible. Larger sticks were then strategically placed to facili-tate the bear's placing its foot on the set, which was cleared of debris and on a natural trailway.

under the skin and inserted in fresh carcasses, to kill wolves for bounty or for their fur.

Strychnine powder and tablets were used in the Southwest as early as the 1850s (Baird 1859). By the 1880s strychnine was stocked at most frontier stores. According to Young (1944), there was an unwritten law that no cowman knowingly passed by a carcass without inserting in it a liberal dose of strychnine sulfate in hopes of killing one more wolf and thus reducing the number of predators. Montague Stevens (1943) wrote that in 1896 all his dogs were poisoned by strychnine so planted by an anonymous benefactor, and he commented bitterly on the dangers of the practice.

Although strychnine was used primarily for wolves, its effects on other wildlife could be devastating (Young 1944). Because Southwest grizzlies and wolves usually inhabited the same range, the effects of the poison on the grizzly may have been of some consequence. Because strychnine breaks down in warm weather, it was most effective in winter, when the bears were in hibernation, but because of its lethal properties, its widespread use, and the carrion-feeding habits of spring-emerging grizzlies, strychnine may have been more of a factor in the reduction of bears between 1885 and 1925 than has been recognized. Also, many animals died away from the bait stations, which further complicates any evaluation of the role of the poison in the extinction of the grizzly.

CHAPTER 10

The Undeclared War

Although much of the southwestern landscape lay devastated by clearing and overgrazing (figs. 30a and 30b) at the turn of the century, there was good cause for optimism for at least some measure of recovery. In 1897 eastern sportsmen had pressed Congress to allow the president to establish forest reserves by executive order and to protect Yellowstone National Park. At the urging of a concerned secretary of the interior, John W. Noble, the Boone and Crockett Club, and a handful of professional foresters, President William H. Harrison was persuaded to set aside an additional thirteen million acres of public domain as forest reserves (Trefethan 1961). Western congressmen loudly objected, especially when they found out that these lands were in fact to be reserved for watershed protection. All commercial use was prohibited. There was to be no mining, timber cutting, or grazing, nor were there provisions for hunting and public entry. Fortunately for the political future of the reserves, there was no enforcement of these provisions, and the law was generally ignored. Still the potential for restriction was there, and every rancher, prospector, and homesteader felt his livelihood threatened.

Concern intensified in 1896 when, ten days before leaving office, President Grover Cleveland added another 21,280,000 acres to the reserves more than doubling their size. Much of the added lands were carved out of Arizona and New Mexico territories. Predictably, the citizens of these soon-to-be states exploded in rage. While the action was praised by the new breed of conservationists in the East, the southwestern ranchers and settlers reacted with hatred and suspicion of the forest reserves for years to come. Territorial and

FIG. 30a. *Santa Fe Dam, south of Williams, Arizona, in 1902, with Bill Williams Mountain in the background. Photograph by N. N. Darton, U.S. Geological Survey. The habitat destruction at midcentury is evident. Most of the pine forest has been logged, and grazing has depleted the ground cover, leaving the rocky soils vulnerable to sheet erosion. Such conditions were hard on the grizzlies, depriving them of forage and escape cover and forcing them to use only the steepest slopes and the most rugged canyons.*

FIG. 30b. *The same landscape depicted in fig. 30a, photographed in 1982. A new forest has grown up, and the ground cover shows much improvement. The major change over the eighty years, however, appears to be the general closing in of the forest. Although conditions have greatly improved, the potential for herbaceous vegetation has been reduced by the increase in forest cover.*

western state congressmen demanded that the reserves be returned to the public domain.

To save the reserves, a compromise had to be devised. Thanks to the forward thinking and influence of Gifford Pinchot and Theodore Roosevelt, Congress saw fit to modify the status of the reserves. The result was the Pettigrew Amendment of 1897, which permitted the sale of mature and decadent timber on the reserves, provided free access for all proper and legal purposes, and, most important, permitted bona fide settlers, miners, prospectors, and residents to use the reserves. The forest reserves were also to be reopened for homesteading for one more year before reverting to national forest reservations.

Upon taking office as president in 1905, Theodore Roosevelt prevailed upon Congress to move the forest reservations from the Department of the Interior to the Department of Agriculture. The Transfer Act authorized the reserves to be used for "game and fish protection" and for "other purposes." It also provided for the establishment of the U.S. Forest Service and the hiring of forest guards to protect the reservations. In 1908 the Apache, Coconino, Sitgreaves, Prescott, Coronado, Chiricahua, Garces, Crook, Dixie, Carson, Manzano, Datil, San Mateo, Magdalena, Lincoln, Pecos, and Gila national forests were created from forest reserves in Arizona and New Mexico. Almost all of the remaining grizzly habitat in the United States's half of the Southwest was now in the hands of the U.S. Forest Service.

By this time the grizzly had been much reduced (Bailey 1931) and the pressure was still on. Yet one could still find a grizzly without too much difficulty, as the following item from the *Arizona Daily Star* attests:

Phoenix, June 26, 1912. —With the magnificent pelt of a gigantic silvertip bear as a trophy, W. H. Maxwell has returned from a hunting trip in the country between Winslow and Payson.

Mr. Maxwell, who is the contractor erecting the new federal building, defied all traditions of hunters and took four young women with him on the trip. He left Phoenix with his niece,

Miss Cecilia Campbell and Miss Alice Cooley. At Winslow they were joined by two more young women, relations of Mr. Maxwell from Ohio. They took horses and rode down as far as Payson, returning over practically the same route. Two weeks were spent roughing it in the wilds. The complete story of how he killed the silvertip has not been drawn from Mr. Maxwell by his friends, but there is a well defined suspicion that he had quite a wild adventure before he succeeded in putting a bullet through a vital part of the big brute's anatomy.

THE U.S. FOREST SERVICE LENDS A HAND

Ever eager to please its tenants and develop a political constituency, the administrators of the southwestern forests quickly joined in cooperative agreements with the two territories of New Mexico and Arizona to have the forest guards enforce the game laws and control predatory animals. Wolves and mountain lions were considered the stockman's primary problem, but the "big bears" were also targeted. Federal assistance, it was reasoned, was only fair, since it was the national forests that harbored these large-stock killers.

Most of the forest guards were local men, reared on the frontier. It appears that they were more eager to take up predatory animal trapping than to enforce territorial game laws, since there is no record of any arrests for infractions of the laws before 1915 (Flader 1974). Some national-forest guards took up the trapping of grizzlies both to cement relations with settlers and ranchmen and to earn some of the bounty money that was locally offered (see, e.g., Young and Beyers 1980). Bailey (1931) also reported that forest officers took bears during this period, and Barker (1963) described how he took seven grizzlies when he was a forest ranger in the Pecos National Forest:

> In the spring of 1908 a grizzly bear with two cubs killed three head of cattle that I know of in the Mora Flats area. I took that bear and the cubs and also a large male grizzly. . . .
> . . . In 1911 I was a Forest Ranger on the Pecos with

headquarters at Panchuela Ranger Station. Two grizzlies killed several head of cattle in the . . . area. There were some guests at the Mountainview Ranch from Kansas who were very anxious to kill a grizzly and I went with them and set traps at one of the kills and in a period of two days we took the two grizzlies plus a cub.

Gradually the strategy of cooperation (or appeasement, depending on the viewpoint) took hold, and the Forest Service became an accepted arm of the southwestern society. By 1909 the national forests of the Southwest were being formed into a separate district—District 3—and plans were made for the forests to produce more game. At that time there was much debate about what wildlife-management programs should be initiated in the national forests. Many people, mostly easterners outside the Forest Service, thought that all or large parts of the forests should be set aside as refuges and closed to hunting. Others, including a persuasive recreation planner in Albuquerque, named Aldo Leopold, argued for small sanctuaries within the forest. Those areas, they reasoned, would replenish the hunted areas outside the sanctuaries, and the game would become a crop of no little value to the region's economy. The object of the forests was to raise both livestock and game. If the grizzly and other predators were eliminated in the process, so be it.

At about this time fire protection became a cause célèbre, even to the extent that heavy stocking with cattle and sheep was considered desirable because it would reduce the vegetation that might fuel a fire (see, e.g., Crouse 1904). The end result was a management bias favoring browse and trees at the expense of herbaceous vegetation and herbivores that has continued to this day (figs. 31a and 31b).

In the meantime, the forest watersheds continued to deteriorate. In 1912, for example, the Carson National Forest had 7,000 head of cattle, 200,000 sheep, and 400 homesteads (Flader 1974). The Apache and Gila national forests, which were also prime grizzly country, had been settled later and were consequently in better shape. Game numbers had held up better, too, and these forests were to be the models of a new approach to game management by the Forest Service. Game abundance was to be accomplished through the restriction of hunting, predator control, establishment of game refuges, and restocking—the program was promoted by Aldo Leopold. The refuges were to provide breeding stock for the hunted species and maintain the "variety" of rarer animals (e.g. bighorn sheep). Unfortunately for the grizzly, the efforts of Leopold and the Forest Service to maintain variety did not extend to predators or the big bears. The focus was on deer and turkeys; other wildlife species were downplayed or ignored.

THE FORMATION OF THE PARC

At about that time the fledging movement for wildlife protection, active in the East for twenty years, took hold in the Southwest. In 1911 the American Game Protective and Propagation Association was formed to promote the protection of game species and control of predatory animals. Three years later the New Mexico Game Protective Association was chartered in Silver City to promote the same goals, and New Mexico began taking a lead role in game protection (the Arizona Game Protective Association was formed in 1923). The leaders of this local movement were Aldo Leopold and J. Stokely Ligon, an investigator for the United States Biological Survey.

With the backing of such influential Gila National Forest ranchmen as Victor Culbertson, of the GOS Ranch; Hugh Hodge, of the Diamond Bar Ranch; and G. W. Evans, of the Slash Ranch, and most of the sheepmen, Leopold and his sportsmen pressed for an active program of game restoration through predator control. Both the sportsmen and the ranchers could agree on this, and they thought that the best way to accomplish the program was through the federal government. If the U.S. Forest Service collected grazing fees and provided the deer habitat, the government should remove the predators. Although the U.S. Forest Ser-

Fig. 31a. *The San Francisco Mountains, Arizona, from the vicinity of Hart Prairie, taken in 1872 by J. K. Hillers, photographer for explorer John Wesley Powell. The mountain's lower slopes then were open and clothed in herbaceous vegetation with occasional aspens and corridors of pines and other conifers. Note also the cienega of Bebb willows and marsh plants. Photograph courtesy of U.S. Geological Survey.*

vice was heavily involved in predator control and doing an admirable job of it (see, e.g., Bailey 1907), the agency had other programs to administer. Would not a full-time predatory-animal-control agency do an even better job? Besides, the western states were paying out more than a million dollars a year in bounties. That cost could be eliminated once and for all if the job was done right.

Such sentiments were compelling, and on June 30, 1914, the U.S. Congress authorized the Predatory Animal and Rodent Control (PARC) branch of the Biological Survey of the U.S. Department of Agriculture, and made it responsible for experiments and demonstrations in destroying wolves, prairie dogs, and other animals injurious to agriculture and

IG. 31b. *The same view as in fig. 31a photographed in 1981. The aspens
nd conifers have greatly increased; the herbaceous foreground is much reduced,
nd the aspen-studded meadows of the lower slopes are now completely closed in.
he cienega has disappeared. Photograph courtesy of the U.S. Geological Survey
nd Raymond M. Turner.*

animal husbandry. The sum of $125,000 was appropriated
for 1914–15 to employ three hundred hunters. By the close
of fiscal 1916 the PARC had been organized into control
districts and staffed. The "inspector" for the New Mexico-
Arizona District was J. Stokely ("Stoke") Ligon, a professional field biologist and predatory-animal hunter and a competent administrator (fig. 32). He knew the Southwest and
its people and hired the best hunters, among them Eddy
Anderson, Ben Lilly, C. C. Wood, and T. T. Loveless. In
the first year of operation, 1915–16, Ligon employed thirty-
two men and concentrated his efforts in New Mexico. Seven
"bears" were taken by the force that year, one more than
the number of mountain lions taken (Ligon 1916), but the

program was just getting under way. Many more bears were killed by ranchers and bounty hunters. Walter P. Taylor, another survey biologist, stated in his field notes that fifteen grizzlies were verified as killed that year in the "Nantan" District alone (the Nantanes Mountains, on the San Carlos Apache Indian Reservation).

Twelve bears were taken in the fiscal year 1916–17, and in his annual report Stoke Ligon had this to say about bears:

Damage by bear has also been greatly reduced during the year. Several bear were killed in Eastern Arizona, that were destructive to livestock, and the big male grizzly and female grizzly that were killed on Mt. Taylor and the head of the Pecos, in New Mexico, have proven to be of great importance, since their destruction has put an end to the great loss of cattle in the two districts. There are still a few large bear in some of the higher ranges of the District, —the Pecos Forest, Black Range and Mogollons of New Mexico, and in the White Mountains of and a few other points in Arizona, but the wolf and lion men can easily pick those among them that are a nuisance and kill them when they are located. It is of importance to note here that on July 29, 1916, Ed S. Steele and Bart Burnam, two Government hunters, shot and wounded a large bear in Western New Mexico, about 20 miles North-West of Reserve. On recent visits to that locality we are informed that the great damage done by a certain bear ceased with the wounding of this animal, and the ranchers are quite sure now that the wound was a fatal one. At the time, we were informed by the two hunters that the bear was badly wounded, being shot several times, leaving much blood on the trail, and although it was followed for some time, the hunters failed to find it.

One other bear was not reported in the tally, since neither the skin nor the skull had been received by the district office. Thus it appears that, while the records did not differentiate between species, the difference was appreciated and grizzlies were the "big bears" or "large bears." Ligon's attitude toward bears was actually enlightened for the time. Bears were not considered game animals in either state and

FIG. 32. *Ready for the hunt, Ben Lilly* (left), *Jack Thompson* (center), *J. Stokely Ligon* (right) *at Buckhorn, New Mexico in 1920. Determined men such as these and other PARC hunters drove the grizzly to extinction in the Southwest. Photograph by J. E. Hawley.*

were generally thought of as second-class predators or nuisances (see, e.g., Bailey 1931).

In 1915 the Great War was on in Europe, and American commodities were in great demand. Prices for beef and mutton were good, and the ranchmen who had survived the bad years were riding high. Good times also kindled a demand for access to the remaining open ranges, now confined to the most inaccessible parts of the national forests. New settlers, cow outfits large and small, loggers, miners, and even some old market hunters went to their legislatures and demanded the abolition of the national forests. It seemed that the least that America could do for the war effort was to sacrifice its natural resources—at a profit to its citizens. The response of the Forest Service was to relax grazing restrictions.

The forests were also threatened from another quarter. National parks were coming into vogue, and the conservationists were pushing a bill to establish a national park system throughout the West. Where else would these parks come from but the forest reserves?

The reaction of the Forest Service was to seek expanded use of the forests to build a political clientele. The Agriculture Appropriations Act of 1915 provided for the establishment of summer homes, recreation sites, and campgrounds. Hunting and game management were actively pursued and encouraged; grazing and timber cutting restrictions were relaxed—anything to draw attention to the value of the forests to forest users and differentiate this "multiple use" concept of the U.S. Department of Agriculture from the preservationist program of Interior's Park Service.

This strategy worked: only Grand Canyon National Park and a few minor parks were established in the Southwest. The national forests remained intact; ranching, predator control, and the killing of bears continued.

As America entered the war in Europe, the war on predators intensified. At a conference in Albuquerque on November 1, 1917, the president of the New Mexico Cattle Growers Association, the president of the New Mexico College of Agriculture and Mechanical Arts, and other "interested parties" arrived at the following estimate of damage done to the livestock industry in New Mexico by "wolves, mountain lions, 'big bears,' coyotes, bobcats and wild dogs" during the preceding year: Cattle, 24,350 head lost at a value of $1,374,000; sheep, 165,000 head lost at a value of $1,320,000; and horses, 850 head lost at a value of $21,250; making a total loss of $2,715,250 (Gish 1977 in Brown 1983).

Those figures were repeated often and widely and were used to recruit support for Ligon and his PARC. Thus New Mexico and Arizona began to cooperate with PARC, contributing funds and support. In 1918, Ligon had this to report:

Good progress had also been made in big bear and lion work. We have a close check on the number of big bear in the district as well as being familiar with their exact range. From the fact that those that remain occupy the roughest and most heavily forested mountains makes their capture rather difficult. . . . Progress in bear and lion work has necessarily been slow because the greatest effort has been put forth to get wolves. As the wolves are brought under control attention will be directed to bears and lions. [Ligon 1918]

Six "big" bears (grizzlies) had been bagged by the PARC force, four in July, 1917; one in May, 1918, and one in June, 1918. Two of these were taken in Arizona, and four were taken in New Mexico, all by government hunters. This brought to twenty-five the total bears brought in by the PARC. Damage attributed to predatory bears by the PARC during 1917–18 was estimated at $10,000.

Ligon (1918) went on to discuss depredations by bears in detail, and to caution against the political consequences of the failure to destroy them:

As the wolves and lions are killed out in certain districts, much light is thrown on the case against bears as predatory animals. Guilt is now being placed on them, where in years gone by it was generally supposed that bears did little killing of domestic stock. They are becoming more destructive to cattle in recent years. The dry seasons have probably added to their killing, since the shortage of feed has created a demand for range everywhere, even in the highest and most heavily forested regions—the home of big bears—thus throwing the helpless stock into the very haunts of the animals.

The damage from bears has been greatest in the Taos and Pecos Mountains, and in the Black Range and Mogollon Mountains in New Mexico. In Arizona quite a lot of killing has been reported from the White Mountains and Blue Range, in the southern part of the State and in the central portion south of Williams. West of Chloride, New Mexico, along the crest of the Black Range, many cattle were killed in the early spring. This was probably the work of two or three grizzlies. The heaviest losses, however, were sustained in the Taos and Pecos Mountains about the head of the Pecos River, where the number of cattle killed will be more than a hundred head. We are working after these cattle-killers and expect to have the guilty animals destroyed by the end of the year.

While cattle are the animals usually killed by grizzlies and the larger brown and black bears, it develops, beyond any doubt, that *all* kill domestic stock under certain conditions. The black and brown bears appear to be worse after sheep. Mr. Frank Hoctor, who has summered his sheep on the C.C. Flat in the White Mountains, Arizona, had ninty-seven sheep killed by bears during the season. Our hunter, Mr. Ed. S. Steele, has since killed the bears. Sheep have also been bothered in the Jemez Forest, New Mexico, by the smaller bears.

I feel sure that the losses in cattle alone in New Mexico during the present spring and summer will aggregate more than two hundred head. This is rather a serious matter when we consider the fact that *big bears generally kill big animals*—often cows carrying calves.

To fail to listen to the requests from ranchmen for protection against bears would have a serious weakening effect on our organization. Destructive animals, of whatever species, should be controlled. There is no danger of bears being exterminated so long as we have our parks and wild northern woods. Even our reluctance in killing the smaller bears creates discord between our methods and the interest of the ranchmen.

I am preparing a detailed report on the bear as a predatory animal, in which I hope to show clearly the real status of bears in the district.

Ligon was an astute observer and knew the reasons for the increase in bear depredations but was reluctant to state them. Later he would.

In the meantime, the grizzly was to face a new threat. Ligon reported, "We are making extensive preparations to carry out a poison campaign the coming winter—from November to March" (Ligon 1918). Use of poisons was thus to become the worst predator-control technique yet for the grizzly.

By the end of World War I it was increasingly apparent that Southwest grizzlies were on their way out. In 1917, Ligon estimated that only forty-eight grizzlies remained in New Mexico—in the Sangre de Cristo, Jemez, San Mateo, and Magdalena mountains; the Mount Taylor and Black ranges; and the Mogollon Mountain complex (Bailey 1931). Merriam (1922), using information supplied by Ligon and the U.S. Biological Survey staff, listed grizzlies as extant in Arizona only in the White Mountain region, the area south of Bill Williams Mountain, in two locations below the Mogollon Rim, and in the Catalina-Rincon mountains. Grizzlies were still to be found in Colorado's San Juan and Culebra mountains, and he thought that grizzlies might still inhabit the Pine Valley, Escalante, and Abajo mountains in southern Utah (map 2). These estimates, while based on recent information, were already outdated and too generous. By 1915 the last grizzly in the Mogollon Rim country had been killed (Cline, personal communication), and the grizzly was almost certainly extirpated from southern Utah. All in all, probably fewer than sixty grizzlies remained in the southwestern United States.

The intervening years had also been unkind to the grizzly in Mexico. The chaotic conditions that followed the first revolution in 1911–12 had failed to give the animal a respite from the aggressive settlement policy of the Porfirio Díaz regime. Moreover, the harassment and impending breakup of the large haciendas—the ranches that were as large as small American states, such as Hearst's Rancho Babícora, the Corralitos, and the Palomas—and their apportionment to campesinos (Machado 1981) bode ill for the remaining grizzlies in Chihuahua. Sheldon (1925) on a return trip to Chihuahua in 1921 found that bears had become scarce since his hunting days between 1898 and 1902 and that the grizzlies were "greatly reduced in numbers"; he predicted their extinction in the near future. According to Bahre (1977), the last known grizzly in northern Sonora was killed

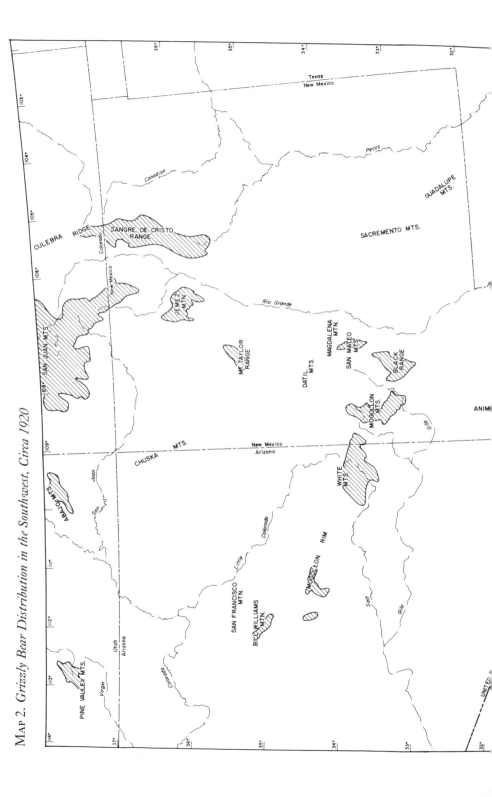

MAP 2. *Grizzly Bear Distribution in the Southwest, Circa 1920*

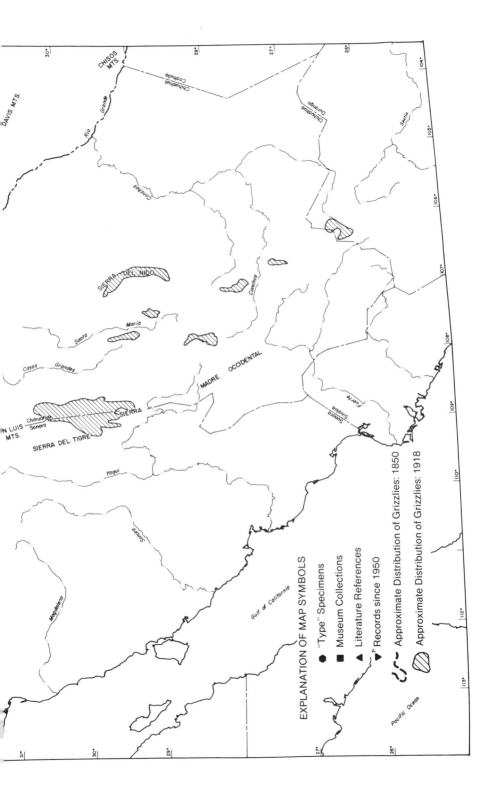

EXPLANATION OF MAP SYMBOLS

● "Type" Specimens
■ Museum Collections
◀ Literature References
▶ Records since 1950
◡ Approximate Distribution of Grizzlies: 1850
▨ Approximate Distribution of Grizzlies: 1918

in 1918 (in Sierra de los Ajos?). Whether most of the great bear's decline in Mexico occurred before or after the revolution is unknown, and it remains for some Mexican historian to document the particulars of the decrease in Mexican grizzlies.

THE LAST HOLDOUTS

Ligon (1919) noted the decline in grizzlies during the war years and considered the PARC at least partly responsible: "The constant trapping and hunting for wolves, lions and big bears in the forests of the state [New Mexico] during the last three years, have greatly reduced these animals." Ligon went on to note that "the stock killing bears have been reduced in numbers, but those that remain occupy practically the same districts." Ligon (1919) was also having some concerns about the prevalent attitude about the taking of bears as stock killers:

The last four years of predatory animal operations have demonstrated conclusively the folly of letting every one destroy bears with the hope of getting the destructive individuals. None but experienced and equipped hunters continuously succeed in getting the cattle killers. Three-fourths of the bears killed during the last fiscal year were harmless as regards destructiveness to livestock, and no bear molests game to any extent. The result is that most of the smaller bears are wasted on account of being killed in summer, when neither meat or hides are of value.

Hunters and others, in their desire to kill bears, report them as being killers of livestock, while the kind and size of the animal disproves their contentions.

Ligon (1919) appeared to be at least temporarily changing his stance on bears:

The smaller bears need protection the same as deer and turkey, leaving the matter of control of individuals in the hands of

Government forces that will operate under permit or agreement.

During the last few months destruction of small bears by citizens of the mountainous districts has been greater than usual, and in but few cases have the hides been worth taking from the animals.

It appears that uniform state laws for the protection of bears, with provisions for the care of destructive animals, be made. Such laws would, no doubt, meet with the approval of both ranchmen and sportsmen of the country.

Few of the black and brown bears are really destructive to livestock, most ranchmen are so unfair as to condemn all of the animals for the crimes of a few. The real mean animals, like the old outlawed wolves and lions, make their kills and rarely ever return to them; the smaller and innocent animals that come to eat from the carcass are those generally trapped.

By recent investigation I found that many cattle, for which bears are credited as having killed, die from effects of poison weeds. This, however, does not remove the guilt from the larger animals, that we know are very destructive to cattle.

Nonetheless, twenty-eight bears were taken in New Mexico during fiscal 1918–19 by PARC and state hunters, eight of them by Ben Lilly (Ligon 1919). Four more were taken by PARC forces in Arizona (Musgrave 1919). At least some of these thirty-two were grizzlies.

An experimental poisoning program in effect in both states was showing promise (Ligon 1919, Musgrave 1919). More strychnine baits were ordered, and a major poisoning campaign was mapped out for the winter of 1919–20.

Then lack of manpower and funds caused the PARC to fall behind in its program against bears during 1919–20. Ligon (1920) reported:

The bear situation is one that has not been met. No concentrated effort has been made to get the depredators; but the time is at hand for our service to add up the heavy losses from this source and this is a more difficult and expensive problem than that of getting other species. Hunting big bear is the most dangerous of predatory work, and requires much experience to make it successful. During the last four months bear have killed no less than 800 head of cattle in the state.

The new poisoning program against coyotes was progressing with promising results, but it too required preparation and attention. Both Ligon and M. E. Musgrave, chief inspector for the Arizona District, considered strychnine a necessary tool if the now-prime targets of the PARC, coyotes, were to be controlled. The use of such a tool was to embark the agency on its most controversial course—and may also have hastened the demise of the grizzly.

Only ten bears had been taken by PARC hunters in Arizona and New Mexico in 1919–20. Another nineteen were killed by state hunters in New Mexico (Ligon 1920, Musgrave 1920). Although there is no way to tell from the record, none of these bears appear to have been grizzlies. Grizzlies and other "big bears" were still on Ligon's (1920) mind, however, and he planned to get them:

> In the future I will recommend that big bear be still-hunted or slow-trailed in order to get those wanted; no other method produces results sought—to get the real depredators and avoid the innocent. Although it is very desirable that the interested public—sportsmen—control the bear situation—such will not occur since the average hunter does not get the destructive individuals. . . .
> Big bear have caused an unusual amount of disturbance in several districts during the last three months. They have not only held their own in some high districts, but their numbers have increased since none of the large grizzlies have been killed by Bureau men or others. There are as many as twenty big grizzlies in the state distributed over the highest portions of the Mogollons, Black Range, San Mateo, and Sangre De Cristo mountain systems; all cattle killers. Definite and expensive methods will have to be followed to get these particular depredators.

Ligon made good on his promise. In July and August, 1920, he personally supervised a few chosen hunters in an organized hunt in the Black Range and Mogollon Mountains region against wolves, lions, and bears. "Many . . . predatory bears were treed and killed" (Bliss 1921). The reference to treeing indicates that these were mostly black bears; moreover, by that time there were no longer that many grizzlies left to be taken. Still, the Black Range and the Mogollons were grizzly strongholds, and an unknown number of grizzlies were taken; the PARC report for 1920–21 is brief and, as usual, vague about the species of bear. All in all, nine bears were taken that year by the PARC force in New Mexico, while state cooperators bagged another eight.

The campaign against bears also intensified in Arizona. Eighteen "bears" were trailed, shot, and trapped by the PARC in that state in 1920–21 (Musgrave 1921). State Supervisor Musgrave (1921) explained the situation:

Owing to the extreme dry condition of the ranges in Arizona this year bear have done more damage than they have ever done before and we have found it necessary to kill them off. Along the Blue Range and around the head of Friscoe and Blue River they have been exceptionally bad, and Mr. Charles Miller was detailed to the work of killing off the most destructive of them. He has succeeded in getting six adult bear in the last two months.

Again, the number of grizzlies killed cannot be ascertained. Musgrave (1921, in Lange 1960), noted that "we also have another grizzly that ranges in the Rincon Mountains, north of Tucson."

The year 1922 marked the beginning of the "last grizzlies." In May of that year, PARC hunter Ramsey Patterson and his friend Jimmy Norman went after an old grizzly that was known to inhabit the Looney Perkins Range south of Williams, Arizona. After a week's work in and around what is now the Sycamore Canyon Wilderness Area, Patterson's dogs brought the big bear to bay in the Bear Canyon–Government Canyon area. The animal, a male, was sent to the National Museum. It was the last grizzly known to be killed in Arizona west of the White Mountains (Housholder 1971).

That there was to be no let up in the war on grizzlies is indicated by State Supervisor Bliss's annual report for New Mexico in 1921–22: "Few brown and black bears are predatory under normal field food conditions, but those of the harmful class along with grizzlies must be dealt with accordingly. Bears, no doubt, should be accepted and more widely appreciated as game animals."

Bliss (1922) estimated that only six grizzlies remained in New Mexico and predicted their extinction: "The few grizzly bears remaining will eventually fall victims to still hunting [baiting] maneuvers. Even a well trained pack of dogs is confronted by a difficult task to bag a powerful grizzly in its flight."

Nonetheless, the beginning of a softened policy on the taking of bears is evident. Only two bears are recorded as having been taken by PARC hunters in New Mexico in 1921–22. New Mexico state hunters took fourteen, however, and PARC personnel in Arizona killed another twenty (Bliss, 1922, Musgrave 1922). Some of these were grizzlies.

Thirty bears were taken by PARC and their state co-operators in New Mexico and Arizona in 1922–23 (Pineau 1923, Musgrave 1923). Musgrave's newsletters to his field men attest that bears were being downplayed as PARC targets (see Appendix C). Hunters were encouraged to concentrate on wolves and lions and to make sure that any bears taken were in fact stock killers—a fine point that was often ignored, of course. Bears were rated at ten points toward the fifteen points required to get on the "honor roll" (a wolf or a lion was worth fifteen points), and in those days a government employee who did not produce was dropped from employment—pronto.

In the summer of 1923 the last Pecos grizzly was bagged. E. S. Barker (1953) described the particulars:

In 1923, I was operating a mountain ranch on Sapello Creek and summer grazing my cattle in the Beaver Creek and Big

Burn country. A big grizzly bear came onto Skipper's range
and killed some cattle. Skipper tried to trap him but the old
bear was a smart one and had learned what traps were and
refused to be caught. When he couldn't find a way to get to
the carcass without getting caught, he would go kill another
cow. I heard of all this and, although it was fifteen miles over
there, I was on the lookout for him to come to my range and
sample some of my beef.

Sure enough, one day I rode over to Beaver Creek and found
he had been there and killed a two-year-old steer near the head
of the north fork of Beaver, and a young cow three miles
below, right near our branding corral. He had eaten a big meal
out of the belly and rump of the first one, but the second he
had just killed for fun. I thought he might come back so rode
to the ranch and got some bear traps and a camp outfit so I
could camp near the cattle. The Koogler boys, neighboring
ranchers, came over and we set the traps. The old fellow didn't
come back that night so the others went home. I took my three
Airedales and tried to follow him, or, at least, find out which
way he had gone and where he might strike next.

We found his big, foot-long track headed right down the
dusty trail along Beaver Creek and followed it four miles to
the junction with Hollinger Canyon. There he had turned
right back up the Hollinger, sticking to the trail most of the
way, his claw marks showing three inches ahead of the toe
pads at every step. At the falls, five miles up the canyon, he
turned out to the right and went up through the Big Burn to
the top of the range. By then it was getting late and the track
was still two days old, so I turned back and rode the eight
long mountain miles back to the ranch.

That night I phoned Skipper Viles to be on the lookout
for the grizzled old stock killer for he was headed back his
way. Skipper reported that the bear had come back to one of
his previous kills the night before and gotten caught in a trap
waiting for his big foot, and that he had shot him that morning.
That, as far as I know, was the last grizzly bear of the Pecos
high country. From time to time, there have been reports of
tracks of a grizzly being seen but certainly none lives there,
and it could be only one occasionally passing through.

At the time I was a bit jealous of Skipper because he, not
I, had killed the bear. Now, since it proved to be the last

one, I am mighty glad I didn't kill it. Mrs. Viles still has the rug and it is really a nice one.

Also in 1923, 103,000 poison baits were distributed to cooperating ranchers in New Mexico, in a program that was to expand greatly in the coming years.

Despite a reported population increase and a more en-lightened PARC policy, 1923–24 was a hard year for bears. At least forty-five were taken by the PARC in New Mexico and Arizona—a new record (Ligon 1924, Musgrave 1924). Some of the animals were known to have been poisoned (Musgrave 1924), and there were undoubtedly others. Ligon had returned from service with the state of New Mexico and was again New Mexico District supervisor for the PARC. As usual, he filed a voluminous report and had plenty to say about bears. The following passage indicates that private hunters with dogs were taking over the control of "stock-killing bears," a role welcomed by the PARC:

Stock-killing bears are becoming scarcer every year. The interest and effort that sportsmen and big game hunters gener-ally put forth in killing bears, especially the larger individuals, relieve the Biological Survey force of much bear killing. It is possible that within another year or two salaried hunters will be relieved of practically all bear hunting even though some damage may be committed so long as there are bears in the mountains. The individual stock-killing bears now at large in the state are well-known and private hunters—not in the or-ganized service—or parties are usually after these during the period that the animals are not hibernating. Guides with equip-ment for taking parties out after bears and mountain lions are becoming established in the state as they have been for years in the northern Rockies; some of these guides at some previous time served as hunters for the Biological Survey. Reliable hunt-ers of this class are being encouraged and when the bears are killed in this way the government-state service is not subjected to the criticism that often results when salaried hunters kill the bears. [Ligon 1924]

Ligon's ambivalence toward bears as valued game animals and the need to satisfy the PARC's ranching political constituency are apparent in the following passages from his report of 1924:

When a bear becomes a killer it seems that the only relief is to kill the bear. However, it must be admitted that bears, large or small, are an asset to any section, a drawing card of no small consideration, and if the destructive individuals can be eliminated by the route of adventure and sportsmanship it is more satisfactory to the general public as they are widely considered game animals. The sportsman, through selfish interests only in his desire to conserve bears is prone to disregard entirely the livestock owner who pays grazing fees in order that his stock may run in the National Forests. . . .

It should not be assumed that all of the few bears killed by government and state hunters are stock-killers, they are not. It is a difficult matter to prevent hunters from killing a few bears while conducting their mountain lion hunting. Good lion dogs, as a rule, are also bear dogs and where lions are scarce it is impossible to keep dogs from running bears occasionally. If a bear is bayed or treed by trained dogs the hunter contends that to call the dog off and let the bear go has a bad effect on the dog. Bear meat is always acceptable as dog food and the fur is not often in such condition that it does not have some monetary value. There is another phase of the bear question that cannot be overlooked; ranchmen who graze stock in sections infested with bear, as a rule, contend that all bears are more or less predatory. For a government or state hunter to kill a bear occasionally pleases them, notwithstanding the attitude of sportsmen, although the bear killed may not always be predatory, and ranchmen often take the attitude that even a small bear may eventually develop into a killer.

As for the declining status of grizzlies, Ligon (1924) reported:

One or more big cattle-killing bears is still at large in the Sangre de Cristo Range, ranging from the head of the Pecos River northward and a few cattle-killers remain in the Black

Range, Mogollon, San Mateo and Zuni Mountains. Even in the mountain ranges mentioned there has not been serious complaint during the past year, although the remaining grizzlies may be expected to kill if cattle are available, no matter where they range.

Ligon (1924) went on seemingly to contradict his earlier statements regarding the efficiency of hunters taking stock-killing bears, noting that, while the grizzlies were becoming scarce, the "smaller bears are rather numerous in all mountainous sections of the state, and unless there is much more effort put forth by sportsmen to kill them than has been the case during the past few years, they will no doubt continue to hold their own."

An increase in bears was also reported in Arizona, and again the PARC considered itself a mediator between bears and stockmen:

Bear are increasing in the State of Arizona. There are perhaps three times as many here now on the range as there were in 1918. Consequently it is becoming necessary for us to pay more attention to the stock-killing bear. In one place near Blue River and about forty miles north at Clifton stockmen located five bear in a canyon and found that they had been slaughtering stock. Cleve Miller was notified and cleaned up the entire bunch in one day[!]

Later an old female with two yearlings were found killing cattle and were also destroyed by Cleve Miller.

We have also found it necessary to destroy several bear in the district south of Springerville and in the Graham Mountains near Safford.

Generally speaking, however, the bear are not so destructive as most stockmen think and we are doing our best to keep them from stampeding against the bear. [Musgrave 1924]

As mentioned earlier, the PARC's expanded use of poison may have been a factor in the demise of the far-ranging grizzly. Ligon (1924) considered poison an indispensable tool for the killing of predatory animals, especially coyotes, and enthusiastically reported that "poison has come to stay."

The poison was again strychnine, rolled in tissue and sand-wiched between pork fat strips or in tallow (Ligon 1924). The strychnine placed at bait stations, while designed for taking coyotes, was not selective, and the bait would have appealed to grizzlies:

Carcasses of animals that die of natural causes make the best poison stations. However, there is so much of the time that dead animals cannot be found that such stations cannot be relied upon. In the fall and early winter, at the time coyotes are most successfully poisoned, it does not often occur that carcasses are available for use as poison stations. While the fetid scent is a fairly good substitute for animal flesh for poison stations the writer has found that scraps of meat or bones from butcher shops or slaughter pens [are also effective.] [Ligon 1924]

Not only was the PARC placing poison and setting out poison bait stations, but "approximately 155,000 poison baits [were] distributed to cooperators free of charge" (Ligon 1924). That more bears were not killed was due to the re-luctance of U.S. Forest Service administrators to condone poisoning in the national forests and the objections of hound men, who were prevented from working lions and bears in poison areas (Appendix C). That this was a real concern was expressed by Ligon (1924):

In actual experience, with but few exceptions, poison has proved to be detrimental on the National Forests in New Mex-ico. Commercial poison has been used by the Manager of the VT Ranch in the Black Range, Datil National Forest, during the last three or four years. The result has been that no Bio-logical Survey wolf nor mountain lion hunters, on account of their valuable dogs (well trained dogs are valued at $100 to $500) could be induced to hunt this range or the country closely adjoining it.

The spring and fall poison campaigns and the large amount of unsupervised poisoning by ranchers undoubtedly killed many bears. The program also had many discrepancies

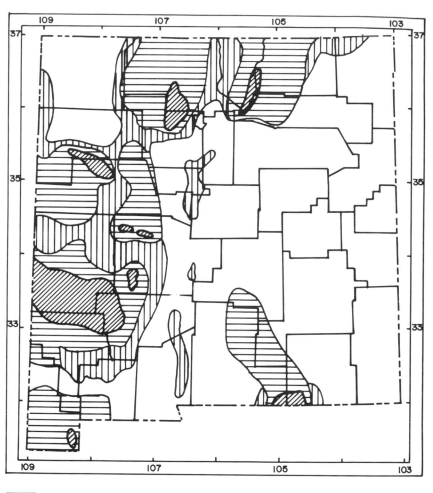

Areas where poison was not to be used under any circumstances

Areas where care was to be exercised in the use of poison

Established hunter control districts where poison operations were to be conducted only by the district hunter and only if necessary

Areas where intensive poisoning was to be conducted

MAP 3. *Designated poison control areas in New Mexico, 1922*

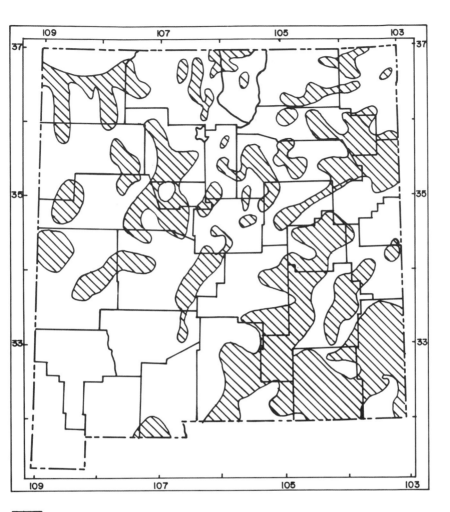

Poison exposed by government hunters and state and cooperative forces

No poison exposed under government supervision

MAP 4. *Areas treated with poison in New Mexico, 1923–24*

between planned operations and the areas where poisoning was actually done (maps 3 and 4).

In 1924 the U.S. Forest Service began keeping estimates of the numbers of big-game species in the national forests. Twenty-seven grizzlies were believed still to exist in Arizona, and six in the southern Colorado forests. Only two bears (no grizzlies) were thought to inhabit the Dixie National Forest, in southern Utah. New Mexico, true to the tradition of Ligon and others, did not separate grizzlies from black bears, a distinction that would be made in subsequent years. These figures were merely educated guesses and were not based on any census techniques other than stock-killing complaints and reports from the Forest Service rangers. They were, in retrospect, optimistic and represent only an idea of the various numbers of grizzlies still extant in the forests, but they are the best information available for the time. Fifty-four grizzlies were estimated to roam the national forests of the Southwest in 1925 (fig. 33).

Almost 162,000 poison baits were issued to cooperators in fiscal 1924–25, and approximately 75,000 square miles of New Mexico were treated (Pope 1925). Sixteen bears were taken in Arizona in 1924–25 (three trapped, six taken with dogs, one shot, one poisoned, and five not reported on), and another sixteen in New Mexico by federal and state hunters (Musgrave 1925, Pope 1925). That the policy of taking only known stock killers was neither popular nor always obeyed is illustrated in PARC hunter Ed Steele's narrative report to District Supervisor, E. F. Pope in 1925:

A few days ago I had four bears up at once. There was an old bear that was fat and I knew she had to be eating beef to be in that shape this time of year so I killed her. She had beef in her stomach and the meat, I don't think if a fried steak was given to anyone to eat, that they could detect it from beef steak. She was by far the fattest bear I ever saw this time of year. The other bear were in good shape, but not as fat and I really had no evidence on them so I just let them go unharmed, but it was about all I could do to leave them for it sure hurts your dogs to tree bear and let them go and my

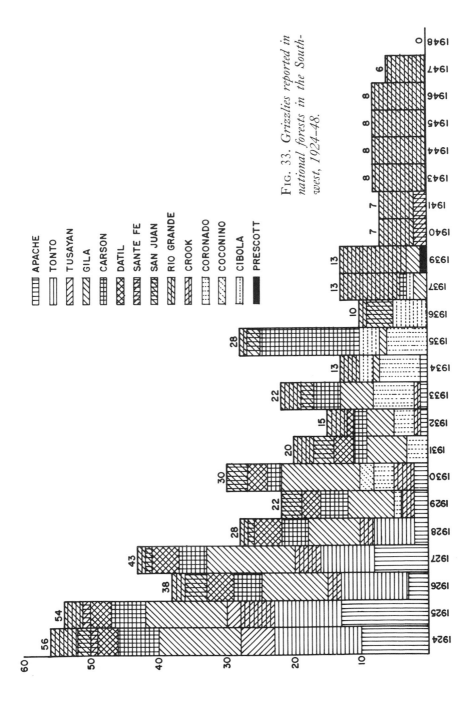

FIG. 33. *Grizzlies reported in national forests in the Southwest, 1924–48.*

dogs have kept away from the small bear and have only run
two or three bad bear and got whipped off till they need some
encouragement. To do good work on the large bear they should
be allowed to work on some small bear and I am inclined to
think that the three I let go will go ahead and kill but I
don't know of course.

I am going to trap the bear at Eagle Peak for I know about
that biggest grizzly for I run him all one day last year and
there has been some better trained bear dogs than mine after
him and they don't have any luck with him. He don't care
for dogs, he just keeps out of the way of the hunters and
fights the dogs off, so I am going to try and hang a trap on
him.

The next year the U.S. Forest Service estimated that
only thirty-eight grizzlies remained in Southwest forests.
Twenty-nine bears (at least four of them cubs) were killed in
New Mexico by the PARC and cooperating New Mexico
state hunters (Musgrave 1926, Pope 1926). Eight of these were
killed by Ed Steele in localities where bears had been killing
livestock (Pope 1926). Pope (1926) went on to elaborate:

During the spring months of the past year many claims
were advanced that bear were killing cattle. Several of the
claims were substantiated and a number of bears were killed
by our hunters. The main cause for so many bear becoming
predatory was attributed to the scarcity, or almost complete
absence, of succulent vegetation on the mountain ranges due to
lack of moisture. During the present spring with these conditions almost exactly reversed, it will be interesting to note the
actions of bear in their relation to livestock as compared with
their behavior last spring. Thus far, during the present season,
only one report of depredations by bear has been received.
This was the case of a large grizzly bear which was killed by
a local hunter near Raton, just after the bear had killed a
steer.

This was the last New Mexico grizzly reported from east
of the Rio Grande. The range of the grizzly became more
restricted each year. Pope (1926) understood the relation-

ship between available forage and stock killing and blamed the dry spring of 1925 for the rash of bear-depredation complaints:

It is believed that an unusual lack of moisture and consequent scarcity of succulent vegetation during the early spring months of the calendar year 1925 was largely responsible for so many bears acquiring predatory habits. . . .

During the latter half of the fiscal year almost no complaint of depredations of bears was received, and only one bear was killed by a salaried hunter during the period from January 1 to June 30. There was no evidence that the bear killed was a predatory animal and the hunter who killed the animal contrary to instructions was promptly dismissed from the service. . . .

The fact that although bear are reported to be very plentiful they evidently are not killing livestock to any noticeable extent may be regarded, we believe, as good evidence that their natural food supply is very largely a governing factor in their relation to livestock.

Bears were now gaining public support as game animals, and there was a general movement among southwestern sportsmen to afford them some protection. The PARC, always attuned to changes in the political wind, reported a total of only ten bears killed by the government and hunters in Arizona and New Mexico during fiscal 1926–27 (Musgrave 1927, Gray 1927).

The movement to afford some protection to bears gained momentum in 1927. In January of that year an editorial in the first issue of *Arizona Wildlife*, the monthly publication of the Arizona Game Protective Association, stated that bears had become scarce and urged the protection of a closed season and a bag limit, at least on black and "brown" bears. Throughout the year and into 1928 there were other articles objecting to the widespread use of poison to kill predatory animals because of the loss of hunting dogs and the destruction of valuable wildlife.

Ligon, now working again for the state of New Mexico and no longer with the PARC, stated a case for the bears

—even grizzlies. A good observer and a truly competent field biologist, Ligon (1927) had known for some time the true reasons behind bear depredations:

> As a group, bears are not livestock killers but individuals, especially among the grizzlies, *occasionally* vary from traditional habits and become serious destroyers of sheep and cattle. Poverty stricken ranges, as result of *excessive range utilization,* and drought often render their usual food so scanty that out of *need* bears become killers; hence, as respects losses from bears, forage conservation would result in increased saving of cattle and sheep. Since bears feed on carrion, they are frequently the victims of circumstantial evidence. Guilt as to having been the killer of livestock is often erroneously charged to them.
> These habitants of the mountains and forests impart a touch of the primitive and a flavor of romance that nothing else can replace. Their absence would take away one of the most interesting phases of the original wild life that all would regret.

Ligon (1927) went on to describe the grizzly's status in New Mexico and expressed the hope that a remnant population might be preserved:

> Unfortunately, the more predatory habits of the grizzlies have resulted in their being almost totally exterminated in the State. Revised policies as affects grazing in the higher portions of the mountains, where these bears make their home, may bring about a situation which will permit a few grizzlies to survive. All true sportsmen of the State hope that such a situation will develop.

In 1927 the New Mexico legislature placed all bears on the list of protected big-game animals, to be taken only during authorized open seasons. Provision was made in the Game Code, however, for stockmen and government hunters to take individual bears that were known to be stock killers. The legislation was enacted with almost no opposition (Ligon 1927). In that year in Arizona, Musgrave (1927) was "glad to report that . . . these animals [bears] are increasing on our ranges." The PARC also acknowledged the changing atti-

tudes by trying to upgrade their field force. A. E. Gray
(1927), the new state supervisor in New Mexico, commented:

One of the most serious handicaps to the speedy conclusion
of our work in the destruction of predatory animals is found in
personnel. With a few exceptions, the men who can be employed to perform the work of trapping are men who have
failed at every other vocation and their sole ambition seems
to be to get along with as little work as possible; they seek
for their hunting grounds places where animals are compara-
tively easy to take, and where the stockman is most liberal
with subsistance, and horse feed. During the last half year an
attempt has been made to weed out this undesirable type of
hunter, and to keep only those who appear to have interest
in the work—men who realize that we are a service organization, and as such must function for the mutual benefit of all.
In spite of care in selecting the best available men, it will
always be a difficult matter to secure a sufficient number of
good men to meet the demands for service.

The U.S. Forest Service estimated that twenty-eight
grizzlies remained in national forests in the Southwest in
1928: sixteen in New Mexico, ten in Arizona, and two in
Colorado (fig. 33). Musgrave (1928) was less optimistic about
Arizona grizzlies: "To the best of our knowledge there is
one large grizzly left in the state. This animal ranges from
the New Mexico line around Blue, Arizona, over into the
White Mountains south and east of McNary."

In New Mexico only one bear was reported taken by
government hunters in fiscal 1928, and that was by a state
cooperator (Gray 1928). Several stock-killing bears were reported, however, and permits were issued by the New Mexico Game and Fish Department for a bear killed in the
Mogollon Mountains, another in the San Mateo Mountains,
and still another that was killed in "self-defense" (Gray 1928).
Gray also reported a general uproar over the continued
widespread use of strychnine poison (now the capsules or
2-D variety) by both stockmen and PARC hunters, and the
widespread use of drop baits and baited carcasses.

Pressure to manage bears, not just kill them, increased. The Ninth Arizona Legislature passed the New Game Code, of which one of the provisions was that all bears were protected as game animals with an October 16 to November 30 hunting season and a bag limit of one bear. Following New Mexico's example, the Arizona legislation provided a clause allowing the state game commission to issue a permit for the killing of any bear that was destroying livestock or was found within a certain distance of human habitation and threatening life or property. No blanket permits were to be issued; each incident was to be evaluated on its individual merits.

A more enlightened public attitude, legal protection, and, most important, improved range conditions served to reduce the kill of bears in Arizona:

It was only necessary for us to take six bear in the State of Arizona during the fiscal year. . . . The fact that a great many thousands of head of cattle and sheep have been permanently removed from the range, giving vegetation a better chance to grow, will give more food for the bear and make him less of a predatory animal. This past year the state legislature put the bear on the protected list in Arizona. However, we are given permission by the State Game Commission to kill any bear that are destroying livestock. [Musgrave 1929]

In 1928–29 only one "stock-killing bear" was taken in New Mexico—by a New Mexico state hunter. The only problem was that sheep were still pastured in bear country: Gray (1929) reported, "The policy relating to the distribution of 2-D poison has been modified so that members of the Cattle Growers and Wool Growers can secure sufficient quantity upon written application approved by the Secretary of these associations."

Bears may still have been a problem in sheep areas, but the U.S. Forest Service was gaining control over the grazing problem on which it had worked so long and which had been set back during the war years. By now, however, it was almost too late for the grizzly; by 1929 only twenty-two animals were thought to remain in Arizona, New Mexico, and southern Colorado. The PARC, in the meantime, appeared to have done a complete about-face. In an article in the September, 1930, issue of *Wildlife Sportsman,* the new Arizona District supervisor of the PARC, D. A. Gilchrist, (1930a) stated:

> The Biological Survey finds that very few bear are stock killers, and are doing all that is possible to discourage the killing of them. Only bear that are known to be killers are taken, the hunter taking them being required to have an affidavit signed by three stockmen that know of the particular bear in question. Hunters are given no credit for taking even a stock killing bear, and when such a killer is apprehended, he must be taken in accordance with the provisions found in the State Game Code.

Gilchrist (1930a) went on to say that the PARC would henceforth use strychnine only in country where sheep and goats were pastured or "where it is not possible to stop severe losses of livestock, game or game birds, rapidly enough by means of traps. Strychnine would not be placed in mountainous countries where lion dogs or fur bearers would be endangered."

The New Mexico District supervisor, J. C. Gatlin (1930), was more circumspect: "In most depredations the ranch men themselves obtain a permit from the State game warden and killed the culprits. We feel that whenever it is possible this method is preferable to having our field force do this work. Adverse criticism is also avoided."

Only five bears were taken by the PARC in Arizona in 1929–30, and none in New Mexico (Gilchrist 1930a, Gatlin 1930). In 1930 the U.S. Forest Service raised its estimate of Southwest grizzlies to thirty. The outlook for the bear in southern Arizona was dire, however:

> Black and brown bear have shown little increase, which is scarcely to be wondered at in view of the fact that until 1929

they were classed as predatory animals and relentlessly hunted. The State Game Commission has also included all species of bear in the region south of the Gila River in the closed-season class for an indefinite period. The sole grizzly bear is reported to be ranging on the Rincon division of the Forest and is credited with having come over from the Graham division of the Crook Forest. If this theory is correct, he is the last and only one of his species on the Coronado Forest.

No mention was made in the New Mexico report of the big male grizzly killed by G. W. ("Dub") Evans in April, 1930, the skull of which was turned in to the U.S. Biological Survey. This grizzly hunt was reported in the *El Paso Times* and in G. W. Evans's *The Slash Ranch Hounds* (1951). The story does little to explain the stock-killing nature of the slain grizzly, but it illustrates the stockmen's attitude toward grizzly killing as duty mixed with sport. The PARC's policies toward bears may have changed, but most ranchers had not changed theirs, and the relaxed control efforts of the PARC were compensated for by their increasing efforts, assisted by professional hunters.

The only bears taken in 1930–31 by the PARC in Arizona and New Mexico were two cubs accidentally caught in coyote traps (Foster 1931, Gatlin 1931). Ranchers were still killing bears, however, as shown by an article in the April 17, 1931, issue of the *Silver City* (N.M.) *Enterprise:*

> To Carl and Blue Rice of Cliff goes the credit for killing one of the largest grizzly bears ever seen in this section. They were riding their range and came upon a dead cow on Rain Creek, and finding the tracks of a big grizzly bear around the carcass, they went to the nearest phone and called up Supervisor James A. Scott and asked him to secure from the state game department a special permit for killing the bear out of season.

As far as I know this is the last written account of the taking of a grizzly in New Mexico.[1]

The Forest Service's grizzly estimates dropped from

twenty in 1931 to fifteen in 1932. Yet during the early 1930s bears were reported to be on the increase (Foster 1932, Gatlin 1933), and fewer bears were taken under permit (Gatlin 1934). By then there was general dissatisfaction with the law requiring a depredation permit: "There is an undercurrent of feeling among stockmen that bear should be taken off the protected list, due to their resentment of being forced to first secure a permit from the State Game Department before we will attempt to take bear. They feel they should be able to take a bear the same as mountain lions or wolves" (Gatlin 1934).

The year 1935 was a drought year; depredation complaints increased, and a number of depredation permits were issued (Gatlin 1935). The PARC again began taking bears; one of them was the last grizzly known to have been taken in Arizona. Housholder (1971) interviewed the hunter who took it, Richard R. (Dick) Miller, and described the event.

Miller, a cowboy turned lion and bear hunter, had only recently been hired by the PARC. He was in Stray Horse Canyon, northeast of Clifton, when his seven hounds picked up a bear scent. In a manner of minutes the trailed bear doubled back and ran right into Miller, who was on horseback. After shooting the bear, later estimated to be two to three years old, Miller looked around and found evidence

---

[1] Nevertheless, there may have been some later records. A grizzly skull in the U.S. National Museum cataloged as collected by G. W. Evans and coming from Magdalena Baldy, New Mexico, is dated 1935. No other accounts of this specimen could be found, however, and in a conversation with the author in 1982, G. W. Evans, Jr., said that he had never heard of his father killing a grizzly on Magdalena Baldy but that he well remembered the grizzly taken earlier, in 1930 on Hillsboro Peak, in the Black Range. The possibility exists that the 1935 skull may have been found or given to the U.S. Biological Survey several years after it was taken. Evans also recalled another grizzly killed before 1935, near Alma, New Mexico. Norman Woolsey (personal communication, 1982) also remembered a grizzly killed about 1933 near Sacaton, near Alma, which was shown to the schoolchildren at Cliff. These animals, however, are thought to be the same one reported in the *Enterprise* account.

Fig. 34. *Dick Miller with the hide of the last known grizzly taken in Arizona. Photograph by Kitt Casto; courtesy of Bob Housholder.*

of another young grizzly and an adult female. The bear was skinned, taken to the Filleman Ranch, and nailed to a cabin wall (fig. 34).

Two days later Kit Casto and a man named Black rode over and positively identified the animal as a grizzly. The other two grizzlies were never seen again, and the date of the last Arizona grizzly of record is September 13, 1935. Dick Miller later told Housholder that he would not have killed the bear if he had known it was a grizzly. No mention of the event is made in PARC's report of 1935–36, and this "last grizzly" is only one of twelve bears reported killed that year. The next year the U.S. Forest Service revised its estimate of the number of grizzlies in the American

Southwest downward to ten, half of them in the San Juan and Rio Grande National Forests in Colorado.

Thus it was that legal protection for the grizzly came too late and was too loosely applied to save these magnificent bears in Arizona and New Mexico. Unlike other wildlife of the Southwest, including the more widespread and numerous black bears, the grizzly's numbers and recruitment rate were too low to make a comeback. If a protected population of even a few bears had been allowed to exist, or if the bears could have held on a little longer, the outcome might have been different.

CHAPTER 11

Ghosts from the Past

Years passed without further verified accounts of grizzlies. The rumors and tales of grizzly sightings that were checked out proved to be imaginings or sightings of black bears. True, there were stories of big bears that would not tree, and of five-inch footprints, but there were no killings of grizzlies—at least not that anyone documented. And how could an animal like the grizzly not make himself known, if not by being taken in combat, or by an act such as killing a cow?

The only grizzlies left in the Southwest were the few the Forest Service estimated to be in southern Colorado and some rumored in Mexico. The bear's status in Colorado was uncertain. The few individuals thought to be present might be a breeding population, or the grizzly might already be biologically extirpated. No one knew for sure.

The situation in Mexico was little better. In 1937, A. Starker Leopold (1959) found the grizzly to be locally extinct in the Colonia García–Colonia Pacheco area, where E. W. Nelson had collected four in 1899. Leopold was told that the last individuals there had been killed in 1928 and in 1932. Leopold found a record of a grizzly killed in 1935 near Los Metates, Chihuahua, but he had no knowledge of any locality where grizzlies definitely persisted until the Lee brothers, professional guides and lion hunters, told him that grizzlies were still to be found in the mountains of the Sierra del Nido.

Then in 1940, in the *Annual Wildlife Report* of the U.S. Forest Service's Region 3, came a report of grizzlies in New Mexico: "Several grizzly bears are reported on the Jemez District of the Santa Fe Forest. On several occasions, bear

160

hunters have had their dogs badly torn up by bears that will not tree. Tracks and feeding habits of these bears along with hair from one animal that one dog got hold of prove the existence of grizzly in this area" [Johnson and Gee 1941].

Whether these were accounts of one or more grizzlies that had wandered down from Colorado is not known. The next year's *Annual Wildlife Report* stated: "The report of a grizzly bear on the Santa Fe Forest made last year caused considerable interest. We have no information concerning this report this year." This was the last official report of grizzlies from New Mexico. Henceforth reports of grizzlies in the American Southwest persisted only in southern Colorado, in the San Juan Mountains, in the upper Rio Grande wilderness of the Rio Grande and San Juan National Forests, and on the Tierra Amarilla Land Grant.

In August, 1951, a sheepherder killed a young grizzly near Plataro, on the headwaters of the Navajo River in San Juan National Forest. More sheep were lost to bears, and the next month Ernie Wilkinson, a predator trapper with the U.S. Fish and Wildlife Service, intentionally trapped and killed a two-year-old male grizzly near Starvation Gulch in the upper Rio Grande Wilderness Area, west of Creede, Colorado. Wilkinson had "never killed a grizzly," and once again the U.S. government had taken a state's last grizzly of record. Another grizzly was also taken just to the north, in Saguache County, in 1954, but that one was "unofficial" (T. Rausch, Colorado Division of Wildlife, 1979, quoted in Bissell 1980). The U.S. Forest Service regularly revised its figures for the number of grizzlies on the San Juan National Forest upward through the 1950s, but no grizzlies were reported taken, officially or unofficially, during the next twenty-five years.

On the basis of the reports by Ernest E. Lee, who had killed grizzlies in the Sierra del Nido through 1941, A. Starker Leopold went to Chihuahua to check on the status of the grizzly there. Leopold (1959) found that grizzlies were still locally known to inhabit the Sierra del Nido and adjoining Cerro La Campana and Sierra Santa Clara. Several

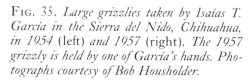

FIG. 35. *Large grizzlies taken by Isaias T. García in the Sierra del Nido, Chihuahua, in 1954* (left) *and 1957* (right). *The 1957 grizzly is held by one of García's hands. Photographs courtesy of Bob Housholder.*

grizzlies had recently been taken there, and Leopold was shown excellent photographs of a big male killed on October 24, 1954, and another grizzly killed on October 4, 1957 (Leopold 1959, 1967; fig 35). Leopold (1959) was also shown hides and photographs of other recently killed grizzlies, and a live animal captured as a cub in 1954 and kept by a taxidermist in Ciudad Chihuahua.

Under Leopold's direction the Museum of Vertebrate Zoology at Berkeley, California, sent four field parties into the Sierra del Nido between 1957 and 1961. On the basis of tracks, other sign, and conversation with the local ranchers, a population of about thirty grizzlies was estimated for the Sierra del Nido complex (Leopold 1967). That small, vulnerable group was the only remaining population of the Southwest's greatest carnivore, and some sound and well-reasoned pleas were presented for their preservation (Leopold 1958, 1959, 1967).

Although the grizzly was technically placed on the list of protected species in Mexico in 1959, some hunting continued. A huge female was killed by a Mexican (Koford 1969), and in July, 1960, a more formal proclamation of protection was issued by the president of Mexico. No one had reported any livestock losses, and it was generally thought that the bears stayed in the mountains most of the time, descending to the lower slopes in the fall to feed on acorns (Leopold 1967). In the same year, in what was said to be unusual behavior, a grizzly began killing cattle in the central portions of the Sierra del Nido (Koford 1969). Invited to take a stock killer, Curtis Prock guided an Arizona hunter, John F. Nutt, to a magnificent male grizzly (fig. 36). Customs agents allowed the animal's carcass to enter the United States, but when it was delivered to a Phoenix taxidermist, a controversy developed concerning the bear's origin and legality. In the ensuing imbroglio the hide and head were sequestered, but fortunately reason prevailed, and the admirably prepared hide has been saved and properly cared for.

The remnant grizzlies may have faced an even greater threat than that from hunters. In 1950, and again in 1955, the U.S. Fish and Wildlife Service, in conjunction with the Pan-American Livestock Sanitary Board, conducted demonstrations of a potent new predacide, Compound 1080, for Mexican ranchers in Chihuahua and made it available to them (Laney 1958, in Brown 1983). At least in part because of the stock-killing bear, poison stations were put out in the Sierra del Nido during the winters of 1961–62 and 1963–64, using 1080-treated baits (Leopold 1967). The effect of the poison on the grizzlies was never documented, but several have thought that it may have played a role in their rapid extinction thereafter (see, e.g., Koford 1969).

There have since been several investigations into the status of the grizzly in the Sierra del Nido and elsewhere in Mexico (e.g., see Jonkel 1980). Rumors persist, and there are unverified reports that grizzlies are still present. Field investigations by competent biologists have been inconclusive, and most, but not all, reports are pessimistic (José Treviño, personal communication, 1983). I found no evidence of grizzlies there in October, 1982, and the foreman at Rancho El Nido told me that no grizzlies had been killed or known there for twenty years. Despite some hope, the chances of a remaining population of grizzlies there, or anywhere else in Mexico, appears increasingly remote. A national park farther south, Parque Nacional, the "Cumbres de Majalca" established by presidential decree in 1939, contains no grizzlies, though one reason for the park's creation was to preserve the area's wildlife (José Treviño, personal communication, 1983).

Throughout the 1960s rumor persisted of a grizzly or two in Colorado's San Juan Mountains. In response to some evidence and public interest, the Colorado Division of Wildlife created a grizzly-management area, and in 1969 an attempt was made to determine whether any grizzlies were indeed present. Several bait stations were established and monitored for grizzly sign; at least one was equipped with a time-lapse camera to record any bears coming to the carcasses. These studies were inconclusive, and the large number of black bears that came to the baits confounded any determination. Although grizzlies were considered a possibility, their special-management status was abandoned. The grizzly was a hope, not a viable management consideration (Tulley 1970).

Then, almost ten years later, an incredible event took place.

THE WISEMAN GRIZZLY

On the evening of September 23, 1979, Ed Wiseman, of Crestone, Colorado, was attacked and seriously mauled by a bear near the head of the Navajo River just northwest of Blue Lake, in the San Juan National Forest in Conejos County, Colorado. The particulars are described by Bissell (1980). Wiseman, an outfitter, was guiding Mike Niederee, of Great

FIG. 36. *John Nutt and Curtis Prock with their male grizzly in the Sierra del Nido in 1960. This was the last grizzly reported taken in Chihuahua. Photograph courtesy of Bob Housholder.*

Bend, Kansas, on an archery elk hunt when the incident occurred. According to testimony, Niederee saw the bear, apparently asleep, about ten to twenty yards away. When the bear detected him, it ran straight into Wiseman, who was several hundred yards away on a trail. The bear knocked down the yelling and waving Wiseman and began biting him on the right shoulder and legs. The man lay still, hoping the bear would go away, but the bear kept mauling him. Wiseman then saw one of his hunting arrows lying within reach. He grasped it and began stabbing the beast in the throat and neck, getting in two good jabs. The bear, apparently weakened, released his victim, went off a short distance, and died.

Wiseman's client, Niederee, did not see the attack but

investigated Wiseman's shouts and came upon him collapsed on the ground. Seeing that Wiseman was badly injured, Niederee, the son of a surgeon, immediately applied first aid. Then he went to get their horses, which had been tethered one and a half miles back, and the men headed for their base camp. Wiseman was unable to complete the trip, so Niederee made camp and left Wiseman there, continuing on.

Arriving at the camp, Niederee told the hunting party about the incident and Wiseman's condition. The camp cook rode out to the trail head; the rest of the party, including Niederee's father, returned to Wiseman, reaching him at about 4:00 A.M. Later in the morning a helicopter took Wiseman to the Alamosa County Hospital. His body temperature had dropped to 94.8°F, he had been bitten many times, and his right leg was broken. Several weeks were spent recuperating in the hospital and at home.

Dick Weldon, district wildlife manager of the Colorado Division of Wildlife, was notified of the attack on the evening of the rescue. On the next day, September 25, he, Bob Rouse, and one of Wiseman's employees traveled to the scene in a Colorado Department of Wildlife helicopter. The helicopter was damaged on landing, and Weldon and the pilot had to walk out, while Rouse and the guide went to skin the bear.

What they found was a full-grown female grizzly. The next day a leased helicopter took out the skull and hide, but the carcass and the all-important reproductive organs were left behind. Had those been saved, it could have been determined whether the bear had bred and if other grizzlies were likely to be present.

On September 29, days after the attack, another helicopter was sent to retrieve the carcass and repair the damaged helicopter. After securing the bear to the sling, the helicopter pilot took off, but his craft crashed on leaving Plataro en route for Alamosa. No one was hurt, and the carcass was placed in the freezer at the La Jara Fish Hatchery. The first Colorado grizzly in almost twenty-five years had been retrieved.

A necropsy showed that the bear probably died from internal hemorrhaging caused by a wound inflicted between the second and third ribs that severed the aortic arch. In short, she had bled to death. That the fatal wound was not described in the testimony and would have been difficult to administer with a hand-held arrow made for some controversy about what had actually occurred (Reed 1980).

The annual rings in a sectioned tooth showed the bear to be more than sixteen years old. Her weight was estimated at between 350 and 400 pounds, and she was considered to have been in "remarkably good condition." Her reproductive history remains unknown; the uterus had spoiled and could not be examined for placental scars. The hide, the skull, and part of the skeleton were placed in the Denver Museum of Natural History (Bissell 1980).

Was this the last Southwest grizzly at long last? Probably so, although no one can say for certain. Grizzlies have been known to live for more than thirty years, and chances are the Wiseman grizzly was the last survivor of the small breeding population still extant in Southwest Colorado in the mid-1950s. Even if other individuals show up, the possibility that there is a small, relict breeding population is exceedingly slim. Until evidence of more grizzlies is forthcoming, it must be assumed that this bizarre incident is the last chapter in the Southwest grizzly's passage into history. But then the grizzly was always a grandstand performer, from his discovery through his decline. There was no reason to expect him to exit without a flourish.

PART FOUR

Lore, Legends, and Adventures

MARILYN HOFF STEWART

CHAPTER 12

On the Ferocity of the Grizzly

I was very proud over my first bear; but Merrifield's chief feeling seemed to be disappointment that the animal had not had time to show fight. He was rather a reckless fellow, and very confident in his own skill with the rifle; and he really did not seem to have any more fear of the grizzlies than if they had been so many jack-rabbits. I did not at all share his feelings, having a hearty respect for my foe's prowness [*sic*], and in following and attacking them always took all possible care to get the chances on my side. Merrifield was sincerely sorry that we never had to stand a regular charge; while on this trip we killed five grizzlies with seven bullets, and except in the case of the she and cub, spoken of furthur [*sic*] on, each was shot about as quickly as it got sight of us.—Theodore Roosevelt, 1885

Although the grizzly was associated with danger and adventure, many were disappointed by their game's behavior. Even at an early date, before grizzlies had become wary of the deadly Anglos, some hunters were so taken aback by the "ungrizzlylike" behavior of the species that they doubted that their animals were indeed grizzlies (Baird 1859). Consider Charles Sheldon's statements concerning the aggressiveness of grizzlies in the Sierra Madre:

They were extremely timid, quickly fleeing if they suspected human presence. In fact, although I have shot, (killing directly or wounding) many of these bears at or approaching their food, and on other occasions, not once have I ever seen one display any trait except extreme fright. On receiving a wound that did not disable them, they always attempted to run away. Twice I have approached badly wounded mature male bears, but in each case they only tried to crawl away. In Mexico, as in every other region, most natives dread an encounter with

171

a grizzly, and one may hear the usual reports of its aggressiveness and ferocity. My efforts were unceasing to find an authenticated case of an attack of any kind of a grizzly, but I never succeeded in doing so. [Sheldon 1925:161–62]

Others reported the grizzly to be as dangerous as advertised. No less a grizzly hunter than Ben V. Lilly had this to say about the subject:

I find a wounded grizzly of mature age more than willing to keep up his or her end of the mix-up. They are not cowards when it comes to defending themselves. They fight fast and have nothing but fighting in view. Man is their choice opponent. They make for his skull. Grizzlies under two years old fight only for liberty. Up to six years old, they fight to protect their young. When they get older, they fight to destroy an enemy. I mean when they are wounded or harried. [Dobie 1981:131]

There are also many verified accounts of bear fights that leave no doubt that the grizzly could be a mean adversary. In what is probably as objective an account as any, Montague Stevens (1943:246) presented his view:

The grizzly, to give him his due, is not often the aggressor, and he will seldom attack a man unless the latter first molests him. As a matter of fact, he would rather run away than fight. On the other hand, if he is wounded, even if he doesn't see you, he is likely to hunt you up to attack you.

There can be no doubt that the grizzly was a potentially dangerous animal. How, then, does one explain the variations in grizzly behavior when met by his opponents? The answer, I believe, lies not in the views but in the character of the beholders.

Most of the Southwest's frontier explorers, hunters, ranchers, and cowboys were southerners, with east Texas heavily represented. Theirs was a culture of single-mindedness and audacity. They had no fear of animals of any kind and were excellent horsemen and cowboys (see, e.g., Roosevelt 1888). Such men were almost fanatical in their mission to rid the southwestern rangeland of wolves, bears, and other varmints. Their response to seeing even the sign of bear was to mount an attack at once. No matter what the circumstance, these men were invariably armed (even if ineffectually), and a bear encounter quickly becomes a scrap. There was no choice for Bruin; when he was caught up with, he was forced to fight for his life. If not wounded in the initial onslaught, the bear was persistently pursued until he was destroyed.

Mexicans and Yankee sportsmen, if no less courageous, were more circumspect. Bears were viewed as occasional adversaries or sport, not as natural enemies. Unlike the Texas-style ranchmen, they were content to wait for fortuitous circumstances before taking on a bear and to shoot him when it was their purpose and the bear was at their advantage.

Given the minimum distance within which a sudden intrusion by man may elicit a threatened reaction or an attack from grizzlies (Herrero 1970), the reasons for the different responses become clear. According to Herrero (1970, 1976) and Mundy and Flook (1973), surprise is an important factor in most man-grizzly confrontations. A surprise intrusion into the bear's individual "space" results in an almost reflexive charge by females with young or by an animal defending a kill or carrion. Even then, the charge might be a bluff. But the object of bear hunters was to kill the bear, not to escape. The wonder is that there were not more people mauled by wounded grizzlies.

DEATHS FROM GRIZZLIES

Except for the probably exaggerated accounts of the beaver trappers, reports of human beings actually killed by southwestern grizzlies are rare. Almost all those accounts are of incidents before 1850 and tell of unarmed or poorly armed people without firearms (see, e.g., Pfefferkorn 1949, Pattie 1833). Pike (1808), writing about his travels south through New Mexico, told of three New Mexicans who attacked two grizzlies. When the fight was over, one bear was dead, two men were dead, and one man was wounded.

Later accounts are more difficult to find. F. M. Young (1980) relates how George Naegle's brother Hyrum was killed by a grizzly near Colonia Pacheco, Chihuahua, about 1885. The Naegle brothers were pursuing a grizzly that they had wounded earlier. They had been briefly separated while George repaired a malfunctioning rifle. Then George heard a shot and went to investigate. He found Hyrum under the bear's forefeet, the animal "tearing at his head." On seeing George, the bear released his victim, only to be felled by George's repaired rifle. With great difficulty George lashed the wounded man to his saddle, and after an interminable trip managed to get his brother home alive. Hyrum lived two days before dying of his terrible wounds and shock. This incident is almost certainly the same one related by E. W. Nelson to Sheldon (1925): a "reliable report of one of them [a grizzly] having killed a Mormon, who had wounded the bear and followed it in thick brush, almost stepping on it, when the bear knocked him down and bit him, driving its teeth through his skull."

A. E. Thompson (1968) relates another encounter in 1885 in which a man was killed by a grizzly. This incident, involving a hunter named Richard Wilson, occurred near Indian Gardens, on a tributary of Oak Creek Canyon above Sedona, Arizona. Wilson wounded a grizzly with a light rifle and trailed it into a thicket of Arizona cypress. There the bear attacked him, and Wilson tried to escape by climbing a small tree. The tree was inadequate, however, and the bear pulled the man down and mauled him severely about the face and head. His body was later found face down in a pool of water, and his friends buried him at the site, in what became known as Wilson Canyon. About fifteen years later the skeleton of a bear was found two miles from the site of the battle, and a large grizzly skull was retrieved from "Wilson Mountain."

M. B. Parker (1979) told about a full-grown grizzly that killed a Mexican deer hunter near Cuchillo, near Ocampo,

Chihuahua. Although the victim was unarmed, his two part-ners had a .44-caliber Winchester and killed the bear after it was "riddled with half a dozen or more bullet holes." Apparently the man had stumbled onto the grizzly and was "torn to shreds" before the brute was dispatched by his partners.

The only other report of a grizzly killing a man in the Southwest was one from eastern Arizona. Fred Fritz, the victim, survived the attack for five years. The interesting details of this encounter are presented in Haynes and Haynes (1966). Again the pattern was the same: a lone man suddenly encountered a grizzly and took it on armed with an inade-quate weapon.

CHAPTER 13

The Bear Hunters

There can be no question that a few specialized bear hunters contributed disproportionately to the demise of southwestern grizzlies. Several of these men devoted a large part of their lives to the removal of what they perceived to be an obstacle to settlement and civilization. Some were fanatics, but most saw themselves as patriots in the mold of Daniel Boone and Davy Crockett and became what could be described as obsessed with their self-appointed mission to "civilize the country."

That such men possessed great hunting ability is undeniable. Most of them had been reared in the South, many in hill country, where they had been imbued with woodcraft from early childhood. Hunting skills were cultural attributes; dogs and the raising and handling of them were a part of life.

The typical bear hunter had at one time or another tried his hand at ranching, farming, or some other occupation. More often than not these attempts at a livelihood failed, and he returned to the way of life he knew best. In the wilderness, beyond frontier society, his superior knowledge of woodcraft and his pack of hounds enabled him to provide a service that was appreciated by rancher and homesteader alike. He thus attained a unique social status while remaining outside society's boundaries.

Some of these men were almost recluses; nearly all of them could be described as nonsociable. All of them were highly individualistic and admirably equipped for their self-proclaimed and single-minded assignment. Possessed of great endurance and undeniable courage, many of the bear hunters were truly remarkable. Self-sufficient and able to spend

176

weeks on a trail, they were able to take after a bear at any notice. They were also expert and fearless horsemen and would not give up until the bear was "brought to justice."

They were also without a conservation ethic and appear to have been uninterested in trying to preserve the frontier way of life at which they were so adept. By their own actions they destroyed the essence of their life-style. By taming a wilderness, they created a home only for others and disinherited themselves. For them, like their grizzly foes, there would be no future. Unlike the grizzly, they sensed their doom, but would do nothing to avert it.

PORTRAIT OF A BEAR HUNTER

Although no one could accuse Ben Lilly of being typical of anything, in many ways he was the archetype of the southwestern grizzly hunter. There was apparently something about "Mr. Lilly," as he was most often called, that made for a legendary quality. He made a memorable impression on all who met him as a mountain man from out of the past. Even during the nineteenth century, his habit of sleeping outdoors, regardless of weather and available accommodations, separated him from other outdoorsmen.

Like his earlier California counterpart, Grizzly Adams, Ben Lilly has had his share of admiring biographers. Some accounts, like Hibben's (1948), are partly fanciful, while those by Winn (1923), Musgrave (1938), Burridge (1954, 1956), and Pickens (1981) are more truthful, though still of a popular nature. Yet, just as Theodore H. Hittell (1860) gave Grizzly Adams to posterity, so did J. Frank Dobie, the famous chronicler of Texas and the Southwest, become Ben Lilly's ultimate biographer. Dobie (1950, 1981) made good use of the many journals, diaries, and manuscripts of Lilly and his contemporaries and did not gloss over "Mr. Lilly's" rough edges. Moreover, Dobie's biography got high marks from those who knew Ben; Norm Woolsey and J. E. Hawley, for example, termed Dobie's account "pretty close to the facts." I have therefore relied heavily on Dobie in the following abbreviated sketch to illustrate those characteristics that made Mr. Lilly a bear and lion hunter extraordinaire.

Benjamin Vernon Lilly was born on December 31, 1856, in Wilcox County, Alabama. Shortly afterward his family moved to Mississippi, where Ben was eventually the oldest of seven children. At age twelve he ran off to join an uncle in Louisiana, but was sent back to receive a rudimentary schooling. Even this was odious to him, and he soon returned to his uncle's farm on the Boeuf River.

There he grew to maturity, learning about woodcraft, wildlife, and hunting. The farm had been carved out of a trackless wilderness of bottomland swamps and hardwood forests in which bears and "panthers" (the southern name for cougars) abounded. Ben grew up with the lore and customs of the region and came to regard panthers as symbols of evil. Like many others he came to regard his own desires as the destiny imposed from on high. And hunting was his life.

Both his father and his grandfather were blacksmiths by trade and worked with steel. Ben too made knives at the crude blacksmith shop on the farm as his forefathers had made blades and swords. Farming was a chore to be done as quickly and as seldom as possible. Mostly he just hunted.

In 1880, at age twenty-four, Ben Lilly married a woman whom he was warned was "teched"—but then his grandfather had been a little queer too. Whether this made his marriage less attractive is not known, but he began to spend even more time hunting, ranging deep into Louisiana. Although all species fell before his gun, he concentrated on panthers and bears and had as many as twenty-five dogs at a time. He was hunting bears for the market in Mississippi's Sunflower Swamp when his frail son took sick and died. This precipitated a final break with his wife, who went insane.

Ben, now in the prime of his young adulthood, was described as being only about five feet nine inches tall but about 180 pounds of muscle and sinew. He had blue eyes, a beard, and a reputation for endurance that was already legendary. Ben was well known for his speed, long-distance running, and energy. He was also a great jumper and even in his later years could jump flat-footed out of a cracker barrel. His only illness was a single bout with malaria, his only infirmity was deafness in one ear, perhaps from always sleeping on the ground. He could not swim.

In 1890 he married again and eventually fathered a son and two daughters. Finding farming too restricting, he took up cattle trading and hunted alligators and other marketable animals. For a while he tried his hand at logging hardwoods, but surprisingly, he was not a good judge of wood. He developed several peculiarities, such as signing his name with a picture of a honeybee and a water lily. He never worked on Sunday, even when it meant hardship for the stock or himself. The same was true when he was hunting. The chase would cease on Saturday night and would not resume until Monday, no matter how close the quarry or how inconvenient the delay.

Several other characteristics were to ensure him a reputation that succeeded him. He was scrupulously honest and always insisted on paying his way, even to reimbursing landowners for forage consumed by his stock. Wine, women, and song held no interest for him. He never drank liquor or even coffee. He never cursed and was always well-spoken and talked softly. His word was his bond.

On the other hand, he took poor care of his animals and lost stock through pique or carelessness. He had no conservation ethic and shot deer and any other creatures that caught his eye for target practice. He was wasteful of the wildlife he bagged, and the game he shipped to market might be spoiled. He never had a favorite horse and shot at least two that gave him trouble. He played practical jokes that were crude, childish, and often dangerous. But mostly he hunted.

In 1901, Ben abandoned his wife and family and left for the wilds of northeastern Louisiana. There he hunted wild honey and waterfowl for the market and continued his vendetta against panthers and bears. In 1904 he met Ned Hollister, of the U.S. Biological Survey. Ned taught him to put up skins and persuaded him to collect some animals for science. In the U.S. National Museum are specimens of the ivory-billed woodpecker, the passenger pigeon, the wolf, and the bear from Louisiana all collected by Ben—and now all extinct or extirpated from that state.

In 1906, when he was almost fifty, Ben entered the Big Thicket, in Texas (fig. 37). In December of that year he took a bear for the U.S. Biological Survey—his 180th. His reputation was such that when President Theodore Roosevelt came to the Big Thicket to hunt bear in 1907, Ben was employed as hunt master. Roosevelt's entourage was large, and such hunts were not Ben's way of hunting. Ben proved a poor guide, being unable to hunt for others, only for himself. Roosevelt described him as a religious fanatic. Dobie considered this unfair and thought of him rather as a hunting fanatic. They were probably both right.

When Ben left the Big Thicket on Christmas, 1906, he estimated that there were only fifteen bears left in the region, and no more than forty in all Louisiana and Mississippi. Since bears were extirpated from all three states not long after, he was probably about right. Ben had never learned how to study wildlife without killing it. It was time to move on.

After spending more than a year hunting in the wilds of the Texas Gulf Coast between the Brazos and Colorado rivers, Lilly again moved west. In July, 1908, now age fifty-two, he entered Mexico at Eagle Pass. He settled for a while on a ranch in the Sierra Santa Rosa, where he supplied the town of Múzquiz with venison jerky and the U.S. National Museum with skins and skulls. Later he hunted and trapped in the Serranías del Burro (Burro Hills) and Sierra del Carmen, where he kept the Fronteriza Mine supplied with venison.

After a year in Coahuila, Lilly moved west into Chihuahua. From there he sent the hide and skull of his first grizzly to the U.S. National Museum. The museum records show only that it was shipped from Gallego, the railroad station closest to the Sierra del Nido.

FIG. 37. *Ben Lilly as he appeared in 1905, when he left Texas's Big Thicket and headed west to South Texas, Coahuila, Chihuahua, New Mexico, and Arizona. Photograph courtesy of* Arizona Highways *and the Arizona Historical Foundation.*

There is no record of Lilly's time in the Sierra Madre, but it is known that he worked westward toward Sonora and reentered the United States by way of the New Mexico panhandle in 1911, a year after the beginning of the Madero revolution in Mexico. It was there that he reported one of his most notable feats.

On March 10, 1911, while searching for a lioness and her half-grown cub, he and his Airedale jumped a full-grown grizzly just out of hibernation. He trailed the animal, which was missing two toes, for three days to the San Luis Mountains, in Chihuahua. Lilly returned to the States, obtained traps and supplies, and about two weeks later went back to the mountains to pick up the trail. Once there he killed a lion, and two black bears and "hung a trap" on the grizzly. Following the drag, Lilly trailed the big male into Sonora before it returned to the San Luis Mountains, where he killed it en route to the Animas Mountains. Lilly could thus claim that he tracked a bear through three states in two countries. The skin and skull reside in the U.S. National Museum.

Lilly went to work on the Diamond A Ranch, in the Animas Mountains, where he "found and killed 13 lions, some nice grizzlies, and 12 bear." After taking a few wolves for bounties, he headed north to Clifton and eventually went to work as a forest guard–trapper in the Apache National Forest. His pay for doing what he had always done for nothing—killing lions and bears—was seventy-five dollars a month. Ben Lilly had found a home.

Ben was fifty-five years old when he entered the country that was to be his final and favorite hunting ground. The great wilderness of the Gila headwaters in New Mexico and the adjacent Blue, Escudilla, and White mountains in Arizona had bear and lions aplenty and was almost big enough for him.

For the next several years Ben hunted the Apache and Gila national forests, collecting up to fifty bears and lions a year and collecting bounties from state, county, and private organizations. He became a man of means and acquired a reputation.

In addition to using a .33 Winchester, Ben reportedly killed a number of bears with a knife to protect his dogs when he could not get a clear shot at the harried animal. Such stories are questionable, but he did make knives, a skill developed in his steelsmithing years. Most were curved, had buckhorn handles, and were tempered in "panther oil" (urine) to a "drake-neck color" before being reheated. Each knife was specially made with its own scabbard. He rarely used a shotgun, and is known to have fired a pistol only once. Although he trapped, he does not appear to have been especially good at it. His preferred method of hunting was to travel alone with three to six hounds, keeping an occasional helper to maintain camp and skin any animals that he bagged.

All who knew him agreed that Ben was eccentric. He believed that one should eat only one dish at a time, and that it was unhealthy to mix foods in the stomach. He bathed once a week but rarely changed clothes; he just put more on or took some off, depending on the vagaries of the weather.

His camp gear was a tin cup, a tin can, and a frying pan. He was known to eat prodigious amounts of food at one time and then go for several days without eating. In the field he ate green corn in season and parched corn the rest of the year. He also reportedly ate mountain-lion meat when he was in the field. When he was hunting, he carried only his gun, an ax, light dog chains, one of his hunting knives, a smaller skinning knife, matches in a waterproof tin, extra cartridges in a tobacco sack, and a little sugar and a sack of cornmeal.

He preferred to camp out winter or summer, and he was well known for his indifference to fatigue and hardship. Unlike most other bear hunters, he disdained the use of horses, preferring to follow his dogs on foot—an impossible feat for the ordinary man, but one that allowed him to trail and read sign as he went along. His trailing ability was truly remarkable. According to J. E. Hawley, one evening a forest ranger returned to camp and discovered that he had lost his watch sometime during the day. Lilly volunteered to find it the next day, seemingly an almost impossible task, for the men had been riding horseback through heavy brush and timber all day. Nonetheless, Lilly took up the trail of the ranger's horse and retraced the tracks until he found the watch. This and other extraordinary trailing feats are also related by Dobie, and Lilly's ability in this regard is beyond question.

There was something about Ben that caused people, wherever he went, to take to him. They automatically called him Mr. Lilly. He was a natural publicity agent for himself. He was soft-spoken and presented a gentle appearance. Yet he was not a kind man: if a dog did not live up to his expectations, he killed it. He was known to beat dogs to death, and he castrated or spayed every dog that he sold.

In 1916, at age sixty, Ben began a sporadic career with the newly organized Predator and Rodent Control branch of the U.S. Biological Survey, under J. Stokely Ligon. As in his former days with the U.S. Forest Service, he worked for a salary, but only for as long as he thought he could not make more in bounties. His years in government service were not always amiable ones. Ben Lilly was not in agreement with the early game laws. To him all bears were stock killers sooner or later, and deer were for the taking. Such an attitude was not in compliance with PARC policy; civilization was coming to the Gila and closing in on Ben Lilly.

Ben killed several grizzlies in Arizona and New Mexico while he was employed by the PARC (fig. 38). How many grizzlies he killed is not known, for like many other hunters of the day he did not always differentiate between grizzly and black bear. What the record shows is that later tales of his kills were exaggerated. His own diaries and the PARC reports show him going weeks without even cutting sign. In twenty-six and a half months with the PARC between 1916 and 1920 he took fifty-five lions and twelve bears. In 1920 his services with the PARC were terminated: hired to hunt lions, he spent too much time killing too many bears.

From 1920 until he ceased to hunt, he headquartered out of the GOS Ranch, where the Gila National Forest was his primary hunting ground. It was reputed that during the

Fig. 38. *Ben Lilly with a grizzly taken in his days with the PARC. Note the dense chaparral and the Winchester .33. Photograph courtesy of Bob Housholder.*

1920s the GOS was cleared of bears and lions, and it was during this period that Ben attained the height of his fame. Again he was appointed hunt master for a grand hunt. In 1921, W. H. McFadden, a multimillionaire railroad magnate, and his party planned to hunt the Rocky Mountain cordillera from the Mexican border to the Canadian Rockies. Again, Mr. Lilly's singular energy and lone-wolf ways made him a poor man for the job. Although McFadden's primary goal was to bag a grizzly, neither he nor any member of his party killed one. The only grizzly they found was one shadowed by Lilly from above Taos, New Mexico, into Colorado while McFadden and the other hunters were elsewhere. But then, grizzlies were getting scarce.

In 1928, Ben Lilly was being paid one hundred dollars for each grown lion or bear that he took on the GOS Ranch and was working with the PARC on an interim basis. Now seventy-one, he was showing his age, and by 1931 he was definitely slowing down (fig. 39). His friends and GOS bene-

Fig. 39. *Ben Lilly, his gun, and his dogs on the GOS Ranch in 1933, when he we*
over seventy. Photograph courtesy of Norman G. Woolsey.

FIG. 40. *Monument to Ben Lilly. The inscription reads: "Ben V. Lilly, 1856–1936. Born in Alabama and reared in Mississippi, Ben V. Lilly in early life was a farmer and trader in Louisiana, but turned to hunting of panthers and bears with a passion that led him out of swamps and canebrakes, across Texas, to tramp the wildest mountains of Mexico, and finally become a legendary figure and dean of wilderness hunters in the Southwest. He was a philosopher, keen observer, naturalist, a cherisher of good hounds, a relier on his rifle, and a handicraftsman in horn and steel. He loved little children and vast solitudes. He was a pious man of singular honesty and fidelity and a strict observer of the Sabbath. New Mexico mountains were his final hunting range and the charms of the Gila Wilderness held him to the end. Erected 1947 by friends."*

factors finally talked him into retiring to the Grant County Farm. There, childlike, without a dog or a gun, he died on December 17, 1936, just before his eightieth birthday.

Dobie's statement that Mr. Lilly "was keen in observing but weak deducing" is most apt. Ben was quoted as saying, "I cannot be happy trying to grasp the future." This lack of vision appears to have been a malady characteristic of his breed. The bear hunters dedicated themselves to a mission that made their life-style ultimately purposeless: the extermination of their quarry. Perhaps Ligon sensed that he too shared this fate when he and his friends erected a bronze plaque to Ben's memory at a turnoff between Silver City and the GOS, overlooking the great Gila watersheds (fig. 40).

BEAR HOWARD

Another prominent bear killer, but one of more local fame, was Bear Howard. Howard was a huge man, 6 feet 8 inches, and possessed of great strength (fig. 41). These attributes alone made him well known in the pioneer days of Oak Creek Canyon and early Flagstaff, Arizona, but it was for his vendetta against bears that he achieved his name and reputation. The following sketch of his life is based on information provided by Joe Meehan, curator at the Northern Arizona Pioneer Historical Society and an unpublished manuscript in their files by John Calhoun Cormium. Howard's storage box, made of a pine log, one of his bear traps, and other memorabilia now reside in the society's museum, just outside Flagstaff.

Not much is known about Bear's life before his arrival in Arizona. He supposedly fought in the Mexican War and received a bullet, which he carried with him to California in 1849. After some successes and misfortunes in the goldfields, he took up a homestead and began farming. He got in trouble with the law after a fracas with sheepherders during which a number of herders and sheep were killed. Like a lot of other men who were hiding out in the post-Civil War period, Howard made his way to Arizona.

FIG. 41. *Bear Howard* (center) *hounds, and two black bears, with a group of Flagstaff citizens about 1889. Photograph courtesy of Northern Arizona Pioneers Historical Society collection, Special Collections Library, Northern Arizona University.*

He and his partner, Richard Wilson (see Chapter 12), built a cabin in Oak Creek Canyon. Together they hunted, grew tobacco, and raised wheat that they milled into flour. For ready cash they ran a pack of broodmares and raised saddle horses and mules for sale and trade.

When Wilson was killed by a grizzly, it was Howard who found his mangled body three days after he was pulled from the tree by the bear. Wilson's black hound was subsisting on his late master's remains. Something inside snapped, and Howard became "Bear" Howard. For the next ten years he relentlessly hunted down bear after bear, killing them for the market and selling the galls to the Chinese apothecary shops, in response to depredation complaints and just for revenge. His size and strength made him an awesome adversary, and he became something of a recluse, visiting Flagstaff only infrequently. Unlike Ben Lilly, however, when he did come to town, he used the money from his bounties and sales of meat and bear galls for whiskey. On these occasions, he, like Mr. Lilly, became "Mr. Howard"—not so much out of respect as out of fear of his wrath. This was a man in his seventies.

When he was in his eighties, Howard killed a large female bear that cooled his drive for revenge. It was also about this time that his old wound began bothering him, and he had the bullet removed. Bear never fully recovered from the operation, and his health declined. Ironically, Howard spent his last months raising an orphaned bear cub. The cub had the run of his cabin, and Howard even bought a nanny goat so that it could have fresh milk. One day in 1899, Bear Howard passed quietly away, his pet bear nestled at his feet. He was ninety-four years old.

BEAR MOORE

What must certainly be one of the most grisly grizzly stories was told by J. E. Hawley, a former employee of PARC. Sometime in the early 1920s he and Albert Pickens were trapping in the vicinity of the Black Range, in west-central New Mexico, when they heard the unmistakable bawl of a bear in pain. As the anguished cries continued, they cautiously approached the source. Peering through the trees, they spied a cabin trap holding a bear that was being tortured by Bear Moore. Moore was heating iron rods at a campfire built for the purpose and driving them through the gunports and into the body of the hapless animal. Knowing Moore and his ways, the men slipped away.

Bear Moore, whose real name was James A. Moore, was a professional hunter and something of a latter-day mountain man. According to Pickens (1980), in 1883, Moore and a partner were camped at the headwaters of the Gila, where they were hunting deer to supply venison for Fort Bayard.

FIG. 42. *Colonel Jesse W. Ellison in one of the few photographs of Arizona grizzlies alive or dead. Shown are a female and two cubs taken on Cherry Creek near Pleasant Valley in the autumn of 1907. Colonel Ellison, owner of the Q Ranch and a famous bear and mountain-lion hunter, is in the center. The man on the left is Bob Devore; Jesse Ellison, Jr., is on the right. Photograph from the Roscoe Willson Collection; courtesy of the Arizona Historical Foundation.*

One morning, hunting alone, Moore spotted a large grizzly behind a fallen tree. Moore shot the animal in the back, and when the bear dropped, Moore thought that he had broken its spine. When Moore went around the base of the log to check his kill, the grizzly was waiting for him.

Moore's partner found him that night. The skin had been ripped away from over half his face, and his jaw had been torn loose. His neck and chest had been raked with claws, exposing his heart. The grizzly lay dead, its intestines draped over the field of battle. Moore's knife was on the ground.

Taken to the hospital at Hermosa and later to Saint Louis,

Missouri, Moore survived. He was horribly disfigured, however, and became a recluse, avoiding settlements and having acquaintances obtain his supplies when they went to town. He was somewhat demented and supported himself by hunting and panning for gold. Like Bear Howard, he devoted his time to taking revenge on the brethren of his attacker. Torturing bears was his standard practice, and he systematically applied his heated rod treatment to any bear he caught.

Hawley and Pickens were also to record the way Bear Moore died. During the winter of 1924, Moore somehow fractured a leg while in a remote area. Unable to travel, he tried to stay alive by remaining next to a fallen pine tree that he kept burning for warmth. When he was found, his frozen body was still next to the tree. Marks showed where he had dragged himself alongside the trunk as the fire worked its way up from the base. The tree had finally burned itself out and finished the job the other fallen tree had initiated years earlier.

There were other bear hunters, less fanatical and thus less famous, who mixed ranching with bear hunting. Colonel Jesse Ellison (fig. 42), Toles ("Bear") Cosper, and Clay Hunter were some of the more illustrious hunters in Arizona, as were Montague Stevens and G. W. Evans in New Mexico. Undoubtedly, there were others in both states and in Chihuahua who left no records.

CHAPTER 14

Captive Grizzlies

Unlike California, where bull and bear fights, Grizzly Adams's circus of two hundred bears, and "Monarch" and other captive bears were major attractions, the Southwest appears to have had little interest in captive grizzlies. A few people tried keeping them as pets, and a few attempts were made to maintain live specimens in zoological parks. The first of these efforts occurred in 1808, when Zebulon M. Pike wrote President Jefferson about two cubs obtained for Peale's Museum in Philadelphia (later the Philadelphia Museum):

His Excellency, Thomas Jefferson
President of the United States

Washington, February 3, 1808.

Sir: I had the honor of receiving your note last evening, and in reply to the inquiries of Mr. Peale can only give the following notes: The bears were taken by an Indian in the mountains which divide the large western branch of the Rio del Norte and some small rivers which discharge their water into the east side of the Gulf of California, near the dividing line between the provinces of Biscay and Sonora. We . . . purchased them of the savages, and for three or four days I made my men carry them in their laps on horseback. As they would eat nothing but milk they were in danger of starving. I then had a cage prepared for both, which was carried on a mule, lashed between two packs, but always ordered them to be let out the moment we halted, and not shut up again before we were prepared to march. By this treatment, they became exceedingly docile, when at liberty following my men (whom they learned to distinguish from the Spanish dragoons by their always feeding them, and encamping with them) like dogs through our camps, the small villages, and forts where we halted. When well supplied with sustenance they would play like young puppies with each other and the soldiers, but the instant they were shut up and placed on the mule they became cross, as the jolting knocked them against each other and they were sometimes left exposed to the scorching heat of a vertical sun for days without food or a drop of water, in which case they would worry and tear each other, until nature was exhausted, and they could neither fight nor howl any longer. They will be one year old on the first of next month (March, 1808) and, as I am informed, they frequently arrive at the weight of eight hundred pounds. . . .

With sentiments of the highest respect and esteem,

Your obedient servant,

Z. M. Pike

W. H. Wright (1909) quoted the report by Godman in his *Natural History* on the problems of captive bear cubs at Peale's Museum:

When first received, they were quite small, but speedily gave indications of that ferocity for which this species is so remarkable. As they increased in size they became exceedingly dangerous, seizing and tearing to pieces every animal they could lay hold of, and expressing great eagerness to get at those accidentally brought within sight of their cage by grasping the iron bars with their paws and shaking them violently, to the great terror of spectators, who felt insecure while witnessing such displays of their strength. In one instance an unfortunate monkey was walking over the top of their cage, when the end of the chain which hung from his waist dropped through within reach of the bears; they immediately seized it, dragged the screaming animal through the narrow aperture, tore him limb from limb, and devoured his mangled carcass almost instantaneously.

Another attempt to raise a southwestern grizzly, this one to be presented to the Zoological Society of Philadelphia, was described by Cook (1923:248–54):

During the year 1882, while acting as manager of H. C. Wilson's cattle ranch in southwestern New Mexico, I was out on the range one day with some of my cowboys. While going through a little brushy canon we came across a grizzly bear cub about three months old. After some scrambling among the live-oak trees and shrubs we succeeded in getting the cub out into open ground, and lassoed him. He was a little fighter, but we soon had him hog-tied and muzzled. I had one of the men carry the little beast on his horse to the headquarters ranch, where he was soon chained to a post. The cub soon became a great pet; but as he grew older we found that he was not exactly a plaything. Ned, as we called him, was always creating a disturbance somewhere.

When Ned was about two years old, Professor Cope of Philadelphia was stopping with me while making a geological survey of that section of the country. One day he asked what I intended to do with the bear. I replied that I should probably continue to harbor him until he had killed somebody, and then I should have to shoot him. He asked if I would not like to present Ned to the Zoological Society of Philadelphia.

The handling of even a young, "tame" grizzly was no easy task, as indicated by Cook's description of the preparations for sending Ned to Philadelphia:

We then drove the dog out of the corral and started in to lasso the bear. We had to stand on top of the fence to throw our ropes. Several times they encircled his neck, but each time the infuriated bear grabbed at the rope with his claws and threw it off. At last, as he passed near me, I threw my rope over his head, letting him jump through it with his head and shoulders, but drawing the noose tight about his flanks. With the help of the other boys, Ned was pulled up into the air, the rope being thrown over the top rail of the fence, and trussed up until only his front feet rested on the ground.

I never saw Ned after he was put aboard the cars at Silver City; but I heard from Professor Cope that he was doing nicely and growing into an immense fellow. The Zoological people had him for many years as one of the chief attractions at Fairmount Park. [Cook 1923:219–20]

Cook (1923) has an illustration of Ned on the porch of the WS ranch house. This is one of the few photos of a live grizzly in the Southwest.

Ned's saga was also charmingly discussed by French (1965), who was a junior partner of the WS Ranch when Cook was manager. French was greatly captivated with Ned and made several attempts to keep grizzlies as pets. His first effort failed when the two cubs he tried to raise became ill and died:

When we first got them, after the death of the mother, they were no bigger than little puppies and were apparently only a few days old, for their eyes were still unopened. . . .

We christened them Bud and Sis. They appeared to be in good health until one day Bud refused to gambol with me and became decidedly sick. He displayed all the symptoms of acute pneumonia and we applied all the known remedies. He was brought into the house and kept by the fire, but he lost all interest in his food, and though we administered small doses of good brandy there was only a slight reaction, and after lingering for a few days he quietly expired. . . .

We hoped that Sis might grow to maturity, but she refused to be consoled for the loss of her brother and also refused to leave the house. She moped and lay all day by the fire in the office and at night followed me to my room and camped in the bed. This continued for over a week, when she began to lose interest in her food and displayed the same symptoms as her brother, and with the same result. [French 1965:230–33]

French did not give up easily, and when an opportunity to purchase a pair of grizzly cubs from an old prospector came along, he took it. The bears became great pets, but like many other wild babies raised in captivity, they changed as they matured and came to a bad end:

We kept those bears for more than two years and I have always regretted having to destroy them. They were a source of endless amusement and the greatest pets I ever had. For about a year after they got to know me, I used to turn them loose to play hide and seek with me. They understood the

Fig. 43. *McReed shortly after his capture in the Sangre de Cristo Mountains of New Mexico in 1918. Note the long claws and chain. Photograph courtesy of John Hibben and Bob Housholder.*

game perfectly. We'd hide behind trees and they'd peep out to try to find you. When they got a peep at you they'd come with a rush, pretend to grab hold of you and then scamper off. After which we'd seek new hiding places and begin over again. [French 1965:40]

V. Bailey (1931) tells about another effort to capture a southwestern grizzly for exhibition; this one took place in New Mexico more than one hundred years after Pike's effort (see fig. 43).

On July 22, 1918, T. J. McMullin caught an old grizzly and killed one of her two cubs, on the head of Rio Chiquito, Taos County. With the help of Bob Reed, a cowman from Taos, the other cub was roped from the top of a small spruce tree that it had climbed and was brought to camp alive. A few days later M. E. Musgrave came along and persuaded the men to send the cub to the National Zoological Park, to which they agreed on condition that he should be given the name of

"McReed." Musgrave packed him out 25 miles on his burro and shipped him to the Zoo, where he arrived in good health on August 10, 1918. [Bailey 1931:366]

Records of the U.S. National Museum show that a grizzly obtained from the National Zoological Park died on May 27, 1936, and that the animal had originally been obtained twenty-two miles southwest of Taos. McReed thus lived eighteen years. This is a relatively short life for a captive grizzly. Brown (1982) cites records of captive grizzlies living forty years and more. The life-span for wild grizzlies is approximately thirty years (Craighead et al. 1974, Pearson 1975).

Leopold (1959) tells of another captive grizzly raised from a cub in Ciudad Chihuahua, but it appears that most efforts to maintain southwestern grizzlies either as pets or for exhibition ended in failure. Now it is too late to seek to improve on previous efforts and maintain captives. Pike, French, and Musgrave were simply ahead of their time.

CHAPTER 15

Southwest Bear Stories

Grizzly stories and accounts of bear fights are as much a part of western Americana as cowboys and Indians. Almost everyone who met a grizzly having a distinctive mark or appearance was promptly given a name and made into a local legend. The only thing better than telling of the killing of a "famous grizzly" was writing about the adventures in the process. That the outcome of some of these confrontations was not always certain gave the tales all the elements of true drama. Nor were the dangers imaginary. There were some who truly had hair-raising tales to tell, and a few men sustained terrible wounds in their bouts with grizzlies.

The following stories describe adventures with bears in Arizona and Chihuahua. The first account is by an American and takes place during the 1880s, in the heyday of southwestern bear killing. The author, William Sparks, was a professional hunter, and although the story is exciting enough, his attitude toward the bear is analytical and somewhat dispassionate. The story of the Mexican's hunt, the success of which was based more on good fortune than on dedication, is a celebration of Bruin himself.

These two stories provide firsthand accounts of grizzly habitats and behavior under hunted conditions. The accounts are quite different, however. In both cases the writer was left with such indelible memories of his experience that he was inspired to pass them along. Perhaps we can learn something of value from these passages besides the greatness of our loss. I hope so, because the tradition of southwestern grizzly stories is about at an end.

"A FIGHT WITH A GRIZZLY BEAR"

William Sparks

1888

William Sparks, or as he was apparently better known, "Timberline Bill," must have been an interesting individual. Tom Rynning, a former captain of the Arizona Rangers, noted in a short biographical sketch of Sparks that he came to the Blue country of eastern Arizona during the winter of 1878–79 as a soldier with the U.S. Cavalry. He spent most of the next twenty years in what is now Greenlee County working as a prospector, miner, professional hunter, cowboy, and packer. It was in the last capacity that he served with revolutionaries in Cuba before the United States entered into their fight for independence. When the U.S. declared war on Spain, Sparks served as an officer with Teddy Roosevelt's First Volunteer Cavalry, the Rough Riders. On his return he served as a first sergeant with the Arizona Rangers and from his writings appears to have served in France during World War I.

Besides his true-adventure stories, Sparks wrote a number of sensitive and charming poems and stories which are presented along with a preface by Rynning, in his book *The Apache Kid, a Bear Fight, and Other True Stories of the Old West*, published in 1926. "A Fight with a Grizzly Bear" is a true story. Sparks's injuries were authenticated by Frank Ringgold, the timekeeper for the Inspiration Consolidated Copper Company, his doctor, and his dentist. No other bear story is as well documented.

In the spring of 1888 my partner, a man named Al Robertson, and I, were camped at the forks of Eagle Creek, near the foot of the Blue Range, and about fifteen miles above the Double Circle Ranch in Arizona.

"Al, if you'll wash the dishes, and bring in the horses, I'll go look at that trap we set down the creek," I said to my partner one morning, as he rose from the ground where we had been squatted beside the canvas manta, or pack cover, on which the tin dishes and plates that had contained our breakfast were spread.

"All right," said Al, "I'll have the horses here before you're back. What horse will I tie up for you? I want to start as soon as I can, for it will take me all day to ride to Slaughters and back, so I won't wait, for if there is anything in the trap it may take quite a while to trail it up and skin it."

After telling Al which horse I wanted tied up, I buckled on my cartridge belt, picked up my rifle and started down the creek toward the place where we had set a large bear trap the day before.

The camp was in a small open space on a point between the junction of two mountain streams, that tumbled noisily over their bed of boulders, between banks that were thickly wooded with black alder, ash, balsam, oak, cherry, walnut and pine trees, which in many places were festooned with wild grapes, Virginia creeper, and honey-suckle vines [fig. 44].

For several years there had been a considerable number of hunters in these mountains, who supplied the new mining camps of Coony, Carlisle, and Clifton, with fresh venison and turkey in winter; and winter or summer, hunted and killed the black-tailed and white-tailed deer, bucks and does alike, that abounded in the forests and hills north of the Gila River.

In summer they cut freshly killed venison into thin strips, which were salted and hung on a line until dry enough to be pulverized into powder when beaten with a hammer. When enough of this, "jerky" it was called, had been accumulated to load the pack horses, it was taken to one of the mining camps and sold to the Mexican workmen who, with their families, were very fond of it.

Bear of several varieties; cinnamon, black, brown and silver-tip, as well as mountain lions, were plentiful, and until the advent of the cattlemen, were only killed when the hunters were in need of bears' oil for cooking; or in the autumn, just before the hibernating animals holed up, when the fur and skins were at their best. . . .

When setting a trap for bear, it was the custom to cut a heavy green pole, and drive it through the ring attached to the trap until only about eighteen inches of the larger end remained on the side of the ring from which the pole had been inserted. Then, if a bear got in the trap, in dragging the pole through the trees and rocks he would leave a plain trail, and could be easily followed.

But if no pole, or clog, as the hunters and trappers called it was fixed to the trap, and it was left loose, a large bear might travel for many miles before lying up. And if the trap was made fast, when it snapped on a bear's leg it might break the bones, as sometimes happened, and in such a case it seemed to deaden the pain to such an extent that often a trapped bear would twist and gnaw off his leg above the trap and escape.

But this was in June; and the bear, as was their habit, had all gone to the higher mountains where there was food in plenty. Up in mountain meadows, surrounded by forests of spruce, and quaking aspen, were many delicacies that appealed to the nose and stomach of a hungry bear. Yellow jackets were storing honey that only had to be dug for to be obtained. In many places the ground was matted with wild strawberry vines that bore countless crimson points of wonderful flavor. Wild oats were in the milk; and there were numberless dead trees covered with rotten bark, that a bear had only to tear off, with his claws, to secure great fat grub worms, that were far more grateful to the taste of an almost satiated bear, than the most tender venison.

On my last trip to town, a townsman had requested me to bring in a lion's skin, which he offered to pay well for. Lion were hard to find without dogs, and the trap had been purchased to trap lion. At the time, the Territorial Legislature had made it mandatory on the supervisors of the different counties to pay a bounty on both bear and lion. But the counties of Arizona were very sparsely settled at that time, and were very poor; and the hunters brought in so many scalps of bear and lions that the different supervisors petitioned the next Legislature to repeal the bounty law, which was done.

As a lion caught in a trap would seldom travel farther than the first dense thicket, and the bear, as we supposed, were all higher in the mountains, we put no clog on the trap, but set it between two ash trees, and a few feet in front of another tree that was well covered with grape vines. A little basin, just large enough to secrete the trap in, was scraped away with a stick, and when the trap had been placed in it and covered with twigs and leaves, the bait, a deer's head and liver, were hung on the tree on which the grape vines grew, and the vines were drawn to and around each of the other trees, so that an animal

FIG. 44. *Riparian deciduous forest once inhabited by grizzlies, upper Eagle Creek, Apache National Forest, Greenlee County, Arizona. The trees are sycamore* (Platanus wrightii), *walnut* (Juglans major), *maple* (Acer grandidentatum), *ash* (Fraxinus velutina), *cottonwood* (Populus angustifolia), *and Arizona alder* (Alnus oblongifolia). *The vines are wild grape* (Vitus arizonica) *and Virginia creeper* (Parthenocissus inserta). *Note the dense screening cover.*

intent on investigating the bait would have to step in or over the trap to get to it. Soon after I left camp I came to a place where the creek ran against a bluff. Pulling off my moccasins, and rolling up my trousers, I waded through the swiftly flowing water, slipping on the round boulders at times, but managing to keep my rifle and clothing dry. At several more crossings I repeated this; but at last came to the mouth of a small creek where the trap had been set. Stealthily approaching the place, I saw that the vines were torn, and the bark on several small trees broken and bruised by the teeth of some enraged animal.

When I stood over the spot where the trap had been set, I found that the ground had been almost ploughed up in places by a bear, whose footprints proved him to be a silvertip of enormous size. Different bear, when wounded, or caught in a trap, have no hard and fast rules in regard to their actions. One bear, suddenly finding himself gripped in the torturing jaws of a clattering steel trap, may skulk noiselessly away, while another may frighten all the wood folk within hearing distance with his bawling.

But this bear had acted different from any that I had encountered before. The ground and trees showed plainly where he had swung and struck with the heavy trap, regardless of the pain he must have endured. In places the trap springs had dug holes in the soil that looked like a shovel had been thrust into it by some careless gardener, and saplings five or six inches in diameter were almost bare of bark in places, where he had snapped and torn with teeth and claws.

The "sign" or appearance of the torn vines and bark, and the tracks, proved that the bear had been caught not long before daylight, and as the sun was now not more than an hour high, I reasoned that the enraged animal would not travel after daylight, and might be in any brushy thicket, nursing his hurt, and the hatred that all bear must feel for a trap, and the men who set them.

So I slowly circled around among the trees until I found where the bear, evidently hopping along on three legs and holding the front paw on which the trap was fastened, above the ground, had left the narrow canyon valley, and started straight over a ridge that was covered only with scattered pine trees, and short grass, that made no covering in which a bear could hide.

Though there was no danger of coming suddenly upon the

bear here, I climbed the ridge slowly, halting at times to re-
cover my shortened breath. For a rifle is an arm of precision;
and the man who has swiftly climbed a steep hill, whose breast
is heaving, and nerves jumping from the exertion, cannot pull
the trigger with any certainty, as the sights align on a moving
or distant target.

And although the bear was encumbered with a heavy trap,
I knew that when I came face to face with his bruinship there
would be a reckoning on the part of the bear, if my bullets
were not sent to the only immediately vital spot in a bear's
anatomy—the brain.

The part of a bear's skull that contains the brain is long,
and almost round, like a curved cylinder in profile, with a thick
ridge of bone running from just in front of its junction with
the spinal column to below a line drawn between the eyes.
The frontal part is thickest beneath this ridge, and as the skull
rounds, or curves, away from the ridge, it becomes thinner, but
is still very thick, and in grizzlies often covered with several
inches of hair, hide and gristle. This was long before the day
of high-powered guns, and even the heavy caliber black powder
impelled bullets of those days would often glance and fail to
penetrate the skull of a large bear, unless they struck it squarely.

But a bullet from a .45-90 that I carried would knock any
bear down that it struck in the head; and neither I nor my
companion hunters felt the least fear of any bear if we had a
few yards of open ground to pump our rifles at him before he
could reach us.

It was for this reason that, after reaching the top of the hill,
I descended very slowly, always avoiding every clump of brush,
and circling around through the openings until I had again
picked up the trail, when it went into places where the bear
might be hidden. I finally came to the bottom of the hill and
a small stream of crystal clear water that gurgled between open
groves of small timber. The bed of the creek was sandy, and from
twenty-five to seventy-five feet wide. The bear turned directly
up the creek, and I followed, still carefully avoiding thickets
and turns in the bank, where the bear might have laid up for
the day. At last I found where the bear had left a thicket
and crossed the creek, leaving a string of still wet tracks in
the sand; which the sun had now heated so warm that it was
evident the bear had heard me, and probably thinking the

clump of brush he had laid down in was not so well situated for an ambush as he wished, had silently sneaked away while I was reconnoitering a short distance down the creek.

Presently the tracks led up a gently sloping hill, bare of underbrush, but covered with pine trees. As I slowly neared the top, I heard the rattle of a rattlesnake off to one side, and stepping a few feet towards the sound, I saw a small rattler coiled beside a hole near a large rock. Grasping a small boulder I flung it at the snake, but missed my mark, and as the snake began to disappear beneath the rock, I hurled missle after missle [*sic*], but without effect.

When the snake had disappeared, I slowly climbed to the top of the hill, and passing through the open pines, which grew so thickly here that it was slow trailing over the mat of pine needles, I picked up the trail where the bear had started down the farther hillside, which was pretty well covered with scrub oak and buck brush.

I did not follow the trail here, but traveled parallel with it, when I could see it in the soft volcanic ash which covered the hillside, or, when I could not see it, cut across where the course the bear was taking led me to believe it should be, still keeping in the open spaces until I could see the trail ahead of me.

At last I came to a belt of thick brush, and leaving the trail, I skirted this until I came to an opening, which I entered, and winding from opening to opening, came at last to a clear space about sixty feet in length, up and down the hill, which at that place sloped at an angle of almost 45 degrees. As I stepped out into this clear space near its upper end I could see the bear's track where he had hopped, and slid, down through the soft, ashy soil, and entered the brush at the lower end of the opening.

Thinking the bear was ahead of me, and holding my rifle in the hollow of my left arm, with my right hand holding its grip, my thumb on the hammer, and the trigger-finger in the trigger-guard, I stepped over into the bear's track just below the fringe of brush the bear had come through. Though I was gazing intently across the gulch, hoping I might see the bear ascending the opposite hillside, I had already chosen my route through another break in the brush just beyond the bear's tracks. As I stepped in the trail I heard the rattle of a trap-chain above and behind me, and before I could turn, the bellow of the bear, not unlike the bawl of an enraged bull.

I could not turn my feet on the steep hillside as swiftly as my body, and as I tried to face the bear, for I knew there was absolutely no chance for escape by flight, the bear came charging over the brush, snapping at my head, and striking with its unencumbered paw. Both myself and the bear were at a disadvantage on the steep hillside, and attempting to dodge a stroke from the bear's paw, I threw myself to one side and down the hill. As I did so, the rifle, which I had cocked as I tried to turn, was accidently discharged, leaving it with the chamber of the barrel empty.

I fell with such momentum that I turned over and over several times, like a boy turning back-somersaults, while the bear, his beady, bloodshot eyes flashing malignant rage and hatred, his ears laid back, and his grizzly gray mane standing erect, tried to check himself as he slid and rolled by me. Snapping like a monstrous dog, just as I stopped rolling, he sunk one tusk, all he had left—he had broken the others off biting at the trap—in my thigh, and dragged me along as he slid down the hill.

When bear and man had stopped the bear was standing diagonally over me. The beast's tusk had penetrated my thigh and tore loose a whipcord looking muscle; and snapping again, the bear caught me by the same thigh. After some effort to balance himself, he rose up on his haunches and shook and swung me like a cat might shake a mouse. At last he slowly came down on his feet, and still holding me in the grip of his great jaws, flung or jerked me until my head lay down the hill, while the bear's rump was up the hill, but his head, his jaws still grasping my leg, was turned almost at right angles toward his right, and my left.

I still grasped my rifle, for there was nothing else to hold onto. As the bear, still snuffing, clamped down again and again on my thigh, I slowly at first, and then with a quick sweep, brought the rifle around until it touched the side of the great brute's head. As I swung the gun, I worked the lever. The bear saw, or heard, and let go his hold on my leg. Just as his head turned and the muzzle of the rifle touched its side, a little below and back of the eye, the lever snapped, my finger gripped the trigger, and the crash and smoke that flamed out told me, even before the bear had fallen, that the scrap was over, for there were still several cartridges in the magazine, and even if the bullet did not reach the bear's brain, it would stun him into helplessness for several moments. But as my right hand jerked the lever and threw another cartridge into the barrel, I saw the bear collapse. His feet seemed to give way under him, and with a sort of convulsive shudder of the muscles, he sank to the ground and rolled over against the brush at the lower side of the open space, just as I, with a great effort, threw myself out of the way. When the bear stopped rolling, he lay on his back with his great paws sticking up, and the trap dangling from one of them. Man and bear were not far apart, and as bears have been known to play 'possum, I rose to a sitting position, and poked the bear with the muzzle of my rifle. But there was no doubt that he was dead. A look at the eyes, and the great hole in the side of his head where the powder had burned the hair off, made that certain.

The bear had evidently heard me throwing rocks at the snake, and had circled around through the brush and waited beside his own tracks for his enemy. Had I followed the trail through the brush there can be little doubt I would have fallen an easy victim to the enraged animal. For, as it was, the steep hillside, and loose ashy soil that ran down the hill at every touch of bear or man, was the only thing that saved me.

I now thought of my leg. It felt numb and dead; but I soon found there were no bones broken; but the blood was flowing freely from the wound made by the bear's gnashing tusk. Pulling out my pocket knife, I cut and tore from my cotton flannel undershirt—all I had on except trousers, moccasins and hat—enough strips to tie a bandage around my leg tightly above the wound. Then, picking up my rifle, I looked again at the magnificent animal that luck alone had enabled me to conquer; and limped down the hill to the bottom of the gulch, and then on down to where I knew there was an almost ice-cold spring.

When I arrived at the spring, which bubbled up from a small fern-covered cíenega, or marsh, I lay face down and drank my fill. Then, slowly limping, I went down the gulch until I came to a place beneath a giant mountain cypress where the bear had dug out a wallowing hole. In spring, when the bears begin to shed their winter coats, they greatly enjoy a mud and water bath, and into one of these wallows I scrambled, not without considerable difficulty. I had observed that although I had tied the bandage tightly above the principal wound—for the broken tusks had done little damage, and the grinding teeth had bruised and not cut—with every limping step the blood spurted out afresh. So, after sitting in the cold water for perhaps twenty minutes, I rebandaged the leg tightly, and finding a dead sapling with a fork about the right size for a crutch, I broke it to the right length. Then, leaving my rifle and cartridge belt, I started for the camp.

It was now about an hour before sun-down; and I was about five miles from where the trap had been set, and about six and a half miles from the camp. Leaning on the improvised crutch, I limped down the canyon to the creek as I had come. Dark came on, and the rough and narrow fork of the sapling rubbed and chafed my armpit until I stopped and tore most of what remained of my shirt into strips, and wound it around the fork of the crutch. Then I hobbled on, hour after hour, through the darkened woods.

Limbs, and vines, and thorns reached out and tore and scratched my exposed skin, but I did not care. I did not think my wound was serious; and while other men of my acquaintance had killed bear in hand-to-hand conflict, none had ever met such a monster as I had—except for the slight handicap of the trap for the bear—fought and killed in a fair fight.

Bear, like hogs, are very heavy for their size. But this bear was larger-bodied than a fair-sized cow pony; and although it was June, the season of the year when bear in the foothills are usually poor, he was fat and sleek; a meat-eater that had not gone to the high mountains, but had remained in the lower country to prey on the cowmen's cattle.

Finally I came to the main creek, and stumbling along to the accompaniment of the cries of night animals and birds, wet, weary and sore, came around the point only a hundred yards or so from the camp. Through the trees I could see Al standing by the campfire. At last I crossed the smaller stream and climbed up the bank to the welcoming fire, and the well-meaning but clumsy ministrations of my partner, who finding on his return after dark that the horse he had tied up for me was still unsaddled, knew something had happened, but could do nothing until daylight made it possible to follow a trail.

Next morning, long before daylight, Al saddled up and went after the gun, rifle, trap and hide. At that altitude the nights were cold, and he found the skin still in good condition. After skinning the bear, he returned to the camp, and, loading me on an easy gaited horse, started for the nearest town, about sixty miles away. That night we stopped at the Double Circle Ranch;

the next at McCarthy's Mine, and on the following day we arrived in Clifton, where we sold the bear's hide; and I remained until the wound in my thigh had healed.

THE GREAT GRIZZLY TAKEN BY ISAÍAS T. GARCÍA IN THE FRIAR MOUNTAINS OF CHIHUAHUA, MEXICO, IN 1954

Carlos Mateo Bailón
1954

The following account is one of two articles by Carlos Mateo Bailón, of the Hunting and Shooting Club of Chihuahua, that were sent to me by Ing. José Treviño F., a biologist in Chihuahua for the Secretaria de Agricultura Recursos Hidráulicos. This narrative, translated by James K. Evans, relates the taking of a large male grizzly in the Terrentes region of the northern Sierra del Nido, which had recently been opened to the public. Bailón had just missed getting a cinnamon-colored black bear there a year earlier. García, a druggist and hunting enthusiast, also killed a large female grizzly in 1957, and these were among the last grizzlies of record from Chihuahua. Bailón's other article mentions encountering large numbers of hunters. His accounts are informative in that they suggest that unregulated hunting by even nonprofessional bear hunters may have contributed to decimating a grizzly population past the point of recovery.

The joy and excitement of the hunt is apparent in Bailón's account, as is his appreciation of the grizzly. His celebrations, the employment of the guides, and the interest in the bear in Ciudad Chihuahua illustrates the potential value of the grizzly to the Mexican people. There are no references to saving cows and doing good by killing the bear. One can only wonder what might have been the outcome if such an attitude had prevailed in the Southwest generally, and if effective hunting regulations had allowed such interests to continue and develop.

Isaías García, T. and I planned to hunt the steep and inaccessible canyons of the Friar Mountains of Chihuahua, where we had the best chance of finding a good specimen of the scarce and difficult "barfoot." I had the good fortune to encounter a fine specimen of black bear there last year, although I did not have luck good enough to bag him; however, it served to indicate that in this country, one can find one of the hairy beasts. Besides the individual I saw, I also found many tracks of big, heavy bears. A trip into the same formidable mountain area seemed in order.

On Saturday, October 25 of this year, my companion, Isaías, and I left Chihuahua City for the mountains that we had selected for this hunt. We were to arrive early at a ranch near the mountains we were to hike through, and where our good friend, Mr. Pedro Moreno lived. Mr. Moreno was to lend us the horses and mules necessary to transport us to the top of the mountain. Long before we arrived at the ranch, we had a serious mishap with the steering apparatus of Isaías's pickup. After about three hours of hard work, and with few tools, we were able to improvise a steering system that enabled the pickup to take us and our hunting gear to the ranch.

Shortly after noon we arrived at the ranch. As bad luck would have it, Mr. Moreno had been obliged to make an urgent trip to Colonia Aldama, taking his family with him. There was no one at the ranch except a man and a boy who had not been notified of our impending arrival, nor of our intentions; so, no horses, mules, or guides were ready or even available for us.

Disappointed by so much failure and misfortune, we decided to go on to Colonia San Lorenzo, where we were sure we could get horses and a couple of men to serve as guides. As soon as we found out how to get to C. San Lorenzo, we started anew, so to speak. We followed the road we were told to take for about an hour and a half, and little by little it became more and more untravelable. In fact, the "road" got so bad we opted not to go any farther and, to prevent getting stuck or hung up in a bad spot, we turned around and went back. Now discouraged by so many foul-ups, we went back down the same road with the intention of going to the Sierra Namiquipa of Chihuahua.

On our return over this road, we had the good fortune to run across some gentlemen who were putting up a barbed-wire fence. We stopped and asked them if they knew of anyone in the area who would rent us some horses that could take us and our gear into the mountains. They told us that there was no one around there with any such animals available. Without giving up hope, we kept after them to talk them into taking us into the mountains using the animals they were using on their fence-building job. After a lot of chitchat and several shots of the good brandy that we carried as a barrier against the cold, they began to show encouragement to serve as our guides. The plan was that they were to pick us up early Sunday and take us to a campsite very near where we could pursue the "hairy buggers." Anyway, thank heaven, we had managed to gain our first triumph—that of convincing these gentlemen to guide us into the mountains.

We got as close to the hunting area as the rough terrain allowed, and made camp at the mouth of a canyon. While Isaías arranged a canvas to protect us from the wind while we slept, I went about preparing some supper to restore the strength we had lost through all the troubles on the road. With dinner ready and between sips of rich, hot coffee and the snapping of jaws, Isaías and I rehashed the misadventures and incidents of our first day. I told Isaías that it was hard for others to believe that one who enjoys hunting leaves all the comforts that the city has to offer—his business and his family, to endure thousands of discomforts in the mountains—always with the optimistic hope of being compensated by the taking of a magnificent specimen of game animal. One thus feels the immense satisfaction of compensation for all the work, troubles, and dangers when he is rewarded by seeing the tracks of deer, javelina, or the scarce and large grizzly bear.

And, with our bellies well repleted and satisfied, we continued talking for a while longer about the shelter of our home, until weariness caused us to give it up. Isaías went straight to bed while I stayed up a little longer in the light of the fire to attend the pot of beans so they would finish cooking without burning. When they were almost done, I put in some more water and stoked up the fire and went to dream about those big hairy buggers.

At the crack of dawn we were on our feet again, poking up the fire and preparing breakfast—ranch-style eggs with green chili and cheese, crock-cooked beans, and hot coffee—the mouths of my hunting buddies who read these lines will water upon remembering similar banquets in the mountains; and, when you add to this menu a side of rich-tasting barbecued javelina ribs—or venison jerky roasted on the coals with the ashes and a hot tortilla, you know glory. This is the life, fellow hunters!—and you will agree with me.

We had finished eating when our good guides arrived with the animals and gear. They were three cowboys named Manuel Pedroza, Miguel and Pepe (I don't remember their last names). We invited them to have breakfast and, after they had finished, we got ready to leave camp and go into the mountains.

Bear Ho!

It was about 9:30 in the morning when we began to enter into bear country—lots of manzanita thickets, madrono, agoriz, etc. We traveled quite a ways scrutinizing inch by inch every foot of ground and thicket, which, in this part of the Friar mountains is badly broken and difficult to travel. We went very slowly on foot because we were finding fresh tracks and scat of an enormous bear. Isaías was walking behind Manuel, the guide, when suddenly the eagle eyes of Isaías distinguished a shadowy object in the manzanita thicket on the hillside across from us. The huge object was moving little by little, slowly up the hillside and because of the thickness of the manzanita, he was unable to identify the kind of animal—it looked like it could be a big wolf, judging by its pelage which, at that distance, seemed to be a brownish color.

Isaías, without haste or hesitation, raised his 'scoped .30-06 Winchester to his shoulder, aimed carefully, and fired. A hoarse and formidable growl reverberated through the canyon—then we realized that it was a "hairy bugger" and that the soft-nosed bullet had found its mark. The beast rolled over a few times in the manzanitas and disappeared from our sight. Pretty soon he started going uphill again and was lost in the thicket.

We waited a good long time with our rifles ready in case he should reappear, but—nothing! All was silence around us. The beating of our hearts, which wanted to jump out of our chests, were the only noises heard. We got a fix on the last place we had seen the beast and began working toward it, little by little, with thousands of precautions—well, we didn't know if he was badly hurt, in which case it was dangerous to get too close without due caution. We climbed up on the high boulder above the spot to see if we could locate him with binoculars. Nothing could be seen through the thickness of the manzanita.

We went on, getting closer and closer toward the spot—with rifles and pistols ready for any sudden emergency. Finally, we located him—he was sitting up behind some clumps of manzanita. Since his eyes were open, he seemed to be alive, but he wasn't moving. With our firearms at the ready, we went closer, protecting ourselves behind the manzanitas, until we were able to see him completely. He was sitting up, but lifeless, which was no great relief to us, now that we were so close to the once formidable animal. He was a huge grizzly! A magnificent old bear who, with his astuteness, had managed to survive being sought by all the hunters who, year after year tramp through these mountains in search of "barfoots." There is no doubt that luck had been with us in a special form, especially, with Isaías García, since it was his first bear in his life as a hunter—and since his first shot from his .30-06 was successful in making a killing shot through the lungs with a soft-nosed bullet, ending forever the life of such a large and formidable specimen.

Perhaps equally important is the fact that he set the record for time required to take a grizzly bear, from the time he left Chihuahua City—one day on the road to the mountains, and two hours after leaving camp to the moment he knocked him down. A great dose of luck on this happy hunt.

The next step was the hardships and work we had to go through to get the tremendously precious and coveted trophy down off that mountain—after we contemplated and examined the grizzly. The impact of the bullet had passed it through the right side, through the lung, and into the left forearm, where it lodged. We found it between the meat and the fat when we dressed it out in Chihuahua in preparation for having the meat cured. It made a fine, rich ham.

Once we had opened it up and taken out the entrails, we started the titanic task of raising the carcass up high enough to get it on the mule. The combination of the five of us and the saddle horn was required to raise it up, first the front, then the back, then one leg at a time; all the time being careful to keep it well secured to a thick pine limb with ropes. When the carcass was high enough, we led the biggest and strongest mule under it, which was no easy task. He had to be blindfolded and, even then, he balked and snorted when he sniffed the scent of the bear carcass. Nevertheless, we were able to lead the mule into position, after some little difficulty, and the mule was kind enough to allow us to lower the hairy and bloody brute down onto him. Slowly and carefully we slackened the moorings until the bear was resting on the packsaddle.

Once the carcass was well balanced and lashed to the pack-saddle, we started our perilous journey to camp. The route back was a long one and it got dark before we got very far. From there on it was "Way of The Cross" traveling. We pitched the reins to the horses and let them find their own way through the boulders and brush, thereby allowing us to ward off the assault of the branches that were hitting us in the face and all parts of the body. Every now and then we had to stop and rebalance the load on the poor beast, which weighed little more than its cargo, which we judged to be about 300 kilo-grams [about 685 pounds]. In this fashion we continued our progress in the darkness of the night until finally—we arrived at our camp—safe and sound—thanks be to the good Lord!

Once in camp, we hung the bear up again so it would air out throughout the night and thus be prevented from spoiling, since it was so fat—there was a covering of about two inches of fat over the entire carcass. We unsaddled the horses and mules and turned them loose because we didn't need them any longer (they would return to the ranch unguided). We could carry the bear, the camp gear, the saddles, and the guides back to the ranch with us in the pickup.

After having revived our strength with an abundant dinner, we talked about the good fortune of the day and, around our campfire, which burned with the same enthusiasm as did our hearts, we lasted well into the night. The slices of "Dorado" we were nibbling at awakened the poet in us. Following is what my friend, Isaías's feat inspired in me:

As a druggist he is very famous!
As a pill peddler, that is!
He sells violets for mallow
To whoever will buy them.

As a hunter—now he is famous!
Because with great bravery he attacks

As though to milk the bear
Believing it was a cow.

Poor Isaías was scared as he approached it.
He ran for three days
Until finally he got discouraged.

We have been throwing
Cold water on him to wake him
And running, from fright,
He went falling.

With a shot of booze
In the act he was revived
And now he is so smiling
That he gets close to look at the bear.

At night when he goes to bed
Many shouts has he loosed
Thinking that he is being attacked
By the huge grizzly.

Sugar water we give to him
To calm him down
Why, he has so many spasms
That he wants us to join him.

And with cradle songs
We have been able to lull him
So he will not keep dreaming
About that ferocious animal.

When he wakes early
All the fear has passed
Now he is at peace
And calmed down
And I can relate to his fear.

With music and song
And a few shots of booze
We all celebrate this happy experience.

Now for Isaías's inspiration, dedicated to me, along with the rejoicing of the guides. It goes like this:

Para Bailón

As a hunter he is more of a duck
And is not better as a cook
He wants to serve us cat meat
bled with nixtamal*!*

That sly dude tells us
That they are T-bone steaks
Scrambled with heart
and slices of ham

He has left the restaurant
To go after the bears
But, with such bad luck
That he has done us all wrong

"There will be a next time,"
He tells us optimistically.
"Better luck will come fast
And I will sharpen my vision well
So as not to miss seeing the bear."

After having given vent to our thoughts, we allowed ourselves to rest, but when I started to get into bed I noticed that my glasses were missing. I thought that I had lost case and all, and that this had happened when we were being slapped about the face and chest by all those limbs and branches on the trail.

None of us slept much that last night in the mountains because of the high excitement that we had experienced. Before I had shot at a black bear but that excitement was not as great as that of seeing and being involved in the taking of this precious specimen in all his savage, attractive, and dominating aspect as "king of the mountain."

Triumphant Return to Cd. Chihuahua

We got up early Monday, and, while Isaías and the others were getting breakfast, I went back up the trail to look for my glasses, following the tracks of our horses. Good fortune being still with me, I was able to find my indispensable and very necessary glasses and returned happily to camp.

After everyone had breakfast, we went to work raising that woolly bugger up high enough so we could get the truck under it, as we had done with the mule. The object here was to put it on the rack on top of the cab. We fought and struggled with all our strength and ingenuity until we got him up on a good, heavy oak limb. Then we were able to drive the pickup under it and lower it to the cab rack.

A word about our ingenuity: In order to raise that heavy carcass that high off the ground, we had to load the back of the pickup with rocks, since the truck wasn't heavy enough without the extra weight, and the wheels only spun when pulling on the ropes.

After we finally got the big carcass in place on top of the cab, we loaded all our gear and headed back to the ranch, where we left our guides, then continued on into town.

We arrived in Chihuahua City about 3:30 P.M. It was necessary for us to travel slowly to town in order to avoid the immense weight of the bear caving in the top of the cab or breaking the windshield or maybe even falling off.

Our arrival in Chihuahua was a notable event. Hundreds of people came to admire such a precious trophy. The local reporters and photographers had a field day taking pictures and asking questions; the story came out in all the papers the next day.

As the temperature in the city was pretty high, much to our regret, we had to take the carcass to a place where it could be skinned out with the greatest of care. Then the grease was rendered out, the *chorizos* saved for future enjoyment, and the meat cured into ham by the local "Pork Processing Specialist." The hide was taken to the taxidermist, Sr. V. Jesus Macías B., for his treatment, and once finished, it will be put on exhibition in the place called "The Jewel" for everyone to admire and enjoy.

By this conduct, once more my sincerest congratulations go out to my great friend and hunting companion Isaías T. García for the exceptional good fortune that he had on this occasion and that on future hunts he continues to enjoy the same kind of luck, for his personal satisfaction, as well as that of his family; pride for our Hunting and Shooting Club of Chihuahua, and the admiration and appreciation of all his friends and companions of this manly, dangerous, complete, and exciting sport of hunting.

My invitation also goes out to all the other hunting companions of the Republic who wish to make hunting excursions into the mountains of our dear Chihuahua, and remember that they have sincere friends who are willing to help them out in any way possible with anything related to hunting in our mountains.

For those who wish to know, the vital statistics of this rare and valuable trophy are:

Field-dressed weight, 274 kilograms [about 625 lb.]
Length (point of nose to tip of tail) 2.2 meters [7 ft. 4 in.]
Size of front paw claws, 9 cm [3½ in.]
Hind feet: width, 15 cm [5 in.]; length, 26 cm [10¼ in.]

Chihuahua, Chih., October 31, 1954

CHAPTER 16

Epilogue

A dozen years have passed since I drafted the Wildlife Society Resolution supporting the reintroduction of grizzlies to the Southwest; three years have gone by since I wrote the introduction to this book. Although I do not think a reintroduction is practical at the present time, I again have hope for a return of the grizzly to the Southwest, however far off that might be.

If there is a future for southwestern grizzlies, it relies not on some new-found relict population but on a planned introduction of bears experienced with man and his ways. Those who undertake such an effort will have to display some courage, and more importantly, they will have to possess foresight and common sense. They must develop a workable game plan and be great salesmen, because public support will be essential to success. It is to be hoped these men and women will also be practical bear biologists and know both the opportunities for dreams and the limitations of practical achievement. If so, someday there just might be a chance to bring Bruin home to the Southwest.

The habitats are there. The great Gila Wilderness Area and Blue Primitive Area that are the legacy of Aldo Leopold's frontier youth are with us yet. These areas, always the heart of Southwest grizzly country, remain relatively pristine and intact. Their greatest economic use now, and in the foreseeable future, is to recreationists and wilderness outfitters. Wilderness pack trips and elk hunts are recreation in the Gila; lion and bear hunts are the business of the Blue. Would not grizzlies be an asset to such users of our public lands?

And grizzlies are potentially available. Not some almost mystical Mexican grizzly, but the same grizzly species that inhabited the Southwest in the historical past. They are still present in the Rocky Mountains of Montana. Not "park bears," but wild bears that have learned to get along with man but without his temptations—as the brown bears of Europe do. Here, on the East Front of the Rockies, outside the national parks, such bears appear to be learning to avoid man. If time permits, and mortality does not overtake them (a too-real possibility), man-adapted bears may be available for transplant.

Time and proper planning are the keys—two ingredients not often present when wildlife-management decisions are made. It would be a fatal mistake to sell the public on the wrong bears too soon. It would also be too easy to procrastinate in perpetuity. Bureaucracies have demonstrated that they are prone to make both kinds of errors.

I recently went to the Arizona Cattlegrowers' convention at Payson. I was impressed at the vintage of my old friends and adversaries. They all seemed so much more rational, and while still haughty and opinionated, we had all mellowed. Corporate ranches and agribusiness had taken a toll of their spirit as well as their numbers. They saw themselves not unlike Ben Lilly and the grizzlies, passing on to a new frontier that they did not much understand or like. Unlike the bear hunters, however, they talked of preserving "working ranches" and maintaining pronghorn antelope for sentimental reasons. I almost asked them about introducing grizzlies.

The time for the grizzly to reclaim his domain may yet return. If it comes, I hope it is done right. The opportunity, for success or failure, will probably come only once.

Appendices

MARILYN HOFF STEWART

Resolution

Submitted by the Resolutions Committee at the Annual Meeting of the New Mexico–Arizona Section of the Wildlife Society on February 2, 1973, in Farmington, New Mexico

Pertaining to the Reintroduction of Grizzly Bear into Arizona and New Mexico

WHEREAS, grizzly bears formerly occupied large areas of Arizona and New Mexico, and

WHEREAS, grizzly bears have been completely extirpated from Arizona and New Mexico since the 1930s; and

WHEREAS, there remain large areas of suitable habitat in Arizona and New Mexico in public ownership within the former distribution of grizzly bears; and

WHEREAS, the New Mexico–Arizona Section of the Wildlife Society is of the philosophy that species diversity and the reintroduction of native fauna are desirable; and

WHEREAS, the grizzly bear was and could be a desirable complement to our faunal realm; and

WHEREAS, grizzly bears are currently available for reintroduction from areas in the continental United States in and adjacent to lands administrated by the National Park Service; and

WHEREAS, the New Mexico–Arizona Section of the Wildlife Society recognizes the inherent problem of anticipated or actual incompatability of grizzly bears with livestock operations;

NOW THEREFORE, be it resolved that the New Mexico–Arizona Section of The Wildlife Society encourages the administrators of the United States Forest Service lands possessing wilderness characteristics, designated or de facto, within the historical range of grizzly bear in Arizona and/or New Mexico to prepare management and contingency plans to provide for the successful reintroduction of this species in limited numbers and area.[1]

---

[1] After considerable discussion the resolution was adopted 23 to 17.

Evaluation of the Gila Wilderness for Re-establishment of the Grizzly Bear

Albert W. Erickson, Ph.D.
Wildlife Management Associates
Bellevue, Washington
and
College of Fisheries
University of Washington, Seattle

September, 1974

ABSTRACT

An evaluation of the Gila Wilderness was made to assess the suitability of the area for the reintroduction of the grizzly bear. This evaluation led to the conclusion that the approximate 300 square miles contained in the Gila Wilderness was sufficiently large to satisfy the spatial requirements of a small population of grizzlies. The habitat of the area was also deemed suitable for fulfilling the food, cover and denning requirements of the species although the current habitat array was believed less attractive for the grizzly than at the time of the species extirpation from the area in the 1930's. The direction of the change was a reduction in the amount of open areas and the development of a closed canopy forest due to intense fire control. As consequence of this, the amount of grasses and early successional plants upon which the grizzly depends for its food appears to be in a declining state.

The attractiveness of the Gila Wilderness as grizzly habitat is judged equivalent to the areas where the species exists in the national forests of the mountain states. As such the Gila Wilderness is perhaps at best only moderately good habitat for grizzlies on a comparison with areas such as Kodiak Island or the Alaska Peninsula.

227

While it is probable that a successful reintroduction of the grizzly into the Gila Wilderness can be achieved, it seems probable that some direct conflict can be expected between livestock grazing use of the Wilderness and the grizzly. Suggestions for reducing this potential conflict are (1) stock reductions in prime grizzly habitats, (2) shifting stocks at critical season, and (3) purposeful control of bears in problem areas.

Recommended habitat management for the grizzly in the Wilderness include (1) directed use of wild fire to create openings and suppress forest regeneration and (2) the creation of unattractive vegetative buffers between prime grizzly habitat and grazing areas.

Recommendations are also given relative to stocking procedures should an introduction be attempted.

INTRODUCTION

This report presents an evaluation of the suitability of the Gila Wilderness of the Gila National Forest for reintroduction of the grizzly bear [*Ursus arctos horribilus)* and presents recommendations as to methodology and management, should an introduction be attempted.

The study was performed under U.S. Forest Service Contract Number 6-369-74 awarded to the author on March 25, 1974. The broad objectives of the study were as follows:

1. To delineate the boundaries of an area within which grizzly bear habitat management could be effected.
2. To identify existing and potential seasonal key grizzly bear habitat within the area established and propose management for these areas.
3. To qualify or rate this grizzly bear habitat with that located throughout the United States, including Alaska.

METHODS

The methodology employed in the development of this report concerned (1) a review of maps and information on the Gila Wilderness, provided by Gila National Forest, (2) a search of literature pertinent to the study objectives, (3) a 5 day field reconnaissance of the Gila Wilderness, and (4) discussions of the project with officials of the Gila National Forest and the New Mexico Department of Fish and Game.

The Forest materials examined included:

1. Grazing allotment map of the Gila Forest, including the Gila Wilderness . . .
2. Vegetative type map of the Gila Wilderness . . .
3. Fire history map of the Gila Wilderness for the period 1961–1970
4. Area maps
5. Check lists of the plants, avifauna, mammals and herbs occurring in the Gila Wilderness.

The field reconnaissance was performed during the period April 5–11, 1974. The effort entailed first an aerial examination of the Gila Wilderness and adjacent areas in the company of New Mexico Department of Fish and Game Officials Messers William Huey, Asst. Director and Richard Brown, Pilot-Conservation Officer.

This reconnaissance provided the contractor orientation and a first approximation of the Gila Wilderness as grizzly bear habitat, particularly the general physiognomy of the area, spatial relationships and area use considerations.

A 4 day horseback trip approximating 80 trail miles was subsequently made into the core of the Gila Wilderness. . . . Personnel participating in this trip and advisory to the contractor were, Mr. Dale Jones, Wildlife Biologist USFS Region 3, Mr. John Ross, Wildlife Biologist, and Mr. Jack Carter, Asst. Ranger, Gila National Forest; Mr. Robert Welch, Game Biologist, and Mr. Hugh Bishop, Conservation Officer, New Mexico Department of Fish and Game; and Mr. John Phelps, Game Biologist of the Arizona Department of Fish and Game.

On this trip, judgements were made of the areas traversed as to their attractiveness as grizzly bear habitat and searches were made for evidence of black bear sign. Particular attention was given in the field effort to judge the suitability of the Gila Wilderness area as grizzly habitat on the basis of both current management and stage of plant succession and possible later use and future successional stages. Consideration was also given to evidence of past, present and possible future Forest management practices as 1) bearing on the attractiveness of the Gila Wilderness as grizzly habitat, and 2) the value of that use relative to that if the grizzly were a species to be given prime management consideration in the Gila Wilderness.

PAST EVIDENCE OF THE DISTRIBUTION AND ABUNDANCE OF THE GRIZZLY IN THE GILA WILDERNESS

Only cursory information exists of the grizzly bear in the Gila Wilderness despite the apparent fact that the species was once judged to be so numerous as to constitute a serious menace to human life and domestic stock (Bailey, 1931). That the species has been extant in the Gila Forest since the establishment of the Gila Wilderness in 1924 seems reasonably certain, although it appears that the species was exterminated from the area by the early 1930's. At the turn of the century, the grizzly bear had already been largely exterminated from the state, principally due to a coordinated and concerted control effort by ranchers (Bailey, 1931). The main residual areas where the species was to be found included the Mimbres, Mogollon and San Francisco Ranges. In 1910 the Forest Service reported grizzlies as still extant in the Taos, San Juan and Gallinas Mountains.

The first concerted attempt to assess the status of the waning grizzly population in New Mexico was by J. S. Ligon, who in a report prepared for the U.S. Forest Service in May of 1917, estimated a state population of 48 grizzly bears and presented a map depicting their distribution. Two of these residuum lie within or impinge upon the Gila Wilderness. In a subsequent report presented in 1927, Ligon stated that the predatory habits of the grizzly had resulted in their almost total extermination from the state.

EVALUATION OF THE GILA WILDERNESS AS GRIZZLY HABITAT

Three prime considerations bear on the suitability of the Gila Wilderness as habitat currently or potentially suitable for the grizzly bear. These include (1) the spatial sufficiency of the area to satisfy the normal mobility traits of the species, (2) the support capability of the area for the grizzly and (3) the compatibility of the grizzly with other resource uses of the area.

These three considerations are not independent, of course, but an attempt will be made to examine each in this analysis.

Spatial Sufficiency.—Not surprisingly, there is not a large body of data detailing the movement traits and home range sizes of brown bears.[1] Sufficient information exists, however, to permit the judgement that the normal movements of grizzly bears are quite limited, despite popularly held views to the contrary. Radio-tracking studies conducted on Kodiak Island by Berns and Hensel (1972) determined that 14 radio-tracked bears confined their principle activities to an average area of only 5.5 square miles. The average maximum between-point movements of these animals was 12.5 linear miles (range 5.0 to 29.4). The maximum movements between points were usually associated with movements between winter dens and the major summer activity centers.

In a study of grizzly bears in the Yukon Territory, Pearson (1972) reported the average home range size of eight female grizzlies as 27 square miles and that of an unstated number of males as 114 square miles. Craighead and Craighead (1962) reported the home range of 10 radioed Yellowstone grizzlies of mixed sexes and ages as averaging 41.9 square miles. The maximum and minimum ranges of these animals were 8 and 168 square miles, respectively.

The spatial requirement of grizzly bears can further be inferred from the minimum sizes of areas where the species persists in relic status. Noteworthy among these populations are the 19 to 20 insular populations extant in Europe (Curry-Lindahl, 1972). Most of these populations occupy areas less expansive than that present in the portion of the Gila Wilderness closed to cattle. Notable among these is a population of 60 to 80 bears occurring in the Abruzzo National Park in the Apennines. This park is only 250 square miles in area or slightly smaller than the non-grazed portion of the Gila Wilderness. Correspondingly, a relic population of approximately 15 bears exists in a 200 square mile area in Norway (Elkmork, 1962). Other examples exist in Asia and in the Americas. The most significant of these as concerns the present study are two

[1] The grizzly is but one sub-form of the European-Asian and American brown bear *(Ursus arctos).*

relic populations of bears reported as existing in Mexico (Leopold, 1967 and 1969). One of these populations exists in the Sierra del Nido, a small, isolated range emerging from the desert of central Chihuahua. This population was apparently sustaining itself in an area of only 5000 acres (Cowan, 1972, page 531) until subjected to a campaign of extermination (Leopold, 1969). The second population exists in the upper Yaqui Basin of Sonora in the Sierra Madre about 100 miles west of the Sierra del Nido (Leopold, 1969). Of the grizzly stocks remaining today, these populations most probably represent the race of grizzly most close genetically and habitat-wise to the stock type which formerly occupied the Gila Wilderness.

The foregoing records suggest that the approximately 360 square miles of area contained in the Gila Wilderness are sufficient to fulfill the spatial needs of at least a small grizzly population, assuming, of course, that the area is suitable grizzly habitat.

Habitat Evaluation.—Inasmuch as the habitat requirements of the grizzly bear are ill-defined (Erickson, 1974), and no hard analytical data exist on the habitat characteristics of the Gila Wilderness, only a judgemental evaluation may be made of the attractiveness of the Wilderness as habitat for the grizzly bear. The generalized type map of the Gila Wilderness shows the Wilderness as fairly well broken into an intermixed array of eight major vegetative types based on dominant species. . . . The preponderant vegetative type is Ponderosa pine which covers the principle high country. The second prominent vegetative type is mixed conifer which together with spruce-fir forests occupies the remaining non-Ponderosa pine high country. The lower ranges and the periphery of the Wilderness area contain a large component of pinyon-juniper with major components of brush.

Conspicuously limited in abundance in the Wilderness are the grass and aspen vegetative types. . . .

Observations during the reconnaisance led me to conclude that the grassland and pioneer vegetative component of the Gila Wilderness was today quite limited in extent over that present in the recent past. This conclusion is premised on three observations. The first of these was the major invasion of prime grassland meadows by forest types. . . . The second was the seeming replacement of a grass-type understory beneath the

Ponderosa forests by shrubs and forest regeneration which often assumed the character of a dog-hair thicket. Lastly was the near absence of the aspen type. Each of these observations supports the view that the vegetative character of the forest today is markedly different from that of earlier times. The prime cause for the change appears to have been intense fire control. The effectiveness of this control is apparent by reference to the fire map . . . , which shows literally hundreds of fire starts. Despite this, evidence of recent fire in the Wilderness during our field reconnaissance was essentially nil. The seeming result of this intense fire control has been a marked diminishment of the grassland area within the Wilderness. Whereas this type appears formerly to have been maintained as a fire dis-climax in forest openings and beneath Ponderosa stands, the absence of suppressing fire has permitted understory shrub and mixed-age stand development.

Assuming the foregoing to be true, does the current vegetative pattern render the Gila Wilderness more or less attractive as grizzly bear habitat? In my opinion, the Wilderness as currently vegetated is markedly less attractive as grizzly habitat than it would be if grasses and herbaceous growth were more prominent features. While no definitive habitat studies of the grizzly have been made, there is little doubt that the species thrives best and reaches its greatest densities in those areas of its range wherein grasses and herbaceous plants constitute a significant component of the vegetative array (Erickson, 1974). Conversely, there is to my knowledge not a single population of brown bears in areas of heavy forests which could be considered abundant on a comparison with those populations found in grassland habitats such as exist on Kodiak Island or on the Alaska Peninsula.

As concerns the Gila Wilderness, it seems unlikely that heavy populations of grizzlies ever existed in the Wilderness proper and it is very likely that the heaviest populations in the area formerly occurred in the foothills. In this regard, I was struck during the field reconnaissance at the attractiveness of the Jordan Mesa as grizzly habitat. This area lies at the northeast edge of the Gila Wilderness in the area currently under consideration for addition to the Gila Wilderness. The area possesses a large grassland component, well interspersed with forest types. . . .

If the judgement is correct that the current vegetative state of the Gila is less attractive as grizzly habitat than during former times, does it follow that the Gila Wilderness is presently unsuitable habitat for the grizzly? In my opinion, this would be exceedingly unlikely. Even in its current state, the Gila Wilderness possesses meadows, openings and pioneer areas equalling or exceeding those extant in other areas where grizzly populations exist. Among these are the populations occurring throughout Southeastern Alaska and in many National Forest areas of the Northwest, notably the Bob Marshall Wilderness. Further, the associated food base extant in the Gila Wilderness appeared significantly more abundant in both abundance and type as compared to the food resources available to more northerly grizzly bear populations. The plant list for the Gila Wilderness number 53 species of grasses, 195 herbaceous species, 50 shrubs and 63 tree species (Hayward, et al. 1974). This vast array of potential plant food items is impressive. Beyond the grasses and herbaceous plants foraged upon heavily by bears as the basic food staple, I was impressed during the field reconnaissance at the abundance of fruit bearing plants. Prominent among these was the abundance of pinyon-juniper berries along the lower fringes of the Wilderness zones traversed. These berries are apparently retained almost year long at certain sites and constituted the bulk of the black bear scats observed during the reconnaissance trip. Reports in the literature identify these berries as important foods of the grizzly in former times (Bailey 1931). Another prominent food available to bears in the Gila Wilderness is acorn mast. Despite the recognized inconsistency of acorn mast production, the presence of eight oak species suggests that some production of acorn mast can be expected as a regular occurrence. The field reconnaissance revealed oaks as a prominent tree type and examination of the trees and ground areas for acorn shell remains revealed that 1973 had been a good mast year. While the dependability of this food item is unknown, the fact that eight oak species exist in the area provides some assurance that at least some mast can be expected each year. A further mast item is pinyon nuts, although the frequency of a significant crop is apparently quite irregular. A number of Rosaceae were also observed during the field reconnaissance, particularly service berry and choke cherry, and whenever present they are avidly fed upon by bears.

Other food items of significance likely included the fruit of the prickly pear and yucca present in the lower fringe area of the Wilderness. Another likely important food item is the fruit of manzanita (little apple) which is mentioned in early accounts as eaten by grizzly bears (Bailey, 1931).

In assessing the attractiveness of the Gila Wilderness as grizzly habitat one must of course consider the year-long character of the area. At the season of the field reconnaissance, the region was exceedingly dry except at the higher elevations. It seems likely, therefore, that the grizzlies formerly occupying the Gila Wilderness area may have exhibited seasonal range shifts as has been reported for grizzly bear populations recently studies by radio telemetry (Berns and Hensel, 1972; Craighead and Craighead, 1969; and Pearson, 1972). In the Gila, it is probable that the bears either migrated to the high country or congregated along water courses during the dry season. Likely, both circumstances prevailed. It is probable also that most of the grizzlies migrated to the high country in the late fall due to the propensity of the species to seek high areas for denning (Craighead and Craighead, 1972 and Lentfer, et al., 1972). A migration to the low country was also a likely event upon arousal as the animals sought food during the meager spring period.

The consequence of these distributional shifts will be discussed beyond.

The suitability of the Gila Wilderness as satisfying the cover, shelter and denning requirements of the grizzly, is a foregone conclusion, in my opinion.

Conflict Problems.—A prime consideration bearing on the suitability of the Gila Wilderness as suitable habitat for the grizzly concerns potential conflicts between the species and other uses of the Wilderness. The obvious and critical factor is the potential conflict of the bears with livestock interests. The current Gila Wilderness comprises an area of approximately 360 square miles of which approximately 300 square miles is closed to livestock grazing. The area closed to grazing measures approximately 13 x 25 miles and encloses the central core high country. As assessed earlier, this block of country is sufficient to satisfy the spatial needs of at least a small population of bears and the habitat of the Gila Wilderness would appear to satisfy the food requirements of the grizzly as well. Despite the adjudged suitability of the area spatially and as grizzly habitat, it would be unrealistic to conclude that the bears would not leave the confines of the Wilderness. This happy state could be expected only if the Wilderness were inclusive of all the area attractive to bears and the fate of the original stock is profound evidence to the contrary. It is assumed, therefore, that some movement of grizzlies can be expected into the portion of the Gila Wilderness open to grazing and into adjacent non-wilderness portions of the forest.

Table 1 presents data provided to the contractor on stocking rates on the portion of the Wilderness open to grazing. These data show that approximately 1400 head of stock are grazed 8 to 12 months a year on that portion of the Gila Wilderness open to grazing. Another 900 head of stock are grazed on the Jordan Mesa, Indian Creek and Canyon Creek allotments adjacent to the Gila Wilderness on the northeast. While not given, equivalent stocking rates can be assumed on the Reading Mountain and Redstone allotments to the southeast, on the Shelton Canyon allotment to the west, and on the T-Bar and 625 allotments to the north. These stock allotments abutting directly upon the non-grazed portion of the Gila Wilderness would undoubtedly experience some livestock depredation should the grizzly bear be successfully stocked in the Gila Wilderness. Much of this area is proposed for addition to the Gila Wilderness. The degree of potential conflict undoubtedly could be minimized, however, according to how the bears were managed and when and how livestock were grazed in the Wilderness (see beyond). The level of the predational conflict is naturally difficult to judge, but I would think that it might approximate that experienced with the cougar. Evidence of this predator was observed during the field study and whatever predational loss being experienced is apparently tolerable.

Other potential conflicts of the grizzly bear with other uses of the Gila Wilderness concern principally direct conflicts with human recreational use of the Wilderness. The portent of this conflict exists in direct relation to the type and management of the recreation use. Greatest conflict can be expected in areas subjected to heavy picnicing or camping. Garbage from these activities attracts bears and almost invariably the animals develop nuisance tendencies. A consequence of this is a buildup of bear-human incident which is usually resolved by stringent actions being taken against the bears (witness the Yellowstone and Glacier parks situations). The net result is a constant wasteful drain on the bear population. The solution is, of course,

TABLE 1. *Grazing Quotas for the Gila Wilderness
and Adjacent Forest Areas*

Allotments	Stock Type		Period	AUM
Wilderness				
803 Rain Creek	302 cattle and	6 horses	8¼ months	2530
801 Davis Canyon	175 cattle and	5 horses	8 months	1440
804 Rough Canyon	63 cattle and	4 horses	12 months	804
802 Mogollon Creek	31 cattle and	4 horses	2½ months	298
807 Watson Mtn.	123 cattle and	5 horses	12 months	1536
800 Brock Canyon	123 cattle and	5 horses	12 months	1524
806 Spar Canyon	165 cattle		12 months	1980
808 XSX	300 cattle and	10 horses	12 months	3720
Hulse		13 horses	12 months	156
Hage		10 horses	12 months	120
Campbell		27 horses	12 months	175
Adjacent Area				
103 Canyon Creek	97 cattle		12 months	1164
105 Indian Creek	150 cattle		12 months	1800
106 Jordan Mesa	580 cattle		12 months	6960

stringent garbage management particularly in areas heavily and regularly impacted by human use.

While I am aware of the existence of garbage dumps in or adjacent to the Wilderness, it should be mentioned also that such sites will pull bears for considerable distances with the same consequences noted above. Further, the wilderness image of the species is diminished when the species is observed in the role of a skid row bum.

Summary Evaluation.—As was indicated in evaluating the habitat character of the Gila Wilderness and the spatial requirements of the grizzly bear, the Gila Wilderness is deemed sufficiently large and capable of providing resource support for at least a small population of grizzly bear. At the same time, there is the near-certainty of some conflict between grizzly bears and other uses, notably livestock grazing, of the Gila Wilderness and Forest, should the grizzly be introduced. The extent of this potential conflict can only be surmised and would be influenced by management practices. Assuming an introduction of the grizzly were to be made, the management options as regards this conflict are four. The first would be to simply permit the normal evolution of events, which might prove tolerable with reasonable accommodations between stock interest and the Forest. The second possibility would be reduced grazing use of the Gila Wilderness and Forest where this use resulted in the development of a problem with bears. A third management option would be to stringently control bears when they impinged upon stock grazing areas. The last alternative would concern a blend of options two and three wherein consideration would be weighted favorably toward the bears in areas of chronic or high attraction for the species and conversely, the bears would be suppressed in areas of low attraction.

With accommodation, the exercise of option four might not prove as grievous as would first appear to be the case. In the first instance, it may very well develop that possible depredations of livestock by bears could be greatly diminished by withholding stock from the range during critical periods. In my experience with this problem on Kodiak Island, the time of principle conflict was in the early spring when the bears migrated to the low lands. Young stock is, of course, particularly vulnerable at this time. Obviously, this conflict could be significantly averted by withholding stock from the range until the bears had moved back to higher elevations or into other areas.

On the flip side of the coin and assuming a bear population buildup, it would seem only practical to direct control or exploitation of bear stocks into areas of the range where conflicts are likely to manifest themselves. During the initial buildup of the bear population, this control might assume the form of actual control actions. Later hunting could be directed into these areas. Particularly to be recommended would be a spring bear season running from normal pre-denning emergence beyond the time of likely predational expression. Such a season would serve to arrest the spread of bears beyond the boundaries desired by 1) removal of surpluses and 2) by displacement harassment.

The Feasibility of an Introduction.—Should it be decided that a reintroduction of the grizzly bear into the Gila Wilderness was a viable consideration, the question remains as to the form of the introduction and the type and availability of grizzly bears for the stocking attempt. The following discussion addresses these questions.

Race Types and Their Availability.—As indicated earlier in this report, the relic grizzly bear populations occurring in Mexico are in greatest likelihood the most similar habitat-wise and genetically to the grizzly population formerly occurring in the Gila Wilderness. Ideally, these populations would be the most desired source from which to obtain animals for introduction into the Gila Wilderness. It is questionable that this race will survive for any lengthy period, however, in view of the persecution the remaining populations are experiencing. On the other hand, there is the possibility that certain of these animals exist in captivity and the possibility of obtaining specimens for introduction from this source should be explored. Beyond this consideration, any of a number of grizzly stocks should be suitable for introduction and obtaining suitable animals for stocking should not be too difficult. Such animals could be specifically trapped or obtained as surpluses from zoological gardens.

There would appear to be some advantage in obtaining grizzlies for stocking from populations occurring in areas where the animals have been subjected to control or harassment pressures once they leave the confines of core mountainous areas. Bears from such areas would seemingly already have begun behavioral adaptations toward survival in marginal and confined habitats due to survival selection. While it could be argued that practically all of the grizzly stocks in the Americas, except Alaska, are of this type, I would suggest that those populations occurring in multiple-use forests would be the most likely to manifest such selection to the greatest degree. Less so would be those populations in areas such as national parks where the species associates with man in near-impunity on one hand and on the other faces animosity and persecution.

While obtaining grizzlies for stocking from an area such as the Bob Marshall Wilderness would be somewhat more difficult than obtaining stock from other sources, the end result might well be worth the increased cost and effort.

Other Stocking Considerations.—Likely to be important to the success of any stocking attempt, are factors concerning the ages, sexes and character of the animals to be released and when, where and how the releases might best be made. In my opinion, it would be foolhardy to use nuisance animals obtained from other areas, particularly national parks, as stock for introductions. The fact that the animals are nuisances elsewhere makes it a near-certainty they will be a cause of difficulties when again released. The prime argument for the use of these animals is their ready availability and the fact that there is little other use for the animals. These considerations shrink in significance when one considers the jeopardy the use of such animals could have on an introductory effort which can be expected to be most controversial, no matter how professionally performed.

As concerns the sexes and ages of bears to be used for introduction, I would suggest that best success would be realized if the animals stocked were either young (yearlings or 2-year olds), pregnant females or females with accompanying cubs. In truly wild bear populations, females and young are quite wary and consequently appear less inclined to become problem animals (Erickson, 1964).

As concerns the best time of the year for a release, I would suggest the fall fruit-producing period. Food type and abundance should be greatest at this time and thus the animals would not have to roam widely to satisfy their food needs. Further, the propensity of the grizzly to seek den sites in high areas (Craighead and Craighead, 1972; and Lintfer et al., 1972) would seemingly orient them into the mountains of the Gila Wilderness immediately following the fall foraging season as opposed to areas off the Wilderness.

As concerns the site of any release, it follows that a release near the center of the Wilderness would be preferable to a release on the periphery of the Wilderness. Such a release could be easily accomplished by helicopter transport of bears in an anesthetized state. The procedures or capture, anesthetization and transport of bears are in a technically advanced state and the physical aspects of release should be able to be accomplished with minimum difficulty unless encumbered by red tape.

Post Transplant Monitoring.—A component aspect of any responsible attempt to transplant the grizzly into the Gila Wilderness would include the provision for close assessment of the releases. This could be accomplished most accurately by marking and radio-tagging all released bears. While the simple tag marking of released bears would provide quite close assessment of the ultimate fate of a majority of the released bears, little information would be developed on the movements and actions of the animals during the critical period immediately following release. This could be accomplished only by radio telemetry whereby the animals could be easily monitored as to general location with aircraft and subsequently monitored from the ground as feasible. The efficacy of this procedure is the fact that hard information would exist concerning the locations and actions of the released bears and thus wild speculations could be curbed or addressed factually. Secondly, should a released animal fail to establish itself suitably, either spatially or habit-wise, it could quite likely be easily located and a recovery effort made. While there would appear to be limited virtue to the non-fatal recovery of an undesirable transplant animal, a live recovery could seemingly be accomplished either by intense trapping following radio-location or the animal could be bayed with dogs and captured with a syringe gun. It is possible too, that released animals could be harassed when they approached off-limit areas and thus be conditioned to avoid such areas. A further virtue of the radio-technique as employed on bears is the possibility of annual re-instrumentation of the animals in their winter dens.

Management of the Grizzly Once Established.—Should a successful introduction of the grizzly in the Gila Wilderness be achieved, consideration will have to be given to the management of the species within the Gila Wilderness and Forest. A first determinant is whether the species is to be given particular or peripheral management consideration. In the latter circumstance, principle management of the species would be directed to population management through game regulations or population control as necessary and little overt actions would be taken to benefit the species. Conversely, if the species were to be given particular management consideration, management would concern aspects both of the population and habitat considerations.

As discussed earlier, the current state of the vegetative types within the Gila Wilderness appears quite changed from the likely character of the Wilderness at the time of the demise of the grizzly from the area. The principle change has been a major loss of grassland and earlier successional stages and the loss of a fire-maintained grass ground cover below the climax ponderosa forests. These types appear attractive to grizzly bears, and their current reduced state would suggest that the Gila Wilderness is presently poorer grizzly range than it was during former times. If this is so, and if the grizzly is to be given major management consideration in the Wilderness, it follows that consideration should be given to breaking up and opening up the heavy forest stands of the Wilderness. In view of the current classification of the Gila Wilderness, the principle vehicle for opening the forest could be natural fire, perhaps coupled with non-control of forest insect infestations within the Wilderness. While this management option would normally be difficult to achieve inasmuch as the forest manager would be dependent upon the vagaries of natural fire occurrences, this would appear to be of limited concern in the Gila Wilderness due to the high and widespread occurrence of fire strikes.

There are, of course, a number of arguments in opposition to the non-control of insect infestations and fires in wilderness areas; however, the options of forest management in wilderness areas pretty much limit habitat manipulation to naturally occurring circumstances. Further, unless these few options are exercised, it seems probable that the resulting character of the Wilderness will be quite different than was formerly the natural state. This changed character of the Gila Wilderness would very likely not only decrease the attractiveness of the area as grizzly habitat, but for many other forms of wildlife as well.

While habitat management within the Wilderness is a logical step for improving the attractiveness and raising the support capabilities of the area for the grizzly, it follows that negative habitat management might be employed at the periphery and adjacent to the Gila Wilderness to discourage the use of these areas by the species. Ideally, the Gila Wilderness would be surrounded by an area highly unattractive to the grizzly. Where possible, such a zone could be realized by encouraging dense timber stands (Erickson, 1974), but this prospect appears limited as regards the Gila Forest. It is possible, however, that harassment conditioning, namely control or directed sport hunting at the periphery of the range, might achieve the same goal.

Literature Cited

Bailey, V., 1931. Mammals of New Mexico. *North American Fauna,* no. 53, pp. 350-68.

Berns, V. D., and R. J. Hensel, 1972. Radio tracking brown bears on Kodiak Island. *Bears—Their Biology and Management. ICUN, Publications,* new series, no. 23, pp. 19-25.

Cowan, I. M., 1972. The status and conservation of bears (Ursidae) of the world-1970. *ICUN, Publications,* new series, no. 23, pp. 343-67.

Craighead, F. C., and J. J. Craighead, 1972. Data on grizzly bear denning activities and behavior obtained by using wildlife telemetry. *ICUN, Publications,* new series, no. 23, pp. 84-106.

———, 1964. Radio-tracking of grizzly bears in Yellowstone National Park, Wyoming, 1964. *Nat. Geo. Soc. Res. Reports, 1964 Projects,* pp. 35-43.

Curry-Lindahl, K., 1972. The brown bear (*Ursus arctos* L.) in Europe: decline, present distribution, biology and ecology. *ICUN Publications,* new series, no. 23, pp. 74-80.

Elkmork, K., 1962. Bjornen i Vassfartraktene, 1954-58. *Saertrykk av Naturen* 1, pp. 36-54.

Erickson, A. W., 1965. The brown-grizzly bear in Alaska, its ecology and management, Alaska Dept. Fish and Game. *Federal Aid in Wildlife Research,* Project Report 5, pp. 1-42.

———, 1974. Grizzly bear management in the Seeley Lake District, Lo Lo National Forest. *Contract Report, Region 1, U.S. Forest Service,* pp. 22.

Hayward, B. J., 1974. Field check lists of plants and animals occurring in the Gila National Forest.

Lentfer, J. W., R. J. Hensel, L. H. Miller, L. P. Glenn and V. D. Berns, 1972. Remarks on denning habits of brown bears. *ICUN, Publications,* new series, no. 23, pp. 125-37.

Leopold, A. S., 1967. Grizzlies of the Sierra del Nido. *Pacific Discovery,* vol. 20, pp. 30-32.

———, 1958. Situacion del oso Plateado in Chihuahua. *Revista de la Sociedad Mexicana de Historia Natural,* vol. 19, pp. 115-20.

Ligon, J. S., 1917. See page 368, of Bailey, 1931.

———, 1927. Wildlife of New Mexico: its conservation and management, being a report on the game survey of the state 1926 and 1927. 212 p. *Illus. New Mex. Fish and Game Comm.,* Santa Fe.

Pearson, A. M., 1972. Population characteristics of the Northern Interior grizzly in the Yukon Territory, Canada. *ICUN Publications*, new series, no. 23, pp. 32–35.

Hunters News Letters

Issued to PARC Field Personnel by M. E. Musgrave, Predatory Animal Inspector, U.S. Department of Agriculture, Bureau of Biological Survey, Phoenix, Arizona, State Livestock Sanitary Board Cooperating

December, 1921

The Hunters' News Letter is gotten out for the information of the hunters in order to convey news to them from other parts of the State, to show what each man is doing and to give general instructions from this office when necessary.

During the month of December 15 hunters worked a total of 361 days taking 191 predatory animals, which included 1 Bear, 19 Bobcats, 136 Coyotes, 27 Foxes, 4 Lion and 4 Wolves.

Had it not been for the storms that drove Fredricks out of the mountains before he had a chance to look over his poison line we would have had several more coyotes.

Taking the catch as a whole it was not bad, still we find four men that were not on the honor roll.

Kenneth P. Pickrell, Assistant Inspector, heads the list with 52 coyotes and one fox for the month's work. Mr. Pickrell used nothing but poison. Poison is proving to be the most practical way of controlling predatory animals, and I wish the hunters, if possible, to work on the poisoning of mountain lions. I appreciate the fact that men using dogs are not in a position to use poison on the same range. However, we wish to develop poisoning methods against Mountain Lions and would like very much to have hunters try that out on ranges where they are not using their dogs and where they can pick up the poison or burn it after they are thru.

Our Honor Roll is as follows:

K. P. Pickrell, Willcox, 31 days—52 coyotes, 1 fox (poison)
W. A. Knibbe, Amado, 31 days—2 wolves, 6 coyotes, 1 cat (poison)
Cleve Miller, Metcalf, 30 days—2 lions, 1 Bear, 3 bobcats (dogs)
Fred Ott, Arivaca, 13 days—1 wolf, 1 fox (trap)
O. H. Glaze, Douglas, 27 days—11 coyotes, 9 bobcats (trap)
Robt. Bergier, Patagonia, 30 days—1 wolf, 3 coyotes, 1 fox (trap)
C. L. Walker, Holbrook, 16 days—12 coyotes, 1 bobcat (poison)
E. A. Terry, Payson, 18 days—12 coyotes, 1 bobcat (trap)
J. M. Wilson, Ft. Grant, 25 days—1 lion, 1 bobcat, 11 fox (traps, dogs)
C. A. Miller, Flagstaff, 30 days—1 lion (dogs)
Asa Gardner, Payson, 12 days—6 coyotes (poison)
M. E. Musgrave, Inspector, 2 days—10 coyotes (poison)

Furs are bringing a fairly good price and we sold $585.00 worth of State furs during the past few days. Hunters should save all the skins possible as this means more money in our fund.

All hunters leaving the Service must send in their complimentary trapping licenses to this office as these complimentary licenses are only issued to State and Government hunters.

In a recent letter from the Washington office we were requested to save some bear galls, so I should like to have hunters save the gall of any bear that they get. Remove the gall bladder and hang it up in the shade until it dries, then ship it in to this office.

I have found it necessary to drop two men from the Service on account of their inability to keep up a good catch. This I hate to do but it is necessary unless a man can keep up to a certain standard.

All skins of animals should be saved during the winter months.

November, 1922

The Hunters' News Letter is gotten out for the information of the hunters in order to convey news to them from other parts of the State, to show what each man is doing and to give general instructions from this office when necessary.

The total catch for the past month was not as large as that of August but there were several contributing reasons causing the smaller amount. We hope to eliminate all of these causes and make the present month's catch larger than any of the past months. We can do it.

The Honor Roll is as follows:

J. M. Wilson, Fort Grant, 20 days—2 bear, 1 coyote (trapped)
Cleve Miller, Clifton, 12 days—1 bear (dogs)
W. B. Ramsell, Esporo, 17 days—15 coyotes, 1 bobcat (traps, poison)
W. L. Saunders, Young, 30 days—2 bear, 1 bobcat (trapped)
J. R. Patterson, Prescott, 30 days—2 lion (dogs)
C. W. Carter, Clifton, 30 days—1 wolf, 6 coyotes (traps)
Chas. Miller, Greer, 30 days—1 lion, 2 bobcat (poison, dogs)
C. L. Walker, Heber, 30 days—14 coyotes, 5 bobcats (poison, traps)

It is difficult to say who should be at the head of the list for the past months as several hunters have made almost equally good catches, considering the number of days they worked. While the number of lion and wolves destroyed is not equal to that of last month, there have been more stock-killing bear killed. While it is greatly desired that all stock-killing bear be killed, all hunters will determine that stock is being destroyed by the bear before killing it as you are instructed not to kill other bear.

Hunter Carter reports the finding of a carcass of a wolf that he trapped several months ago. It had escaped from the trap and died several miles away.

Hunter Knibbe is still on the sick list due to an injury to his eye.

There will be a very good exhibit by this Bureau at the Fair at Prescott as well as the State Fair in Phoenix. The exhibit will consist of a large amount of the results of the work of this Bureau and will include several live specimens which will be of interest to the public. We feel that all hunters will feel personally interested in these displays as they are a result of the successful efforts made by the entire force.

Our motto is still "BRING THEM IN REGARDLESS OF HOW."

October, 1922

The Hunters' News Letter is gotten out for the information of the hunters in order to convey news to them from other parts of the State, to show what each man is doing and to give general instructions from this office when necessary.

There has been some very creditable catches made this month but no one exceeded the speed limit by a great deal.

J. M. Wilson, of Fort Grant, caught four bear that had been killing cattle on the west end of the Graham Mountains and is given first place on the honor roll. However, I wish to mention now so that the men will take it under consideration in the future that we do not feel that bear are as great a credit to a hunter as the wolves and lions although sometimes they are just as destructive as either of the other two animals but they are much easier to get. Notwithstanding this we congratulate Mr. Wilson on his catch.

Fred Willis, who has become one of our veteran poisoners, deserves congratulations on getting an old renegade wolf in the vicinity of Nelson. This was a good piece of work as the wolf was very sly and covered a large range.

The Honor Roll is as follows:

J. M. Wilson, Fort Grant, 25 days—4 bear, 1 coyote (traps)
G. W. Carter, Clifton, 31 days—2 wolves, 2 coyotes (traps)
Fred Willis, Nelson, 31 days—1 wolf, 9 coyotes (poison)
W. B. Ramsell, Esporo, 17 days—12 coyotes, 1 fox (poison)
C. L. Walker, Navajo, 22 days—13 coyotes (poison)
W. A. Knibbe, Amado, 22 days—9 coyotes, 3 bobcats (poison)
Cleve Miller, Metcalf, 14 days—1 bear (dogs)
W. L. Saunders, Young, 31 days—1 lion, 1 coyote, 6 fox (dogs, traps)
Lee Parker, Parker Canyon, 31 days—1 wild dog, 2 coyotes (poison)
Chas. Miller, Alpine, 31 days—1 lion (dogs)

W. A. Knibbe has again returned to the Service and will, we hope, get back to his old stride.

C. W. Carter was compelled to lay off for the month of November and probably longer, owing to rheumatism. We are sorry to hear this as Mr. Carter was an old standby on wolf work, always bringing in a few wolves.

We had a splendid exhibit at the State Fair this year, and I wish to call attention to the hunters now that we will want as many young animals as possible for the State Fair next year. . . .

References

ALLEN, G. M.
1942   Extinct and vanishing mammals of the Western Hemisphere. Amer. Comm. Internatl. Wildl. Protection. Special Publ. 11:1–620.

ALLEN, J. A.
1895   On a collection of mammals from Arizona and Mexico, made by Mr. W. W. Price with field notes by the collector. Bull. Amer. Mus. Nat. Hist. 7:193–258.

ANDERSON, S.
1972   Mammals of Chihuahua. Bull. Amer. Mus. of Nat. Hist. 148:377–78.

ANONYMOUS
1871   A bear fight in Arizona. Army and Navy Journ. 8:830.

ANONYMOUS
1883   The fauna of Arizona. Mining and Scientific Press, San Francisco. 46:146.

ARMSTRONG, D. M.
1972   Distribution of mammals in Colorado, Univ. of Kansas, Mus. Nat. Hist. Mongr. 3:1–415.

AUNE, K.
1981   Rocky Mountain Front grizzly bear monitoring and investigation. Annual Report. Bur. of Land Manage. and Montana Dept. Fish, Wildl. and Parks. 68 pp.

AUNE, K. and T. STIVERS
1982   Rocky Mountain Front grizzly bear monitoring and investigation. Annual Report. Bur. of Land Manage., Montana Dept. Fish, Wildl. and Parks, U.S. Forest Serv., Williams Exploration Co., Sun Exploration Co. 143 pp.

BAHRE, C. J.
1977   Land use history of the Research Ranch, Elgin, Arizona. J. Ariz. Acad. Sci. 12 (Suppl. 2):1–32.

BAILEY, V.
1905   Biological survey of Texas. U.S.D.A., Bur. of Biol. Surv., N. Amer. Fauna 25:1–222.

1909   Key to animals on which wolf and coyote bounties are often paid. U.S.D.A., Bur. Biol. Surv. Bull. 69:1-3.

1931   Mammals of New Mexico. U.S.D.A., Bur. of Biol. Surv., N. Amer. Fauna 53:1-412.

1935   Mammals of the Grand Canyon region. Grand Canyon Nat. Hist. Assoc., Nat. Hist. Bull. 1:1-42.

BAIRD, S. F.
1859   United States and Mexican boundary survey: Part 2— Zoology of the boundary. Mammals: 1-62. U.S.D.I., Wash., D.C.

BAKER, R. H.
1956   Mammals of Coahuila, Mexico. Univ. of Kansas. Publs. Mus. of Nat. Hist. 9:125-335.

BAKER, R. H., and J. D. GREER
1962   Mammals of the Mexican state of Durango. Publ. of the Mus. Michigan State Univ. Biol. Ser. 2:25-154.

BARKER, E. S.
1953   Beatty's cabin. Univ. of New Mexico Press, Albuquerque. 220 pp.

1963   Letter to Levon Lee, Chief of Game Manage., New Mexico Game and Fish Dept. *In* B. D. Haynes and E. Haynes, The grizzly bear: portraits from life (1966). Univ. of Okla. Press, Norman.

BARTLETT, J. R.
1854   Personal narrative of explorations and incidents in Texas, New Mexico, California, Sonora, and Chihuahua, connected with the United States and Mexican Boundary Commission during the years 1850, '51, '52, and '53. Vols. 1 and 2. Appleton and Co., New York. 1,125 pp.

BEALE, E. F.
1858   The report of the Superintendent of the Wagon Road from Fort Defiance to the Colorado River. House Ex. Doc. no. 124, 35th Congress, 1st Session, Washington, D.C. 87 pp.

BECK, W. A.
1962   New Mexico: a history of four centuries. Univ. of Oklahoma Press, Norman. 363 pp.

BISSEL, S. J.
1980   Grizzly bear incident, September 1979 summary report. Colorado Division of Wildl. Compendium of reports, correspondence and newspaper columns.

BLISS, C. F.
1921   Predatory animal control. New Mexico District Annual
        Report. U.S.D.A., Bur. Biol. Survey.
1922   Predatory animal control. New Mexico District Annual
        Report. U.S.D.A., Bur. Biol. Survey.
BORDER GRIZZLY PROJECT
1982   B.G.P. Research Papers, agency reports, working papers
        and theses, 1975-1982. BGP Spec. Rep. 45:1-13. Univ.
        of Montana, Missoula.
BROWN, D. E., ed.
1982   Biotic communities of the American Southwest United
        States and Mexico. Desert Plants 4:1-342.
1983   The wolf in the Southwest: the making of an endan-
        gered species. Univ. of Arizona Press, Tucson.
BROWN, D. E., and D. H. ELLIS
1977   Status summary and recovery plan for the masked bob-
        white. U.S.D.I., Fish and Wildlife Service, Office of
        Endangered Species, Region 2, Albuquerque. 18 pp.
BROWN, D. E., and C. H. LOWE, JR.
1974   The Arizona system for natural and potential vegeta-
        tion—illustrated summary through the fifth digit for
        the North American Southwest. J. Ariz. Acad. Sci. 9,
        suppl. 3:1-56.
1980   Biotic communities of the Southwest. U.S.D.A., For.
        Serv., Gen. Tech. Report RM-78. Map.
BROWN, D. E., W. L. MINCKLEY, and J. P. COLLINS
1982   Historical background to Southwestern ecological stud-
        ies. In Brown, D. E., ed., Biotic communities of the
        American Southwest—United States and Mexico. Des-
        ert Plants 3:1-56.
BROWN, D. L.
1982   The grizzly bear recovery plan. U.S. Fish and Wildl.
        Serv., in coop. with Montana Dept. Fish Wildl. and
        Parks. 195 pp.
BROWN, H.
1900   Conditions governing bird life in Arizona. Auk 17:
        31-34.
BURRIDGE, G.
1952   Ben Lilly last of the Mountain Men. Ariz. Wildl.
        Sportsman 5:20-24, 64-67.
1954   Lilly's big grizzly. Ariz. Wildl. Sportsman 7:16-17,
        60-62.

BURT, W. H.
   1938   Faunal relationships and geographic distribution of mammals in Sonora, Mexico. Univ. Mich. Mus. Zool., Misc. Publ. 39:1-77.
CARY, M.
   1911   A biological survey of Colorado. U.S. Biol. Surv. N. Amer. Fauna 33:1-256.
CHURCHER, C. S., and A. V. MORGAN
   1976   A grizzly bear from the middle Wisconsin of Woodbridge, Ontario, Canada. J. Earth Sciences 13:341-47.
CLARK, F.
   1952   The killing of old Ephraim. Utah Fish and Game Bull. 9(8):4-5.
CLARKE, A. B.
   1852   Travels in Mexico and California. Wright's and Hasty's Steam Press, Boston. 138 pp.
COCKRUM, E. L.
   1960   The recent mammals of Arizona: their taxonomy and distribution. Univ. of Arizona Press, Tucson. 276 pp.
COOK, J. H.
   1923   Fifty years on the old frontier. Yale Univ. Press, New Haven. 291 pp.
COSPER, J. A.
   1969   Highlights of the Cosper family migration to Arizona. Unpubl. typescript of memoirs of James Cosper to Phil Cosper. 13 pp.
COUES, E.
   1867   Notes on a collection of mammals from Arizona. Proc. Acad. Sci. of Philadelphia. 19:133-36.
COUES, E., and H. C. YARROW
   1875   Report upon the collections of mammals made in portions of Nevada, Utah, California, Colorado, New Mexico, and Arizona during the years 1871, 1872, 1873, and 1874. Chapter 2, vol. 5, Zoology. Pp. 65-66 *in* Report upon U.S. geographical and geological explorations and surveys west of the one hundredth meridian, in charge of 1st Lieut. G. M. Wheeler. U.S. Govern. Print. Office, Wash., D.C.
CRAIGHEAD, F. C., JR.
   1979   Track of the grizzly. Sierra Club Books, San Francisco. 261 pp.
CRAIGHEAD, J.J., J. S. SUMNER, and G. B. SCAGGS

1982 A definitive system for analysis of grizzly bear habitat and other wilderness resources. Univ. of Montana Foundation, Wildl.-Wildlands Monogr. 1:1–251.

CRAIGHEAD, J. J. and F. C. CRAIGHEAD, JR.
1971 Grizzly bear-man relationship in Yellowstone National Park. Bio Sci: 21(16):845–57.
1972 Grizzly bear prehibernation and denning activities as determined by radio-tracking. Wildl. Monogr. 32:1–35.

CRAIGHEAD, J. J., J. VARNEY, and F. C. CRAIGHEAD, JR.
1974 A population analysis of the Yellowstone grizzly bears. Montana Forest and Conserv. Exper. Sta. School of Forestry, Univ. of Montana, Missoula. Bull. 40:1–20.

CROUSE, C. W.
1904 *In* Mixed-bloods, Apaches, and cattle barons: documents for a history of the livestock economy on the White Mountain Reservation, Arizona, by T. R. McGuire. Cultural Resour. Manage. Section, Ariz. State Museum. Univ. of Ariz. Archaeological Series 142:84.

DAVIS, G. P., JR.
1982 Man and wildlife in Arizona: the American exploration period 1825–1865. Ariz. Game and Fish Dept., Phoenix.

DAVIS, W. B.
1966 The mammals of Texas. Texas Parks and Wildl. Dept., Austin. Bull. 41:1–265.

DOBIE, J. F.
1950 The Ben Lilly legend. Little, Brown & Co., Boston. 237 pp.
1966 Juan oso: bear nights in Mexico. *In* B. D. Haynes and E. Haynes, The grizzly bear: portraits from life. Univ. of Oklahoma Press, Norman. Pp. 266–95.
1981 The Ben Lilly legend. Univ. of Texas Press, Austin. 237 pp.

DURRANT, S.D.
1952 Mammals of Utah: taxonomy and distribution. Univ. of Kansas Publs. Mus. Nat. Hist. 6:1–549.

DYKES, J. C.
1965 Introduction. *In* W. French, Further recollections of a western ranchman. Argosy-Antiquarian, Ltd., New York.

EDWORDS, C. E.
1893 Camp fires of a naturalist: the story of fourteen expeditions after North American mammals from the field

notes of Louis Lindsay Dyche. D. Appleton and Co., New York. 304 pp.

ELLISON, G. R. ("SLIM")
   1968   Cowboys under the Mogollon Rim. Univ. of Arizona Press, Tucson. 274 pp.
   1981   More tales from Slim Ellison. Univ. of Arizona Press, Tucson. 195 pp.

ERICKSON, A. W.
   1974   Evaluation of the suitability of the Gila Wilderness for re-establishment of the grizzly bear. Typewritten report to U.S. Forest Service Contract #6-369-74. 36 pp.

EVANS, G. W.
   1951   Slash Ranch hounds. Univ. of New Mexico Press, Albuquerque. 244 pp.

FARRAR, H. R.
   1968   Tales of New Mexico Territory, 1868–1876. New Mexico Hist. Rev. 43:147–49.

FAULK, O. B.
   1970   Arizona: a short history. Univ. of Oklahoma Press, Norman. 267 pp.

FINDLEY, J. S., A. H. HARRIS, D. E. WILSON, and C. JONES
   1975   Mammals of New Mexico. Univ. of New Mexico Press, Albuquerque. 360 pp.

FLADER, S. L.
   1974   Thinking like a mountain. Univ. of Missouri Press, Columbia. 284 pp.

FOSTER, B. E.
   1931   Predatory animal control. Arizona District Annual Report. U.S.D.A., Bur. Biol. Survey.
   1932   Predatory animal control. Arizona District Annual Report. U.S.D.A., Bur. Biol. Survey.
   1933   Predatory animal control. Arizona District Annual Report. U.S.D.A., Bur. Biol. Survey.
   1934   Predatory animal control. Arizona District Annual Report. U.S.D.A., Bur. Biol. Survey.
   1935   Predatory animal control. Arizona District Annual Report. U.S.D.A., Bur. Biol. Survey.
   1936   Predatory animal control. Arizona District Annual Report. U.S.D.A., Bur. Biol. Survey.

FRENCH, W. J.
   1965a   Some recollections of a western ranchman: New Mex-

ico, 1883–1899. Argosy-Antiquarian Ltd., New York. Vol. 1. 283 pp.

1965b   Further recollections of a western ranchman: New Mexico, 1883–1899. Argosy-Antiquarian Ltd., New York. Vol. 2:285–521.

GARDNER, JENNIE

1893   Story of a bear. Juvenile Instructor, 28:270–71.

GATLIN, J. C.

1930   Predatory animal control. New Mexico District Annual Report. U.S.D.A., Bur. Biol. Survey.

1931   Predatory animal control. New Mexico District Annual Report. U.S.D.A., Bur. Biol. Survey.

1932   Predatory animal control. New Mexico District Annual Report. U.S.D.A. Bur. Biol. Survey.

1933   Predatory animal control. New Mexico District Annual Report. U.S.D.A., Bur. Biol. Survey.

1934   Predatory animal control. New Mexico District Annual Report. U.S.D.A., Bur. Biol. Survey.

1935   Predatory animal control. New Mexico District Annual Report. U.S.D.A., Bur. Biol. Survey.

1936   Predatory animal control. New Mexico District Annual Report. U.S.D.A., Bur. Biol. Survey.

GEHLBACH, F. R.

1981   Mountain islands and desert seas—a natural history of the U.S.—Mexican borderlands. Texas A & M Univ. Press, College Station. 298 pp.

GILCHRIST, D. A.

1930a   Arizona Wildlife Sportsman. Sept., p. 27.

1930b   Predatory animal control. Arizona District Annual Report. U.S.D.A., Bur. Biol. Survey.

GILLESPIE, O., and C. JONKEL

1980   Grizzly bear denning in the South Fork of the Flathead River. Pp. 178–95 *in* Ann. Report no. 5. Border Grizzly Project, University of Montana, Missoula.

GOLDMAN, D. M.

1969   Arizona Odyssey: bibliographic adventures in 19th century magazines. Ariz. Historical Foundation, Tempe. 360 pp.

GOLDMAN, E. A.

1951   Biological investigatins in Mexico. Smithsonian Misc. Coll., Washington, D.C. 115:1–476.

GRAY, A. E.
  1927 Predatory animal control. New Mexico District Annual
        Report. U.S.D.A., Bur. Biol. Survey.
  1928 Predatory animal control. New Mexico District Annual
        Report. U.S.D.A., Bur. Biol. Survey.
  1929 Predatory animal control. New Mexico District Annual
        Report. U.S.D.A., Bur. Biol. Survey.
GREGG, J.
  1844 Commerce of the prairies. M. L. Moorhead, ed. Univ.
        of Oklahoma Press, Norman. 1973 ed. 469 pp.
GULDAY, J. C.
  1968 Grizzly bears from eastern North America. Amer. Midl.
        Natur. 79:247-50.
HALL, E. R.
  1946 Mammals of Nevada. Univ. of California Press, Berke-
        ley and Los Angeles. 710 pp.
HAMER, D., S. HERRERO, and L. ROGERS
  1981 Differentiating black and grizzly bear feces. Wildl. Soc.
        Bull. 9:210-12.
HANCOCK, J. C.
  1930 Around the campfire—reminiscences of the "Good Old
        Days." Arizona Wildlife, June, pp. 14, 17.
HARDING, A. R.
  1942 Steel traps. A. R. Harding Publ. Co., Columbus, Ohio.
        324 pp.
HARDY, R. W. H.
  1829 Travels in the interior of Mexico, in 1825, 1826, 1827,
        and 1828. Henry Colburn and Richard Bentley, London.
HASTINGS, F. R., and R. M. TURNER
  1965 The changing mile: an ecological study of vegetation
        change with time in the lower mile of an arid and
        semiarid region. Univ. of Arizona Press, Tucson. 317 pp.
HAURY, E. W.
  1950 The stratigraphy and archaeology of Ventana Cave.
        Univ. of Arizona Press, Tucson.
HAYNES, B. D., and E. HAYNES
  1966 The grizzly bear: portraits from life. Univ. of Okla-
        homa Press, Norman. 370 pp.
HERRERO, S.
  1970 Man and the grizzly bear (present, past, but future?).
        Bio. Science 20 (21):1148-1153.

1976   Conflicts between man and grizzly bears in the National Parks of North America. Pp. 121–45 *in* M. R. Pelton, J. W. Lentfer, and G. E. Folk, Jr., eds., Bears — their biology and management. IUCN Publ. Ser. (new) 40.

HERRERO, S. and D. HAMER
1977   Courtship and copulation of a pair of grizzly bears, with comments on reproductive plasticity and strategy. J. Mammal. 58:441–44.

HIBBEN, F. C.
1948   Last of the mountain men. Outdoor Life. 101:47–53.

HINTON, R. J.
1878   The handbook to Arizona: its resources, history, towns, mines, ruins and scenery. Payot, Upham & Co., San Francisco and American News Co., New York. 431 pp.

HITTELL, T. H.
1860   The adventures of James Capen Adams, mountaineer and grizzly bear hunter, of California. Towne and Bacon, San Francisco; and Crosby, Nichols, Lee, and Co., Boston. 378 pp.

1911   The adventures of James Capen Adams, mountaineer and grizzly bear hunter of California. Chas. Scribners and Sons, New York.

HOFFMEISTER, D. F.
1985   Mammals of Arizona. University of Arizona Press, Tucson.

HOUSHOLDER, B.
1966   The grizzly bear in Arizona. Bob Housholder, Phoenix. 39pp. 2d printing, 1971.

HUBBARD, W. P., and S. HARRIS
1960   Notorious grizzly bears. Sage Books, Swallow Press, Inc., Denver. 205 pp.

IVES, J. C.
1861   Report upon the Colorado River of the West. Govern. Print. Office, Wash., D.C. 31 pp.

JOHNSON, F. W., and M. A. GEE
1941   Report on wildlife within National Forests of Arizona and New Mexico, 1940. U.S.D.A., Forest Service, Region 3, 46 pp. and tables.

1942   Report on wildlife within National Forests of Arizona and New Mexico, 1941. U.S.D.A., Forest Service, Region 3, 29 pp. and tables.

JOHNSON, S. J., and D. E. GRIFFEL
  1982   Sheep losses on grizzly bear range. J. Wildl. Manage.
          46:786–90.
JONKEL, C.
  1980   Mexican grizzlies: 1977–79 studies; status; habitat; rec-
          ommendations. Border Grizzly Proj., Final Report no.
          58:1–47.
KEARNEY, T. H., and R. H. PEEBLES
  1960   Arizona flora. Univ. of California Press, Berkeley, Los
          Angeles, London. 1085 pp.
KENNERLY, C. B. R.
  1856   Report on the zoology of the expedition. *In* Reports of
          exploration and surveys, etc., 1853–1854. Vol. 4. Ex-
          pedition under Lt. A. W. Whipple, Corps of Topo-
          graphical Engineers, upon the route near the 35th paral-
          lel. Wash., D.C.
KLUCKHOHN, C.
  1946   The Navajo. Harvard Univ. Press, Cambridge. 355 pp.
KOFORD, C. B.
  1969   The last of the Mexican grizzly bear. Intern. Union
          Conserv. Nature and Nat. Resour. Bull: 95.
LANGE, K. I.
  1960   Mammals of the Santa Catalina Mountains, Arizona.
          Amer. Midl. Nat. 64:436–58.
LECOUNT, A.
  1977a   Some aspects of black bear ecology in the Arizona
          chaparral. Bear Biol. Assoc. Conf. Ser. 3:175–79.
  1977b   Using chest circumference to determine bear weight.
          Ariz. Game and Fish Dept. Wildl. Digest 11:1–2.
LEE, L.
  1967   Bear. Pp. 83–87 *in* New Mexico Wildlife Management.
          New Mexico Dept. of Game and Fish, Santa Fe. 250 pp.
LEOPOLD, A.
  1966   Sand County almanac. Oxford Univ. Press, New York.
          269 pp.
LEOPOLD, A. S.
  1958   Situacion del oso plateado en Chihuahua. Rev. Soc.
          Mexicana Hist. Nat. 19:115–20.
  1959   Wildlife of Mexico. Univ. of California Press, Berkeley,
          Los Angeles, London. 2d printing, 1972. 568 pp.
  1967   Grizzlies of the Sierra del Nido. Pacific Discovery 20:
          30–32.

LIGON, J. S.
    1916   Predatory animal control. New Mexico District Annual Report. U.S.D.A., Bur. Biol. Survey.
    1917   Predatory animal control. New Mexico District Annual Report. U.S.D.A., Bur. Biol. Survey.
    1918   Predatory animal control. New Mexico District Annual Report. U.S.D.A., Bur. Biol. Survey.
    1919   Predatory animal control. New Mexico and Oklahoma-Arkansas sub-district Annual Report. U.S.D.A., Bur. Biol. Survey.
    1920   Predatory animal control. New Mexico and Oklahoma-Arkansas sub-district Annual Report. U.S.D.A., Bur. Biol. Survey.
    1924   Predatory animal control. New Mexico District Annual Report. U.S.D.A., Bur. Biol. Survey.
    1927   Wildlife of New Mexico: its conservation and management. New Mexico Dept. of Game and Fish, Santa Fe.

LINDSAY, E. H., and N. T. TESSMAN
    1974   Cenozoic vertebrate localities and faunas in Arizona. J. Ariz. Acad. Sci. 9:3-24.

LINDZEY, F. G.
    1981   Denning dates and hunting seasons for black bears. Wildl. Soc. Bull. 9:212-16.

LOPEZ, C. M., and C. LOPEZ
    1911   Caza Mexicana. Libreria de la Vda. de C. Bouret, México and Paris. 629 pp.

LOWE, C. H., and D. E. BROWN
    1982   Introduction *in* D. E. Brown 1982. Biotic communities of the American Southwest—United States and Mexico. Desert Plants 4(1-4):1-342.

LUMHOLTZ, K. S.
    1902   Unknown Mexico: a record of five years' exploration among the tribes of the western Sierra Madre; in the Tierra Caliente of Tepic and Jalisco; and among the Tarascos of Michoacan. 2 vols. Charles Scribner's Sons, New York. 1,013 pp.

McGUIRE, T. R.
    1980   Mixed-bloods, Apaches, and cattle barons: documents for a history of the livestock economy on the White Mountain Reservation, Arizona. Cultural Resour. Manage. Section, Ariz. State Museum, Univ. of Ariz. Archaeological Series 142:1-227.

MACHADO, M. A., JR.
    1981   The north Mexican cattle industry, 1910-1975. Texas
            A & M Univ. Press, College Station. 152 pp.
MARTIN, P. S., and F. PLOG
    1973   The archaeology of Arizona: a study of the Southwest
            region. Amer. Mus. of Nat. Hist., New York.
MARTINKA, C. J.
    1974   Population characteristics of grizzly bear in Glacier
            National Park, Montana. J. Mammal. 55(1):21-29.
MARTINKA, C. J., and K. L. McARTHUR
    1980   Bears—their biology and management: a selection of
            papers from the fourth international conference on bear
            research and management. Kalispell, Montana, 1977.
            Bear Biology Association. 375 pp.
MEALEY, S. P.
    1980   The natural food habits of grizzly bears in Yellowstone
            National Park, 1973-74. In Bears—their biology and
            management. Bear Biol. Assoc. Confer. Ser. 3:281-92.
MEARNS, E. A.
    1907   Mammals of the Mexican boundary of the United States.
            U.S. National Museum Bull. 56:1-530.
MERRIAM, C. H.
    1918   Review of the grizzly and big brown bears of North
            America. North Amer. Fauna 4:1-136. U.S. Govern.
            Printing Office, Wash., D.C.
    1922   Map of the distribution of grizzly bear. Outdoor Life 12.
MILLER, G. S., JR., and R. KELLOG
    1955   List of North American recent mammals. U.S. Govern.
            Print. Office, Wash., D.C. Pp. 696-711.
MILLER, J.
    1956   Arizona: the last frontier. Hastings House, New York.
MILLS, E. O.
    1919   The grizzly: our greatest wild animal. Houghton Mif-
            flin, Boston and New York.
MÖLLHAUSEN, H. B.
    1858   Diary of a journey from the Mississippi to the coasts
            of the Pacific with a United States Government expe-
            dition. 2 vols. London. 749 pp.
MUNDY, K. R. D., and D. R. FLOOK
    1973   Background for managing grizzly bears in the National
            Parks of Canada. Canad. Wildl. Serv. Rep. Ser. 22:1-35.

MURIE, A.
  1948   Cattle on grizzly bear range. J. Wildl. Manage. 12:
          57–72.
  1981   The grizzlies of Mount McKinley. U.S.D.I., Nat. Park
          Serv., Sci. Monog. Ser. 14:1–251.
MUSGRAVE, M. E.
  1919   Predatory animal control. Arizona District Annual Re-
          port. U.S.D.A., Bur. Biol. Survey.
  1920   Predatory animal control. Arizona District Annual Re-
          port. U.S.D.A., Bur. Biol. Survey.
  1921   Predatory animal control. Arizona District Annual Re-
          port. U.S.D.A., Bur. Biol. Survey.
  1922   Predatory animal control. Arizona District Annual Re-
          port. U.S.D.A., Bur. Biol. Survey.
  1923   Predatory animal control. Arizona District Annual Re-
          port. U.S.D.A., Bur. Biol. Survey.
  1924   Predatory animal control. Arizona District Annual Re-
          port. U.S.D.A., Bur. Biol. Survey.
  1925   Predatory animal control. Arizona District Annual Re-
          port. U.S.D.A., Bur. Biol. Survey.
  1926   Predatory animal control. Arizona District Annual Re-
          port. U.S.D.A., Bur. Biol. Survey.
  1927   Predatory animal control. Arizona District Annual Re-
          port. U.S.D.A., Bur. Biol. Survey.
  1928   Predatory animal control. Arizona District Annual Re-
          port. U.S.D.A., Bur. Biol. Survey.
  1929   Predatory animal control. Arizona District Annual Re-
          port. U.S.D.A., Bur. Biol. Survey.
  1938   Ben Lilly—last of the mountain men. *Amer. Forests*,
          Aug.
NENTVIG, J.
  1980   Rudo Ensayo: a description of Sonora and Arizona in
          1764. Trans., clarified, and annot. by A. F. Pradeau
          and R. R. Rasmussen. Univ. of Arizona Press, Tucson.
O'CONNOR, J.
  1945   Hunting in the Southwest. Alfred A. Knopf, New York.
          Pp. 213–16.
OPLER, M. E.
  1941   An Apache life-way. Univ. of Chicago Press. 500 pp.
PARKER, M. B.
  1979   Mules, mines and me in Mexico: 1895–1932. J. M.
          Day, ed. Univ. of Arizona Press, Tucson. 230 pp.

PATTIE, J. O.
  1833   The personal narrative of James Ohio Pattie of Ken-
          tucky. T. Flint, ed. John H. Wood, Cincinnati.
PEARSON, A. M.
  1975   The northern interior grizzly bear (*Ursus arctos* L.).
          Canad. Wildl. Serv. Rep. Ser. 34:1–86.
PFEFFERKORN, I.
  1949   Sonora—a description of the province. Transl. and an-
          notated by T. E. Treutlein, from the 1875 German
          edition. Univ. of New Mexico Press, Albuquerque. Pp.
          106–108.
PICKENS, H. C.
  1980   Tracks across New Mexico. Bishop Publ. Co., Portales,
          N.Mex. 121 pp.
PICTON, H. D., and I. E. PICTON
  1975   Saga of the Sun: a history of the Sun River elk herd.
          Game Manage. Div., Montana Dept. Fish and Game.
          55 pp.
PIKE, Z. M.
  1808   Letter to Pres. Thomas Jefferson. Pp. 32–33 *in* Wright,
          W. H., 1909.
PINEAU, E. L.
  1923   Predatory animal control. New Mexico District Annual
          Report. U.S.D.A., Bur. Biol. Survey.
PLATT, V.
  1952   Combat with a grizzly. Ariz. Wildl. Sportsman 5:26–28.
POOLE, A. J., and V. S. SCHANTZ
  1942   Catalog of the type specimens of mammals in United
          States National Museum, including the Biological Sur-
          veys collection. Govern. Print. Office, Wash., D.C.
          Pp. 88–100.
POPE, E. F.
  1925   Predatory animal control. New Mexico District Annual
          Report. U.S.D.A., Bur. Biol. Survey.
  1926   Predatory animal control. New Mexico District Annual
          Report. U.S.D.A., Bur. Biol. Survey.
RASMUSSEN, D. I.
  1941   Biotic communities of Kaibab Plateau, Arizona. Ecol.
          Monogr. 3:229–75.
RAUSCH, R. L.
  1963   Geographic variation in size in North American brown
          bears, *Ursus arctos* L., as indicated by condylobasal
          length. Can. Jour. of Zool. 41:33–45.

REED, P.
1980   Attorney denies bear was shot before attack. Rocky
        Mtn. News (Denver, Colo.), Feb. 3, p. 9.

REGIONAL FORESTER
1951   National Forest facts—southwestern region—Arizona
        and New Mexico. U.S.D.A. Forest Service, Region 3.
        35 pp.

ROOSEVELT, T.
1885   Hunting trips of a ranchman, sketches of the northern
        cattle plains. G. P. Putnam's Sons, New York and
        London.
1888   Ranch life and the hunting trail. Reprinted *as* Ranch
        life in the far West, in 1981, by Outbooks, Golden,
        Colo.

ROY, L. D., and M. J. DORRANCE
1976   Methods of investigating predation of domestic live-
        stock: a manual for investigating officers. Alberta Agric.
        Plant Industry Lab., Edmonton. 54 pp.

RUSSELL, A.
1976   Grizzly country. Alfred A. Knopf, New York. 302 pp.

RUXTON, G. F.
1847   Adventures in Mexico and the Rocky Mountains. 1973
        ed., C. R. Buell, ed. Rio Grande Press, Inc., Glorieta,
        New Mexico.

SAMSON, J.
1979   The bear book. Amwell Press, Clinton, N.J. 250 pp.

SCHORGER, A. W.
1955   The passenger pigeon: its natural history and extinc-
        tion. Univ. of Wisconsin Press, Madison. 2d printing,
        1973, Univ. of Oklahoma Press, Norman. 424 pp.

SCHULTZ, J. W.
1920   In the great Apache Forest. Houghton Mifflin Co.,
        Boston and New York. 225 pp.

SERVHEEN, C.
1981   Denning ecology, food habits, habitat use, and move-
        ments of grizzly bears in the Mission Mountains, Mon-
        tana. Ph.D. diss., Univ. of Montana, Missoula.

SETON, E. T.
1900   The biography of a grizzly. Century Co., New York.

SHELDON, C.
1925   Big game of Chihuahua, Mexico. *In* Hunting and con-

servation, C. Sheldon and G. B. Grinnell, eds. Boone and Crockett Club and Yale Univ. Press, New Haven.

SITGREAVES, L.
1853   Report of an expedition down the Zuni and Colorado Rivers, ed. Robert Armstrong. Wash., D.C. 190 pp.

SONNICHSEN, C. L.
1974   Colonel Greene and the copper skyrocket. Univ. of Arizona Press, Tucson. 325 pp.

SPARKS, W.
1926   The Apache Kid, a bear fight and other true stories of the old West. Skelton Publ. Co., Los Angeles. 215 pp.

SPRING, J.
1966   John Spring's Arizona. A. M. Gustafson, ed. Univ. of Arizona Press, Tucson. Pp. 112-13, 302-305.

STEELE, E.
1925   May narrative report. In Pope, E. F., Predatory animal control. New Mexico District Annual Report, U.S.D.A., Bur. Biol. Survey.

STEVENS, M.
1943   Meet Mr. Grizzly: a saga on the passing of the grizzly. Univ. of New Mexico Press, Albuquerque. 281 pp.

STORER, T. J., and L. P. TEVIS, JR.
1955   California grizzly. Univ. of California Press, Berkeley and Los Angeles. 2d printing, Univ. of Nebraska Press, Lincoln and London. 1978. 335 pp.

TAYLOR, W. P., W. P. McDOUGALL, C. C. PRESNALL, and K. P. SCHMIDT
1945   Preliminary ecological survey of the northern Sierra del Carmen, Coahuila, Mexico. Texas Coop. Wildl. Research Unit Rept. 48 pp.

THOMSON, A. E.
1968   A bear hunter who lost. Pp. 132-35 in Oldtimers' memoirs—Oak Creek, Sedona, and the Verde Valley region of northern Arizona. Sedona Westerners.

THOMSON, WILLIAM
1895   Beset in Aravaipa Canyon. Lippincott's Magazine 55: 845-51.

TINKER, G. H.
1969   Northern Arizona and Flagstaff in 1887: the people and resources. Arthur H. Clark Co., Glendale, Calif. 62 pp.

TREFETHEN, J. B.
1961   Crusade for wildlife. Boone and Crockett Club, and Stackpole Co., Harrisburg, Pa. 377 pp.

TULLY, R. J.
1970   Status of the grizzly bear in Colorado. Report to the Special Grizzly Bear Committee, Intern. Assoc. of Game, Fish and Conservation Commissioners. Mack's Inn, Idaho, 7 July. 3 pp.

WADDELL, T. E., and D. E. BROWN
1984   Black bear population characteristics in an isolated Southwest mountain range. J. Mammal. 65:350-51.

WAGONER, J. J.
1952   History of the cattle industry in southern Arizona, 1540-1940. Univ. of Arizona. Social Sci. Bull. 20. Univ. of Ariz. Press, Tucson.

WARREN, E. R.
1942   The mammals of Colorado. Univ. of Oklahoma Press, Norman. 2d ed. 330 pp.

WAUER, R. H.
1973   Naturalist's Big Bend. Peregrine Productions, Santa Fe, N.Mex. 159 pp.

WAY, P. R.
1865   Overland via jackass mail in 1858: the diary of Phocian R. Way. W. A. Duffen, ed. Arizona and the West, 2:35-43, 147-64, 279-92, 353-70.

WINN, F.
1923   Ben Lilly, a twentieth century Daniel Boone. Amer. Forestry. July.
1930   Annual and Five Year Game Report. Coronado National Forest files.

WINSHIP, G. P.
1896   The Coronado expedition, 1540-1542. Bur. of Ethnol. 14th Ann. Report, Smithsonian Inst. (1892-93). Pp. 329-613. Trans. of the narrative of Castañeda.

WRIGHT, W. H.
1909   The grizzly bear—narrative of a hunter naturalist. Charles Scribner's Sons, New York. 1977, Univ. of Nebraska Press. 273 pp.

YOUNG, S. P., and E. A. GOLDMAN
1944   The wolves of North America. Amer. Wildl. Inst., Wash., D.C. 636 pp.

YOUNG, F. M., and C. BEYERS
    1980   Man meets grizzly. Houghton Mifflin Co., Boston.
            298 pp.

Index

The Grizzly Bear in the Southwest,

designed by Bill Cason, was set in Caslon by the University of Oklahoma Press and printed offset on 60-pound Glatfelter's Smooth Antique, B-31, a permanized sheet, by Cushing-Malloy, Inc., with case binding by John H. Dekker & Sons.